INSTRUCTOR'S MANUAL
to accompany

CALCULUS
PRELIMINARY EDITION

Deborah Hughes-Hallett
Harvard University

Andrew Gleason
Harvard University

et al.

Prepared By: **William G. McCallum**
University of Arizona

Brad G. Osgood
Stanford University

Jeff Tecosky-Feldman
Haverford College

Karen R. Thrash
University of Southern Mississippi

Eric K. Wepsic
Harvard University

John Wiley & Sons, Inc.
New York • Chichester • Brisbane • Toronto • Singapore

ISBN 0-471-58598-X

Printed in the United States of America

10 9 8 7 6 5 4 3

Printed and bound by Malloy Lithographing, Inc.

CONTENTS

INSTRUCTOR'S MANUAL
to accompany

CALCULUS
PRELIMINARY EDITION

The best way to get a feel for what we have done, and to get excited about it, is to read the book; above all to read and try the problems. One teacher was reading them aloud in bed to her husband! But if you are the sort of person who always reads the manual first, here it is. It is organized into three parts: The Book, The Chapters, and The Sections and Exercises. Read the first part to get a general idea of our approach. Then, as you read through the text, you should refer to the second part for comments on particular chapters, and do the suggested exercises for each chapter; if you have a computer or graphing calculator, do the suggested computer exercises. Finally, when you are preparing individual classes, refer to the third part for tips on each section and comments about specific exercises. There is also an appendix which gives sample syllabi.

I   The Book

We have tried to produce a textbook that

- demands greater understanding and less routine manipulation,

- covers less material in greater depth,

- presents concepts graphically and numerically as well as algebraically,

- develops concepts from common sense investigations rather than abstract definitions,

- incorporates the use of computers and calculators,

- is written to be read, and is written for students.

Greater understanding, less manipulation

We expect the students to understand the derivative and definite integral beyond the purely symbolic level; in return we don't ask them to perform great feats of symbolic manipulation.

For example, rather than requiring them to reproduce $\epsilon - \delta$ proofs with no understanding, we require them to show a genuine understanding of the difference quotient underlying the definition of the derivative; rather than making

$$\int_a^b x^2 \, dx = \frac{1}{3}(b^3 - a^3)$$

into a difficult but mindless algebra exercise using summation formulas, we require them to genuinely understand why the definite integral of a rate of change is the total change.

Less material in greater depth

We have omitted:

- introductory chapters on precalculus material,

- the formal definition of limit,

- limits as a separate topic,

- continuity as a separate topic,

- related rates,

- the mean-value theorem,

- convergence of series of constants.

Further,

- curve sketching has been replaced with a section on the graphs and qualitative behavior of parametrized families of curves,

- integrals using partial fractions, inverse trigonometric functions, integrals of powers of sine and cosine, and reduction formulas have been replaced with a section on tables of integrals,

- there is less material on volumes of revolution and arclength.

In turn, we spend more time introducing the key concepts of the derivative and definite integral. Further, the applications of these concepts are not categorized into templates to be imitated and require more prolonged thought than in the conventional curriculum.

The Rule of Three

The Rule of Three is that every concept should be introduced graphically, numerically, and analytically. This means more than throwing in a few graphs when you feel like it, or calculating a few difference quotients. It means giving equal time to all three components of understanding. It means expecting and accepting geometric explanations: for example, giving full credit to a student who can give a clear graphical explanation of why $f'' > 0$ means the graph of f is concave up. It means giving at least partial credit for correct numerical calculation of the answer. For example, you ask two students for the derivative of x^x at $x = 2$. One says

$$\frac{d}{dx}(x^x) = x(x^{x-1}) = 4 \quad \text{when } x = 2.$$

The other says

$$\frac{d}{dx}(x^x)\bigg|_{x=2} \approx \frac{2.01^{2.01} - 2^2}{0.01} \approx 6.8.$$

If they have had a conventional calculus course, the first student will be outraged at receiving no credit. You won't find the second student in a conventional calculus course; the rule of three means teaching in such a way that you might.

The Way of Archimedes

The Way of Archimedes is to let formal definitions and proofs *evolve* from a long process of common sense investigation, rather than to start with abstract definitions. Or, in Archimedes' words:

> ...I thought fit to write out for you and explain in detail ...the peculiarity of a certain method, by which it will be possible for you to get a start to enable you to investigate some of the problems in mathematics by means of mechanics. This procedure is, I am persuaded, no less useful even for the proof of the theorems themselves; for certain things first became clear to me by a mechanical method, although they had to be demonstrated by geometry afterwards because their investigation by the said method did not furnish an actual demonstration. But it is of course easier, when we have previously acquired, by the method, some knowledge of the questions, to supply the proof than it is to find it without any previous knowledge.

This is from *The Method*, in *The Works of Archimedes* edited and translated by Sir Thomas L. Heath (Dover, New York). In the spirit of Archimedes, we have tried to ignore the mathematician peering over our shoulder. For example, we introduce Taylor series as a natural consequence of the observation that the Taylor polynomials of successive degree all have the same initial terms; only after that do we begin to investigate the question of convergence. Also, we have thrown out the $\epsilon - \delta$ definition of the limit, and have given only informal proofs of many theorems. We have tried to give proofs that, while mathematically sound, are comprehensible to the student; we would expect the better students to actually read the proofs and understand them.

Not being bound by mathematical rigor also means a different approach to the various transcendental functions. Rather than putting them off until they can be rigorously defined, we have introduced all the functions we will need for the course in the first chapter. Each function is introduced in the context of its real-life uses, not as an abstract function.

We also often give real numbers as approximations in this text: 3.63, not $\frac{\pi^2}{e}$. This is because decimals conform to experiential reality; when you measure a board, your tape measure does not read $\frac{\pi^2}{e}$, it reads 3.63. Most importantly, we want to "loosen up" students so that they will be willing to apply their common sense.

Technology

If you mistrust technology, listen to this student, who started out the same way:

> Using computers is strange, but surprisingly beneficial, and in my opinion is what leads to success in this class. I have difficulty visualizing graphs in my head, and this has always led to my downfall in calculus. With the assistance of the computers, that stress was no longer a factor, and I was able to concentrate on the concepts behind the shapes of the graphs, and since these became gradually more clear, I got increasingly better at picturing what the graphs should look like. It's the old story of not being able to get a job without previous experience, but not being able to get experience without a job. Relying on the computer to help me avoid graphing, I was tricked into focusing on what the graphs meant instead of how to make them look right, and what graphs

symbolize is the fundamental basis of this class. By being able to see what I was trying to describe and learn from, I could understand a lot more about the concepts, because I could change the conditions and see the results. For the first time, I was able to see how everything works together . . . .

That was a student at the University of Arizona who took calculus in Fall 1990, the first time we used the text. She was terrified of calculus, got a C on her first test, but finished with an A for the course.

The text assumes the students have access to:

- A program or calculator that finds roots of equations

- A program or calculator that draws graphs of functions

- A program or calculator that can numerically integrate functions.

Programs

Calculator programs for several types of calculators are provided later on in this manual.

A book to be read as a book

There is nothing in the book that's there because we were afraid of what mathematicians and teachers might say if we left it out. It is not a reference book, it is not an encyclopedia, it is an account of the basic ideas of calculus. The writing is informal because we want students to read it; however, we have intentionally made it difficult for students to do what they normally do, which is to look first at the homework exercises, then to look for a worked example that fits the template, and only as a last resort to read the pieces of text between the examples.

Exercises

The exercises are the heart of the text. Assign fewer of them than you normally would, and give the students more time. There are fewer rote exercises than in a traditional text, and more requiring thought and the ability to write clearly. There are some essay questions, questions that require graphical and numerical work rather than algebra, and questions that require use of a calculator or computer program.

Although many of the exercises are not difficult, students are not accustomed to reading and interpreting math problems. They are used to seeing problems which mimic the examples—and have unique answers in the back of the book. The initial shock (perhaps even hostility) at finding these conditions changed needs to be dealt with. Constantly reassure students that indeed, these problems are different, but that efforts to deal with them will pay off in the end. Not only does it work for the most part, it turns out to be true advice. More detailed comments on some of the exercises are included in the Sections and Exercises portion of this guide.

The first three chapters

If you are used to teaching a traditional calculus course, you may be tempted to go too fast through these chapters. We know from experience that the course is a disaster if students don't have a thorough grasp of the material in Chapter 1. Although much of the material should be familiar to the students, it is presented in a sufficiently different manner that most will find it quite new. It is crucial that students get comfortable with graphical and numerical work early on. The idea of Chapter 1 is to make the students thoroughly familiar with functions from all points of view, e.g., to be able to recognize that a function is linear from a table of its values, or to understand in graphical terms the relative growth rates of functions.

Chapters 2 and 3 introduce the key concepts of derivative and definite integral in parallel, in order to show clearly the relation between them. It is only after this introduction that we get into the details of techniques of differentiation and integration, and how to use the key concepts in applications. They are crucial to the spirit of the book. You should cover them slowly enough for the students to think about what the key concepts really mean, so that they may ultimately use them for themselves. There aren't many exercises for these sections, but there is a lot of thinking to be done in reading them.

Sections called "Notes on"

These sections are generally more theoretical or philosophical reflections on earlier material; they are optional.

A Few Warnings

Students are reasonably proficient at what is usually emphasized in mathematics courses: using rules to manipulate formulas. They are much less proficient at understanding and critically interpreting mathematics, as well as applying it to practical situations.

On the Rule of Three: Students have much more difficulty with tables and graphs than they do with formulas. They confuse functions with their formulas, the rules that generate them. Tables are foreign to them; they need time and practice getting used to them. Graphs are also difficult; while most of them will have seen graphs before, they may not be used to the idea of interpreting them. For example, many students will have difficulty interpreting a graph of distance versus time, confusing it with a trajectory, for example. A graph of velocity versus time causes even more trouble. This difficulty with interpretation is part of the reason for the sections on "Interpreting the Derivative" and "Interpreting the Definite Integral".

Often, students are also not yet very geometrically adept. Many of them, for example, cannot read the slope of a line from its graph. Try to wean them away from depending on formulas to see such things. Often, they will also have problems interpreting geometric objects: they confuse the secant line itself with average rate of change (which is the slope of the secant line), and they confuse the tangent line with derivative (which is the slope of the tangent line).

Many students have difficulty with basic material, such as exponential functions and logarithms, or even percents or fractions. We suggest that you not spend too much time at the beginning going over manipulative rules but instead review whenever there is difficulty or confusion.

Often students misinterpret results on their graphing calculators or computers. This is often due to the computer's tendency to deal badly with the very large (say, asymptotes) and the very small (roundoff error). Finding an appropriate viewing region for a graph is difficult for students as well; once again, they have difficulty critically interpreting mathematics. (What is important about this graph?) They often give up too easily when graphing to find points of intersection, especially when very large values are involved (for example, $y = e^x$ and $y = 2 + 1000x^8$). Students sometimes also assume that if the cursor is on top of the point of intersection then the (x, y) values are exact, whereas these values can actually be off by ridiculous amounts, depending on the window settings.

In the spirit of this book, try to make your class interactive; make it a class rather than a lecture.

II The Chapters

Chapter 1: A Library of Functions

Overview

This chapter was the most difficult to write and is probably the hardest to teach. The differences in students' backgrounds and the universal resistance to being asked to think about math in new ways can be frustrating for you and your students. Try not to get bogged down on any particular section; keep the flow as fast-paced and lively as possible. Syllabi from different institutions indicate that the time to cover the material in the first eleven sections can range from around eight to twelve class meetings. An extremely fast class for well-prepared students might cover the material in as few as six meetings. Be assured (and assure your class) that the time spent on these sections will pay off when you do get to the "calculus".

All the elementary functions to be used in the book are introduced in this chapter. Our purpose is to acquaint the student with each function's individuality: the shape of its graph, characteristic properties, comparative growth rates, and general uses; and to give the student the skill to read graphs and think graphically, to read tables and think numerically, and to apply these skills, along with their algebraic skills, to modeling the real world. Further attention is given to constructing new functions from old ones—how to shift, flip and stretch the graph of any basic function into a new, related function.

Description

The first 11 sections of this chapter are of fundamental importance. Although the functions are probably familiar, the graphical, numerical, and modeling approach to them is fresh.

In Section 1.1 we discuss the concept of a function and introduce three ways of representing it: by tables, graphs, and formulas. Then in Section 1.2 we introduce linear functions and characterize them in terms of the basic property that they change by an equal amount in equal times. Following this line of thought we introduce exponential functions next, in Section 1.3, since they have the equally simple defining property of changing by an equal ratio in equal times. We give modeling applications of both linear and exponential functions. We discuss the particular choice of the base e in Section 1.4, because it is the most commonly used exponential function; we promise an explanation later. In Section 1.5 we introduce power functions, and compare the growth rates of different powers, and of power functions and exponential functions. The discussion of inverse functions in Section 1.6 leads naturally to the introduction of logarithms and the natural logarithm in Sections 1.7 and 1.8. Section 1.9 on combining functions gives a graphical interpretation of addition and multiplication by a constant. Later come trigonometric functions, again with modeling applications, in Section 1.10, and polynomials and rational functions in Section 1.11.

The final section on roots, continuity, and accuracy is optional. It is important if you plan to give real-life max-min problems, where the roots of the derivative are not easy to find analytically. The idea of accuracy to some number of decimal places is important in Chapters 2 and 3, but can be covered then. Whether or not you want to cover a numerical method to finding roots (like bisection) depends on what technology you have.

Computer or Calculator exercises

1. Graph x, x^2, x^3, and x^4 on scales $[-5, 5] \times [-10, 10]$ (to illustrate the general shape, and the behavior of even versus odd), then $[0, 1.2] \times [0, 2]$ (to illustrate small scale behavior), then $[0, 10] \times [0, 10^n]$, $n = 1, 2, 3, 4$ (to illustrate large scale behavior). (If you are doing this in the class room, get the students to tell you what the y-scale should be to clearly separate the various powers.)

2. Graph x^3 against 2^x on $[0, 10]$. Which one is dominant? Which one *looks like* it will dominate ultimately? Change the x-range change to $[0, 100]$, then to $[0, 1,000]$, each time asking the same questions. (Answer: ultimately 2^x dominates, although it doesn't look like it on a small scale.)

3. Plot $f(x) = x^3 - x + 83$ and $g(x) = x^3$ on $[-10, 10]$, then on $[-100, 100]$. What do you see on the larger scale? What point does this illustrate? (Answer: that on a large scale, a polynomial looks like its leading term.)

Exercises

Page 6 # 1; Page 15 # 7; Page 16 # 12; Page 27 # 5; Page 29 # 18; Page 49 # 17; Page 87 # 42; Page 93 # 1.

Chapter 2: The Derivative

Overview

Our purpose is to give the student a practical understanding of the limit definition of the derivative, and its interpretation as an instantaneous rate of change, without muddying the waters with differentiation rules. The student should finish this chapter able to find derivatives numerically by taking arbitrarily fine difference quotients, and to visualize derivatives graphically as the slope of the graph when you "zoom in" (using a calculator), and to interpret the meaning of first and second derivatives in various applications. The student should also understand local linearity and to recognize the derivative as a function in its own right.

Description

The first six sections, up to and including the section on local linearity, form a coherent account of the key concept, and are crucial. In Section 2.1 we show how to capture the concept of instantaneous velocity as a limit of average velocities. Then we formalize this into the definition of the derivative in Section 2.2, and interpret it as a general rate of change and as a slope. We give examples of computing the derivative numerically, estimating it graphically, and deriving it algebraically. In Section 2.3 we introduce the derivative function, and relate the global behavior of the derivative to the global behavior of the function; we go beyond

$$f'(a) > 0 \Rightarrow f \text{ is sloping upward at } x = a$$

to

$$f' \text{ is a spike function} \Rightarrow f \text{ is a step function.}$$

We discuss the standard interpretations of the derivative in Section 2.4, but also give advice on how to interpret it in non-standard situations, and discuss the uses of the Leibniz notation, dy/dx, in thinking about what the derivative means. This section flows naturally on to Section 2.5, where we discuss the second derivative and concavity. In Section 2.6 we introduce the idea that the derivative gives a local linear approximation to a function.

The last two sections are optional digressions on limits and differentiability. Section 2.7 moves the reader a bit closer to the formal definition of limit; Section 2.8 explores points of non-differentiability.

Computer/Calculator exercises

1. Use a graphing program to zoom in on e^{ax} at $x = 0$ for various values of a, and make a conjecture on what the derivative is at $x = 0$.

2. Using your calculator, compute the derivative of $\log(\log(\log x))$ and x^x at $x = 2$.

3. Using your calculator, estimate the rate of change of 10^x with respect to x, when $x = 1, 10$, and 100. Formulate a conjecture and test it out on some other values of x.

Exercises

Page 126 # 8; Page 146 # 14; Page 153 # 7; Page 167 # 9, Page 167 # 10. Page 179 # 20;

Chapter 3: The Definite Integral

Overview

Our purpose is to give the student a practical understanding of the definite integral as a limit of Riemann sums, and to bring out the dualism between the derivative and the definite integral, culminating in the Fundamental Theorem of Calculus. We use the same method as in Chapter 2, of introducing the fundamental concept in depth without going into technique. The motivating problem is computing the total distance traveled from the velocity function. The student should finish the chapter with a good grasp of the definite integral as a limit of Riemann sums, the ability to compute it numerically, and an understanding of how to interpret the definite integral in various contexts.

Description

Note the parallelism between the development here and the development in Chapter 2. In Section 3.1 we introduce the thought experiment of estimating total distance traveled from velocity measurements, the converse of Section 2.1. This leads very naturally to left and right hand sums, and even to accuracy estimates in the case that the velocity function is monotonic. In Section 3.2 we give the precise definition of the definite integral using left and right hand sums and interpret it geometrically as an area. We give all the standard interpretations, including average value, in Section 3.3, and also discuss how to use the notation of the definite integral to interpret its meaning in exotic situations. In Section 3.4 we give the Fundamental Theorem of Calculus in the weak form: if $F'(x) = f(x)$, then

$$\int_a^b f(x)\, dx = F(b) - F(a).$$

This is almost a tautology, given our distance interpretation of the definite integral. In Section 3.5, which is optional, we go into the nature of the limit defining the definite integral.

Computer/Calculator exercises

The students should use a computer or a programmable calculator to calculate lots of Riemann sums with enough subdivisions to give accurate answers. This reinforces the notion that the definite integral is a number, not a strange symbolic object.

1. Page 195 # 5.

2. Page 209 # 6.

Exercises

Page 201 # 2; Page 210 # 13; Page 210 # 14; Page 210 # 15; Page 216 # 16.

Chapter 4: Short-Cuts to Differentiation

Overview

The title is intended to remind the student that the basic methods of differentiation are not to be regarded as easier definitions of the derivative. We find the derivatives of all the functions introduced in Chapter 1, and the rules for differentiating the combinations discussed in Chapter 1. Implicit differentiation is introduced and used to find derivatives of several basic functions. We give informal but mathematically sound justifications, introducing graphical and numerical reasoning where appropriate. The student should finish this chapter with basic proficiency at differentiating, and an understanding in terms of the definition of why the various rules are true.

Description

In Section 4.1 we introduce the notion of having a formula for a derivative function, and illustrate this idea with the example of the derivative of a linear function and the rule for differentiating sums and constant multiples. In Section 4.2 we derive the power rule and show how to differentiate polynomials. In Section 4.3 we show that the derivative of a^x is of the form: (constant)$\cdot(a^x)$, at first by experimenting with the case $a = 2$ and then by a general argument. We define e to be the base that makes the constant 1; otherwise the constant is not identified at this stage. We use a graphical argument in Section 4.4 to suggest the product rule, and then give a formal justification. In Section 4.5 we give an informal justification of the chain rule. In Section 4.6 we find the derivatives of trigonometric functions, at first giving some numerical and graphical evidence for the general formula. Then, in Section 4.7, we give some applications of the chain rule. In Section 4.8 we show how to get derivatives of implicitly defined functions using the chain rule, in particular inverse functions. We find the derivatives of $\sqrt{x}$, $\ln x$, a^x (defined by $\ln f(x) = x \ln a$), and the inverse trigonometric functions. Section 4.9, on the tangent line approximation, is optional but important to those who are looking ahead to Taylor series.

Computer/Calculator exercises

1. How would you use a graphing program to graph the derivative of a function if you don't know a formula for the derivative? Try this out with $f(x) = \sin x$. (Answer: graph $(f(x + 0.0001) - f(x))/0.0001$.)

2. Using the method suggested in (1), graph the derivative of a^x for various values of a. Try to find a value that makes the derivative equal to the original function.

3. (Variation on 2.) Using a spreadsheet, produce a table of values a^x and, in the next column, a table of values of the derivative of a^x (by tabulating $(a^{x+0.001} - a^x)/0.001$). Vary the value of a until the two columns are the same.

Exercises

Page 238 # 28; Page 245 # 31; Page 271 # 23.

Chapter 5: Using the Derivative

Overview

Our aim in this chapter is to train the student to use the derivative in solving problems, rather than to learn a catalogue of application templates. It is not meant to be comprehensive, and you do not need to cover all of it; the student should finish this chapter with the experience of having successfully tackled a few problems that required sustained thought over more than one session.

Description

In Sections 5.1 and 5.2 we discuss how to use the first and second derivatives to analyze the basic global properties of a function: where it is increasing or decreasing; where it is concave up or down; where it has maxima and minima; and where it has inflection points. If your students have thoroughly grasped the material in Chapter 2, you may be able to go quite quickly through these sections. If not, they will be useful review. In Section 5.3 we apply this knowledge to a qualitative analysis of families of curves, such as $e^{-ax} \sin bx$, by seeing how varying the parameters affects the position of the critical points and inflection points. In Section 5.4 we introduce some examples from economics of graphical, qualitative reasoning using the derivative. Section 5.5, on optimization, also contains some non-standard problems where the answer is determined by graphical reasoning. Section 5.6 is an optional supplement to 5.5. Section 5.7 is on Newton's method. Section 5.8 introduces the ideas of antiderivative, differential equation, families of solutions, and initial conditions, through equations of motion. The last section, 5.9, which discusses the equations of motion, is optional.

Computer/Calculator exercises

Use a graphing program (preferably one that accepts parameters, such as University of Arizona's TWIDDLE) to graph $e^{-x^2/a}$ for various different values of a. Describe in a brief sentence the effect of varying a on the shape of the graph. Now find the inflection points of $e^{-x^2/a}$, and relate them to your description.

Exercises

Page 289 # 29; Page 296 # 12 Page 296 # 14; Page 310 # 11; Page 327 # 14; Page 350 # 29 through 31; Page 359 # 40.

Chapter 6: The Integral

Overview

This rather long and complex chapter threads practical skills with theoretical understanding, and needs to be treated with care. The first two sections recapitulate Chapter 3 and state the basic properties of the definite integral. Then come two groups of sections on computing definite integrals: using the fundamental theorem (Sections 6.3–6.7), and by numerical methods (Sections 6.8–6.9). Sections 6.10 and 6.11 are on improper integrals. Having seen that antiderivatives cannot always be found in elementary terms, students with a more theoretical bent will be ready for the triumphant final section on constructing new functions using the definite integral.

Description

In Section 6.1 we recall the definition of the definite integral, and in Section 6.2 we give its basic properties, using graphical reasoning where appropriate. In Section 6.3 we recall the Fundamental Theorem of Calculus, and introduce the notation for the indefinite integral; we then embark on a series of sections dealing with the problem of finding antiderivatives. We treat standard substitutions in Section 6.4, and more complicated ones in Section 6.5, where we also discuss how to change the limits of integration in a definite integral. Section 6.6 covers integration by parts. Section 6.7 shows how to use tables of integrals, with a few examples of how the formulas in such tables are obtained. This concludes the part of the chapter dealing with indefinite integration.

In Section 6.8 we introduce the simpler numerical methods for computing definite integrals, then in Section 6.9 we go into error analysis, and use this analysis to derive Simpson's Rule.

Section 6.10 and 6.11 form a digression on improper integrals. In Section 6.10, antiderivatives are found explicitly; in Section 6.11, convergence is determined by comparison.

Finally, Section 6.12 tackles the problem of finding antiderivatives of functions that do not have antiderivatives in elementary terms. First we show by a graphical argument, using direction fields, that such functions must have antiderivatives, and then we show how these functions may be defined precisely and in a computable way using the definite integral.

Computer/Calculator exercises

For Section 6.11, use SLOPES (from the University of Arizona software) or one of the calculator slope field programs to draw the slope field corresponding to

$$\frac{dy}{dx} = \frac{1}{x}.$$

Draw the curve that follows these slopes and passes through the point $(1, 0)$. What is the y-coordinate on this curve at $x = 2$? Do you recognize this number? Should you?

If you do not have software available, later in the manual copies of the slope fields programs are provided for photocopying.

Exercises

Page 365 # 7; Page 373 # 5; Page 402 # 48; Page 440 # 33; Page 456 # 1.

Chapter 7: Using the Definite Integral

Overview

This chapter has parallel aims to Chapter 5: to show some ways the integral is used without resorting to templates. We start with a discussion of how to set up definite integrals that represent given physical quantities, and then give examples from geometry, physics, probability, and economics. The same comments apply as to Chapter 5: cover a few problems in depth, and encourage the students to make extended and repeated attacks on those problems.

Description

We start in Section 7.1 with a discussion of how formulating the solution of a problem in terms of a definite integral can be useful, and then give in Section 7.2 a number of examples of how to set up such a definite integral. In Section 7.3 we give some standard applications to geometry: volumes and arclength. Since the student by now can integrate numerically, we don't limit the arclength problems to those artificial ones that can only be done in elementary terms. In Section 7.4, we give some applications to physics: work, escape velocity, and fluid pressure. Section 7.5 gives some applications to economics. Section 7.6 explains probability density and its relation to cumulative probability distributions.

Computer/Calculator exercises

Derive the formula

$$A = cr^2$$

for the area of a circle, where

$$c = 2 \int_{-1}^{1} \sqrt{1 - x^2} \, dx.$$

Evaluate the constant c numerically.

Exercises

Page 469 # 15; Page 476 # 4; Page 487 # 22; Page 521 # 8.

Chapter 8: Differential Equations

Overview

This is a brief introduction to differential equations, without too many technicalities. It is intended to show the power of the methods we have developed, in more realistic and complex applications than we have hitherto explored.

Description

Differential equations are introduced in Section 8.1. In Section 8.2 we discuss the general first order differential equation from a graphical point of view using slope fields, and in Section 8.3 we do the same thing from a numerical point of view using Euler's method. Then we introduce the analytic method of separation of variables in Section 8.4. 8.5 covers growth and decay, and 8.6 introduces the use of differential equations for modeling. 8.7 and 8.8 explore models of population growth, including the logistic equation and interacting populations. 8.9 and 8.10 look at oscillations and damped oscillations, respectively. 8.11 discusses the solution of a particular differential equation, using the characteristic equation. 8.12 is an appendix on complex numbers.

Computer/Calculator exercises

A program to draw slope fields and integral curves can be used here to find graphical solutions of differential equations and analyze their behavior as initial conditions are changed.

Exercises

Page 543 # 5; Page 548 # 3; Page 569 # 1; Page 583 # 1 through 7.

Chapter 9: Approximations

Overview

This is a brief introduction to Taylor series and Fourier series via the idea of approximating functions with simpler functions; the Taylor series is a local approximation, the Fourier series a global one. The notion of a convergent series is permitted to evolve naturally out of the investigation of Taylor polynomials. The graphical and numerical points of view are kept at the forefront throughout.

Description

Section 9.1 introduces Taylor polynomials as local approximations, obtained by matching higher derivatives at a point; it shows the approximations graphically and numerically, and brings out the fact that the approximation is better if you take a higher degree polynomial, and if you are closer to the point of expansion. Section 9.2 starts with the natural observation that the Taylor polynomials all fit together in the sense that each is obtained from the last by adding one more term; this leads naturally to the idea of a Taylor series. Intervals of convergence are shown graphically. Section 9.3 is about how to find and use Taylor series. First it discusses (without proof) some methods of deriving new Taylor series from old (e.g. by substitution, multiplication, or integration); then it shows how Taylor expansions are used in physics to analyze physical laws. Section 9.4 discusses the error in the Taylor approximation , and gives Taylor's form of the error. This is used to determine how high to go in the Taylor series to obtained prescribed accuracy over an interval. Finally, Section 9.5 is a brief introduction to Fourier series from a graphical point of view. They are introduced as a global approximation over an interval, as opposed to the local approximation represented by the Taylor series. The justification for the formula for the coefficients is given in an appendix.

Computer/Calculator Exercises

Graph successive terms of the power series for $\sin x$; see the function itself emerge. Graph successive terms of the power series for $\ln x$; the higher you go, the clearer the interval of convergence becomes. Calculate numerically the values of higher and higher Taylor approximations to $\cos(0.1)$ and $\cos 2$; notice how the convergence is much faster closer to 0.

Exercises

Page 633 # 11; Page 634 # 27; Page 635 # 34; Page 642 # 20; Page 642 # 22; Page 649 # 17; Page 649 # 18; Page 656 # 1; Page 656 # 5; Page 657 # 14; Page 665 # 3; Page 665 # 5.

III   The Sections and Exercises

There are many different teaching styles; if you have your own ideas on how to teach a particular section, ignore this and try them out (but let us know how they work). On the other hand, if you have trouble knowing what to do with a particular section, or what the main point is supposed to be, consult the relevant part below. There you may find a suggestion on how to introduce the topic, some extra examples to show, tips on what the students find particularly hard, or a suggestion for a computer lab.

There are many good exercises in the text; hopefully you will be able to use them all eventually. The exercises in the sample syllabi were chosen to reflect (wherever possible) the Rule of Three. Some may also be used as in-class examples. They are *not* necessarily a reasonable number of problems to assign. You may need to adjust the number of problems up or down depending upon the needs of your class and the speed at which you intend to cover the material.

1.1: What's a Function?

Half a class.

Key points

The Rule of Three: representing functions by tables, graphs and formulas.

Ideas for the class

Start with the concept of function, and play around with different examples. Emphasize from the outset that a function is nothing but a rule that uniquely assigns to one number some other number: this rule is not necessarily a "math formula". Students often believe functions and formulas are one and the same, so you could lead off by defining functions in terms of tables and graphs as well, in accordance with the Rule of Three.

To start the ball rolling, take a familiar function, such as $f(x) = x^2$, and present it as a table. Have students guess what rule of assignment the function follows, and then draw the graph. Discuss the merits of each method of representation. The graph is good for seeing global properties at a glance; for example, the function in question, $f(x) = x^2$, can be seen to take only nonnegative values because its graph never goes below the x-axis. Now ask the students to explain how this property shows up in the table (answer: notice that all the numbers in the right hand column are positive). Explain to the students that you would like them to become proficient at noticing properties of a function from a table of its values. (Tables are important because they are often the way that functions arise, for example as tables of measurements of a physical quantity.) Finally, introduce the formula, $f(x) = x^2$, and derive the positivity property from the fact that the square of a negative number is always positive. This illustrates the power of formulas; they are exact and subject to analysis.

Students have trouble reading tables. You have to go quite slowly at the beginning, getting them to observe extremely simple properties such as positivity of the values. Another good thing to do is to give them a table of values and ask them to say where the function is increasing and where it is decreasing. Then graph the same function and check the answer.

Since students are so prone to believing that formulas are the same thing as functions, you might want to deemphasize formulas in your first few classes in favor of tables and graphs.

1.2: Linear Functions

One half to one class.

Key points

Linear functions are fundamental, by virtue of the simple property that characterizes them: they increase by equal amounts in equal intervals.

Ideas for the class

Follow the Rule of Three. Start with a table of values of a linear function, and ask the students to give you the slope, or the equation. It's a good idea to use a real life example such as the Olympic Pole Vault (Page 9) or the success of search and rescue teams (Page 11). Otherwise students will think that you are simply trying to torture them by making a table, then hiding the equation that produced it. You want the class to focus on how the formula is deduced from the table, not on how the table is made from the formula. Students will have trouble at first realizing that they can see the slope (or rate of change) of such a function by looking at the ratio between an increment in y and the corresponding increment in x. (It's important to give some tables whose x-values aren't evenly placed.)

Also, give the students a verbal description of a linear function and ask them to write down its equation. For example: The cost of apples fresh from the orchard is \$20, but it drops by 35¢ a day; write down a function that gives the cost of a case which has been sitting in the store for t days. Again emphasize that the characteristic property of a linear function has been indicated in this verbal description by the constant rate of decrease in the price.

Students should be able to determine from a graph that a slope is approximately 2 or $-1/2$ without computing it from two points. (You might be surprised how many students can't do this.) If you want to calculate some slopes, have different students pick different pairs of points to do so. Point out that a characteristic property of linear functions is that the slope is the same regardless of the points chosen.

Students find it difficult to think of linear functions as functions rather than as straight lines. They find it difficult to recognize linearity from the table of values of a linear function. They also find it quite difficult to model using linear functions; it is worth going over one of the examples from the text in detail.

The terms "increasing" and "decreasing" are also introduced in this section. Be sure to stress that these definitions apply as the independent variable goes from left to right. Some students are confused about this—they say, for example, that $f(x) = x^2$ increases for negative x. After all, the curve is going up from the origin; it's only natural to make this sort of mistake at first.

1.3: Exponential Functions

One half to one class.

Key points

Exponential functions are also characterized by a simple basic property: they increase by equal ratios in equal intervals. (This can be contrasted with the constant absolute change of linear functions.)

Ideas for the class

Start with a table of values of 2^t at $t = 0, 1, 2, \ldots$. This could be the population of a colony of bacteria that is doubling every hour. Point out that the y-values double every time, hence the 2 in the base of the exponential function. Now give a table of values of, say, $2 \cdot (1.1)^t$ for the same t-values, but without the formula. Ask the students how they would decide if this is also an exponential function (answer: take ratios of successive values to see if they are the same each time). One can see that the constant in front is 2 by looking at the value at $t = 0$. (Note: students have particular trouble coming up with a formula from a table when the value at $t = 0$ is not given, and if you have time you may want to do such an example.) Again, an example using real data always helps: perhaps population projections for a local community.

Point out that given a table of values for a mystery function (with equally spaced x-values), you can test it for linearity by subtracting successive y values, while you can test to see if it is an exponential function by taking ratios of successive y-values. Demonstrate the explosive growth of exponential functions both by tabulating values and by examining graphs on different scales using a graphing program. Practice deriving the formula from a table, or from particular values. Be sure to also give examples of exponential functions which are decreasing and ones that increase to a horizontal asymptote.

Concavity is introduced in this section. Give examples of increasing and decreasing functions of all possible concavities (up, down, and straight lines). Try to connect concavity with increasing/decreasing rates of change (this function is "increasing at an increasing rate"), but don't get too technical.

Students often find this material surprisingly hard. They have had little experience with exponential functions, and are often not comfortable with percents, which are important here. In particular, they find the formula for exponential functions (on Page 23) difficult. Familiarize students very well with exponential functions in general before getting to the next section and discussing e.

1.4: The Number e

Half a class.

Key points

The base e is just another number; its naturalness as a base for exponentials will become clear later. By varying the constant k in e^{kt} you can achieve varying growth rates.

Ideas for the class

A practical way of introducing e^x is to point out that it has its own button on the student's calculator. Be honest that there is no great justification *yet* for singling out e as a base and calling it natural. The justification in terms of compound interest is there if you want to use it, but be careful; you don't want students to come away with the impression that the naturalness of e has something to do with its applications to economics. Compound interest *is* useful in explaining why the constant k in e^{kt} is called the exponential growth rate.

Students are bound to confuse the formulas for compounded and continually compounded interest: they don't understand why you must add 1 to r in the former but not in the latter. Explain this by noting that an increasing exponential function (such as a bank balance) must have a base greater than 1. For compounded interest, that base is $1 + r$; for continuous compounding, it is e^r.

Keep the concept of limit informal to the extent that you introduce it here. Let students approach limits (no pun intended!) intuitively. By way of illustration, on Page 36, students are encouraged to use their calculators to show that for very large values of n,

$$\left(1 + \frac{0.07}{n}\right)^n \approx e^{0.07}.$$

Show students how to verify this on their calculators.

Even though we haven't done logarithms yet, it is worth mentioning at this stage that any exponential function can be expressed with base e. A good computer lab or graphing calculator exercise is to find by trial and error the constant k that makes the graph of e^{kt} match the graph of 2^t, or use any type of calculator to approximate k so that $e^k = 2$. Another good exercise is to get the students to find doubling times experimentally.

This section could be covered with section 1.3, if there is time, or in the same session as section 1.5.

1.5: Power Functions

Half a class or a whole computer lab.

Key points

How different powers compare, on large and small scales. Basic shapes of graphs of power functions. Increasing exponential functions grow more quickly than power functions.

Ideas for the class

Ideally, this is a class in which to draw lots of graphs on the computer or the graphing calculator. For example, you can make classroom demonstrations from computer exercises (1) and (2) described in the section of this manual about Chapter 1. Don't be afraid of being too elementary; you would be amazed how little ability the students have to picture even simple functions like power functions. Briefly review odd and even integral powers as well as zero and negative powers and fractional powers.

Even better, if you have the facilities, devote the entire class to a computer lab, where you walk around looking over the students shoulders and getting them to do the work. For example, get them to do the exercise on choosing different viewing rectangles to get different pictures of x^4 and 3^x (Page 49 # 17). Students find it quite hard to understand the way the choice of scale affects the dominance of one function over another; they are used to thinking of functions in terms of a single picture. Demonstrate, that for large x, e^x will overwhelm x^n for all n. Help students select appropriate window settings early on. Don't underestimate the extent to which the computer or calculator can confuse a student!

Unfortunately, you may not have the facilities to give this kind of class. If not, the graphs in the text are good and fairly easy to reconstruct on the blackboard. But, if at all possible, have students use computer labs or graphing calculators.

1.6: Inverse Functions

One class or skip.

Key points

The concept of an inverse function.

Ideas for the class

Too often students have a purely algebraic understanding of inverse functions: they know how to solve an equation for y then swap x and y, but they don't know what they are doing. There are several ways to get around this.

Inverses lend themselves beautifully to the Rule of Three. Draw a mystery function on the board and ask for, say, $f^{-1}(5)$ or $f^{-1}(2)$. Then impress upon them that since the point $(1, 5)$ is on the graph of f, $(5, 1)$ is on the graph of f^{-1}. Sketch the function f^{-1} from this sort of deduction, then draw the reflecting line $y = x$. This will show that the graph of f suffices to determine that of f^{-1}, and will doubtlessly impress everyone. This same interpretation can also be made numerically by simply writing out f and f^{-1} in tabular form, as in the text, and noting that the table for f^{-1} is obtained from that of f by reversing the x and y columns.

Application problems are particularly useful here because we can get away from the x and y and see the reversal more clearly. The section on Page 50, which gives times for Arturo Barrios's world record 10 kilometer run is a case in point. Distance (in meters) in the original function gives elapsed time (in seconds); in the inverse, the elapsed time yields the distance run.

Another way to describe the inverse function is in purely operational terms: the inverse function to f is the function that undoes whatever f does. For example, if f transforms a frog into a prince, then f^{-1} would begin with the prince and return the frog. For a more mathematical example, let $f(x) = 1/(x + 1)$, and determine the inverse verbally without doing any algebra. Just say out loud what f does: it adds 1 to x then inverts the result. So the inverse function must invert first, then subtract 1; i.e., the inverse function is $g(x) = (1/x) - 1$. Note that this requires students to decompose functions. The more practice they get doing this, the better—they'll need it (in spades!) for the chain rule, for example.

1.7–8: Logarithms, Natural Logarithms

One class.

Key points

The logarithm as the inverse of the exponential; using the logarithm to solve equations involving exponentials. Getting practice using the calculator to solve equations which can't be solved analytically.

Ideas for the class

Many students have little or no understanding of logarithms. Start by drawing a graph of 10^x and reading off the values of $\log_{10} x$. Discuss how the slow growth of $\log_{10} x$ follows from the rapid growth of 10^x; illustrate this by asking how large x needs to be to get 10^x equal to a thousand, a million, a billion, etc. Emphasize the inverse relation between the exponential and the logarithm. Compare their graphs and explain why they are symmetrical about the line $y = x$. Make sure that students have a basic picture in their minds of the graph of the logarithm, and compare it with power functions and exponentials. They should be building up a catalogue of graphs to go with their library of functions.

You can give the following rule of thumb to decide whether a graph represents a logarithm or an exponential function: an exponential function has a horizontal asymptote, and a logarithmic function has a vertical asymptote. (This will help students who have trouble telling apart $y = 1 - e^{-x}$ and $y = \ln x$, for example.)

Do a number of examples using the logarithm to solve for an exponent (e. g. "How long will it be until the population reaches. . .?") It's always worth using real data on the population of countries or cities that the students are familiar with.

If you did the exercise suggested under Section 1.4 about experimentally finding k so that $e^{kt} = 2^t$, you can now find the k precisely using natural logarithms and a calculator. It is worth repeating the point here that any exponential can be expressed in terms of one with base e, and showing how this can be done using natural logarithms.

Example 5 of the text (page 59), solving $1 + x = 2^x$ and $1 + x = 5^x$, is a nice assurance that logarithms don't magically erase the need for trial and error techniques. If you have the technology, you can have the students approximate a solution to this equation once they see that logs are of no use here. Discuss how to determine the accuracy of a given numerical solution. When solving $f(x) = 0$, it's easy for students to confuse finding x to 2 decimal places with getting the first 2 decimal places of $f(x)$ to be zero.

1.9: New Functions from Old

One class, or part of a class and emphasize and review material in later sections.

Key points

Graphical interpretation of linear combinations of functions, modeling interpretation of composition of functions. Basic manipulations of graphs, including shifts, flips, and stretches.

Ideas for the class

It's very important for students to recognize basic manipulations of the functions in their library. They should be comfortable with the following facts, and know how to use them: $f(x) + k$ and $f(x + k)$ represent vertical and horizontal shifts; $-f(x)$ and $f(-x)$ represent vertical and horizontal flips; $kf(x)$ and $f(kx)$ represent vertical and horizontal distortions, either "stretches" or "shrinks" depending on the magnitude of k. You can use the Rule of Three to demonstrate these. Starting with a table of values for $f(x)$, make new tables of $f(x+1)$, $f(x)+1$, $-f(x)$, $f(-x)$, etc. Compare the ensuing graphs, and discuss. Then give a formula for f, and derive formulas for related functions. (This also gives a good review of functional notation.) A function like $f(x) = x^2 - 4x + 7$ is a good example, as it is a parabola with vertex $(2, 3)$ and thus undergoes obvious changes when flipped or shifted. Trigonometric functions are also nice, but as they won't have been covered yet, you'll have to rely on calculators to graph $\sin x$.

Have students identify (by eye!) where the functions being studied are concave up or down.

1.10: The Trigonometric Functions

One class.

Key points

The basic picture of a sine curve as an infinitely repeating wave; its use to represent periodic phenomena. Amplitude, period, radians, odd and even functions.

Ideas for the class

Work entirely in radians: make sure that students' calculators are set to radians.

Start by drawing the graph of $\sin x$ on the blackboard. Point out its amplitude (1) and its period (2π). Then ask what you need to do to it to, say, double its amplitude or halve its period. Move on from there to examples where you try to construct sine curves with specific amplitudes and periods. For example, draw a sine curve on the blackboard and ask your students to write down its equation (see Page 85 #35). Or, give a table of values of a sine function and ask for the approximate amplitude and phase shift; get the students to make conjectures on what the function is and then check them on their calculators (the table of values for F, G, and H in Page 87 #42 are examples). Or, ask for the periods of various real-life phenomena (see Page 84 #23–Page 84 #24). For a computer demonstration on composition of functions, compare the graphs of $\sin(e^x)$ and $e^{\sin x}$, and explain their shape in terms of the basic properties of the sine and the exponential: $\sin(e^x)$ is the sine of something which increases more and more rapidly, hence it oscillates faster and faster; $e^{\sin x}$ is the exponential of something which oscillates regularly between 1 and -1, hence it oscillates regularly between e and e^{-1}.

Discuss inverse trig functions and range restrictions. (This has proven so problematic on occasion that professors have resorted to making their students recite the definition of arcsine *out loud!*) If you have time, show them some fun graphs, like Example 5 on Page 83 and Example 6 on Page 83.

1.11: Polynomials and Rational Functions

Half to most of a class.

Key points

Flexibility of polynomial graphs on a small scale; basic resemblance to power functions on a large scale. Varying the coefficients to produce particular graphs.

Ideas for the class

Polynomials are very useful for representing shapes because they are so flexible; you might mention that bits of cubic polynomials form the basic drawing elements in many computer drafting programs. (Curves pieced together from bits of cubics are called "cubic splines".)

Do examples where coefficients have to be varied to fit a quadratic or cubic to a particular situation. For example: say you have a parabolic mirror which is 2 meters wide and 5 cm deep at its center; write down a quadratic polynomial whose graph gives the cross section of the mirror. This is a good exercise because the students are required to set up the coordinate axes themselves.

You will probably find the students are not very familiar with twiddling the coefficients to produce a polynomial with a given shape. They are used to being asked 'What is the shape of $y = -x^2$,' but they are not used to being asked 'How do you make an upside-down parabola?' They may not understand the effect varying the leading coefficient has on the width of the parabola; explain this numerically: if the leading coefficient is large, then only a small x-value is required to produce a large y-value, so the parabola is narrow.

To show that on a large scale polynomials look like their leading terms, get the students to do a computer or calculator lab where they compare the two on various scales. First, give them $f(x) = x^3 - x + 83$ and $g(x) = x^3$ to plot on $[-10, 10]$, then on $[-100, 100]$. Then give them just the polynomial, and ask them to identify the leading term, then plot it on the same axes. If you give them a polynomial where the terms are out of order, so that the leading term is in the middle, it helps get the point across.

Note that many calculators and computer programs give confusing results when asked to graph asymptotes. (They might connect the two branches of the curve, for example.) If students are using a machine to try to produce something like Figure 1.79, Page 93, be aware of, and be sure to discuss, the limitations of their technology.

Again, have students identify (by eye!) regions where the functions studied are increasing, decreasing, and concave up or down.

1.12: Roots, Continuity, and Accuracy

Half a class or a whole computer lab or skip entirely.

Key points

Application of all three viewpoints, algebraic, graphical, and numerical, to the problem of finding roots.

Ideas for the class

Do some of the University of Arizona projects which require a root finder. Give each student a different cubic polynomial (coefficients the last four digits of their social security or college ID number) and get them to find the largest real root.

2.1: How do we Measure Speed?

A half to a whole class.

Key points

Instantaneous velocity as a limit of average velocities, and as a slope on the position-versus-time graph.

Ideas for the class

Focus solely on measuring velocity in this class.

If you want something interesting around which to build a discussion, try the following idea (from David Lovelock). There is a Dover book of the first "motion pictures" ever of animals in motion, by Edward Muybridge. Each page has a series of frames from a movie of some animal running against a grid background, so that you can measure their progress from frame to frame. Make an overhead slide of one of these pages and ask your students how fast the animal is moving in a given frame. It immediately becomes clear that you need *two* frames to get a velocity, and it is natural to choose two adjacent frames.

An easier, and recommended example is something being thrown straight up in the air. The text uses a grapefruit: how fast is it moving at different times.

When you plot your data (height above ground as a function of time), explain the graph very carefully. Some students will believe that what you have drawn is the trajectory of the grapefruit—i.e., its path through physical space. They're (not unreasonably) assuming that the horizontal axis is spatial. Make sure that you convince them that the actual trajectory of the grapefruit is straight up and down, not arch-shaped. (Why not use a real grapefruit?) Mark units on the axes, and ask if the units are realistic; get students to read from the graph how high the object went, how fast it was thrown, if the height and velocity fit their experience and are consistent with each other.

You should probably work with a table of data without using any formula. If you use a formula, students will resort to "short cuts" — applying the rules of differentiation some of them have no doubt memorized. There is also the danger that you could end up trying to justify the formula: good in a physics class, but not so good in a calculus class.

It's important to compute various average velocities on the board, or have students work them out on their calculators, before you get to the idea of instantaneous velocity. Tell your students that the slope of the secant line on your graph represents the average velocity of the grapefruit for some given interval of time. This is not obvious to students. They sometimes identify the average velocity with the secant line itself, rather than with its slope. Of course, this doesn't make sense, but you may often find that students need help in separating one feature of a graph from all the others. Emphasize that the secant line segment represents how the grapefruit would be moving if its velocity were constant over some interval, and that the slope represents this constant velocity.

When you begin to discuss instantaneous velocity, make the argument that looking at the function on smaller and smaller intervals reveals an increasingly linear curve, one that resembles more and more its own tangent line. Here, if you have the technology, it might be useful to have students zoom in on various curved functions on their calculators until they look linear.

Be sure to state explicitly that the difference quotient is just a disguised version of the slope formula they've always known, $\frac{\Delta y}{\Delta x}$. Taking the limit is necessary only because the slope being measured is at a point on a curve and not of a straight line.

In a discussion section, it may be fun to spend some time discussing the paradox of the notion of instantaneous velocity.

2.2: The Derivative

A whole class.

Key points

Practical understanding of the limit definition of the derivative.

Ideas for the class

In today's class, you should consider functions whose rates of change *aren't* velocities. See Example 1, Page 128, and Example 2, Page 129.

It is important to spend some time on this, and do lots of examples, numerical, graphical, and algebraic, along the same lines as the ones given in the text. Begin by reviewing the difference quotient, the secant line, and the idea of rate of change of a function. When you define the derivative of $f(x)$ at a, make sure you emphasize that the definition is at a point, so that the derivative is just a number. If you have the technology, "zoom in" on a graph until it becomes straight; the slope of this line is the derivative. Calculate a few derivatives this way. Your students will begin to feel at sea, especially the ones who have had calculus before. They will want to know when you are going to start teaching them 'real' calculus. Most of the ones with calculus experience will be accustomed to thinking of the derivative as a function of x. Some may be able to find derivatives of very complicated functions analytically and yet be unable to explain clearly what the derivative of a function at a point means. The important thing is not to do everything for them; get them to answer questions. If it takes time, allow the time. Above all, make sure they understand that the derivative is approximated by a difference quotient, and that it represents the slope.

Ask your students for the derivative of x^x at $x = 2$. The ones who have had calculus before might say 4 ($= 2 \cdot 2^{2-1}$). Then do it numerically, by calculating the difference quotient

$$\frac{2.001^{2.001} - 2^2}{0.001} \approx 6.779.$$

Compute derivatives of other functions numerically. Try to avoid "easy" functions like x^2 if possible, as this will confirm the prejudices of the experienced students, who will just scream out, "$2x$!"

Hand out photocopies of a graph drawn on graph paper (for example, $\sin x^2$), and ask your students for the value of the derivative at various points, or at what points the derivative is -1.

Or combine the graphical and numerical approaches: draw the graph of e^{-x} on the blackboard, and ask what you can say about the derivative of e^{-x} at $x = 0$ just from the graph (answer: it is negative, and is about -1). Then compute some difference quotients, with $h = \pm.1, \pm.01, \ldots$.

Do computer exercise (1) from the section on Chapter 2 as a classroom demonstration or a computer lab. (An instructive mistake that can be made in this exercise is to fail to observe that the scales on the x and y axes are different.)

Of course, you should do some simple algebraic examples as well. When going through the examples, and when assigning homework, be sure to remind students that derivatives should be found without "short cuts", at least for the time being.

A word about notation: in sections 2.2 and 2.3, the text writes f' almost exclusively for the derivative of f. The Leibniz notation $\frac{dy}{dx}$ is introduced in Section 2.2 but not used much until section 2.4.

You should not assume that by the end of this class they have completely understood the idea of the derivative. It will need to be repeated many times throughout the course.

2.3: The Derivative Function

A half to a whole class.

Key points

Understanding the derivative function. Seeing how the shape of the graph of a function affects the shape of the graph of its derivative.

Ideas for the class

Draw a graph (for example, a generic cubic) on the blackboard, and ask your students to figure out the general shape of its derivative function. Most students will need a lot of practice moving from point to point along the curve, sketching small tangent lines, estimating their slope, and plotting them on the graph of f'. (It might be useful to hand out photocopies of the graph so that students can measure slopes at their desks, using pencils and rulers.) Each time you do this, point out that the derivative graph is above the axis along the intervals where the function is increasing, below it where the function is decreasing, and crosses it in between, where the function is horizontal. It is also helpful to point out that the slope is steepest (positively and negatively) where the concavity changes. Don't be surprised if you get questions about how one knows the concavity of the derivative graph (the answer is you don't, because one can't "see" the third derivative on the graph of the original function).

Students find graphical differentiation quite difficult. One way of giving them some practice is to ask each student to draw the graph of a function on a piece of paper, put their name on it, and pass it to their neighbor. The neighbor draws the graph of the derivative on a different piece of paper, copying the name of the first person on it. The derivative graph is passed to another neighbor, while the original graph is passed to its author. The third student sketches a graph of the original function from the derivative, and then compares it with the original. (This is an exercise which may be used later in the semester for review; even at the end of the term, it will not be easy for many.) This exercise produces a lot of noise, but also a lot of mathematical discussion.

Sketch the graph of $\tan^{-1} x$ and its derivative on the same axes, without identifying the functions, and ask them which function is the derivative of which. The way to see the answer in a flash is to observe that exactly one of these functions is always increasing, and exactly one of them is always positive.

Try the same sort of thing with tables of values; again, you want them to be able to look for global properties, such as regions where the function is increasing or decreasing.

Find the formula for the derivative of $f(x) = x^2$ quickly. There are two ways to do it: algebraically, and by making a table of f' at different values of x and looking for the pattern. For the sake of students who already know the shortcuts, you may wish to point out that the way you prove that the shortcuts work is to use difference quotients. It's worth making this point because some students have had the shortcuts hammered so forcefully into their heads that they believe such shortcuts represent the underpinnings of all of calculus.

Give them the graph of a sine curve as the derivative of a mystery function, and ask what it tells them about the graph of the original function; then give them the same graph shifted up so that it never dips below the x-axis. Ideally (but this may be difficult) you want to wean them away from a point by point approach to a global approach; you want them to look at the second graph and say: Well, whatever else is going on the function is always increasing because the derivative is always positive. This is also the point of the spike function example in the text; they should look at the spike and say: Oh, it must zoom up at that point.

It takes quite some time for students to come to terms with the graph of the derivative function. For this reason, resist the temptation to make too many connections for them at this point. For example, unless someone in class points out the relation between zeroes of the derivative and extrema of the original function, or between the extrema of the derivative and the critical points of the original function, don't do so yourself. If these issues do arise, don't let them overtake the discussion. Chalk them up as perceptive observations that merit future consideration, and then move on.

2.4: Interpretations of the Derivative

Half a class or assign for reading, then assign relevant homework problems, then spend a class going over the homework.

Key points

Using the difference quotient to interpret the meaning of the derivative.

Ideas for the class

This section is very difficult for the students. It's not that they necessarily have trouble understanding various interpretations of the derivative once you have explained them, but they find it very difficult to come up with their own answers. For example, consider Page 153 #7: if $g(v)$ is the fuel efficiency of a car going at v miles per hour, what is the practical meaning of the statement $g'(55) = -0.54$? We would like the students to be able to seize on the negative sign as the key part of the right hand side of this question, but they are generally so terrified of all those numbers that they don't even notice it. Help students think about what the units of the derivative can tell them.

The students are probably not going to get much out of a class on this section if they don't bring something with them. One possibility is to assign the section for reading, and then get the students to discuss the examples in the text, and air their misunderstandings. Another would be to go over some of the examples, then save most of the talking until after the students have struggled with some of the key problems (Page 153 # 8, Page 154 # 12 and Page 167 # 9). Make sure you have struggled with them yourself first.

If you wish to lecture on this section before assigning homework, you should almost certainly cover acceleration. (Save second derivatives for later!) A good way to do this is to return to the data you used for the grapefruit thrown into the air, since this example is already familiar to students. This time, provide a table of velocity as a function of time, and have them find the average change in velocity over given intervals. Be very careful when you graph your data, because students have not seen a graph of velocity versus time yet. They may confuse it with plots of distance versus time or with trajectories. By clearing up their confusion now, though, you can save them and yourself difficulty later when other "abstract" graphs are drawn.

Stress using the difference quotient when appropriate, and take time to give students some more practice in comparing the graph of the derivative with the original function. The mathematical content of this class should be nearly identical to the content of the last class; only the examples used should be different. Take a look at the $\frac{dy}{dx}$ notation in this class, as it is used quite a bit in this section of the text. Emphasize that although the notation looks like a fraction, it isn't; canceling the d's makes no sense.

2.5: The Second and Higher Derivatives

One class.

Key points

Interpretation of the second derivative as concavity and acceleration.

Ideas for the class

The explanation of why the sign of the second derivative gives the concavity is fun to give and worth going over carefully. Let students write out (in clear, concise English) their own explanation of what the second derivative tells you about concavity.

Mention that a straight line is neither concave up nor concave down, and has second derivative zero.

Draw two possible position versus time graphs of an accelerating car; both increasing and starting from zero, but make one concave up and one concave down. Ask which is correct. Answer: the concave up one, since the acceleration is positive. The other one illustrates something that starts with a positive velocity and brakes.

Keep in mind that students easily confuse *increasing first derivative* with *first derivative of increasing magnitude*. They tend to associate any graph which gets "steeper and steeper" with an increasing first derivative, even if the first derivative is negative and decreasing (say $y = -e^x$).

They also sometimes think that decreasing functions can't have increasing first derivatives, so show them e^{-x} and discuss. If the confusion persists, convince them that it makes sense to say that the sequence $\{-1, -2, -3, \ldots\}$ is decreasing while the sequence $\{-5, -4, -3, \ldots\}$ is increasing; it can help if you draw a vertical number line (like a thermometer) as a reference. Do some examples like Example 1, Page 156.

It would be nice to look at an example in which the acceleration isn't constant.

2.6: Local Linearity and Linear Approximations

One class.

Key points

Local linearization obtained by zooming in on graph at $(a, f(a))$.

Ideas for the class

Once again explain how the graph of any differentiable function looks like a straight line if you zoom in on it at a point. A graphing calculator can make this exercise quite convincing. Then derive the local linear approximation by considering how to compute the y-coordinate of a point on that straight line whose x-coordinate is $a + h$ (start at $f(a)$ and add h times the slope). Tell them that since lines are just about the easiest functions to work with, the idea of local linearization is to approximate a function by a line that closely resembles it.

Explain how to spot the derivative in equations like $(1.01)^2 = 1.0201$, $\ln(1.1) = 0.095$, and $\cos(3.15159) = -1.0000$. Answer:

$$(1.01)^2 = 1 + 2 \times 0.01 + \text{higher order terms},$$

so the derivative of x^2 at $x = 1$ is 2. By similar reasoning the derivative of $\ln x$ at $x = 1$ is 1.

This is a place where you can bring in data from the newspapers, and discuss extrapolating it.

2.7: Notes on the Limit

Brief discussion, skip entirely, or set for reading.

Key points

A discussion of the concept of limit, without ϵ's or δ's.

Ideas for the class

Play around with the idea of limit on a calculator: ask the class to compute

$$\lim_{x \to 0} \frac{\cos x - 1}{x^2}$$

on a calculator. This is a good example because you really need to try a few different x values to see that this limit is approaching -0.5, since it approaches via -0.49, and if you put x too small the calculator will just spit out 0 because of round-off error. Do graphical examples also.

2.8: Notes on Differentiability

Brief discussion, skip entirely, or set for reading.

Key points

Discussion of points of non-differentiability.

Ideas for the class

Zoom in on sharp corners using a graphing program. You can show that $f(x) = |x|$ has no derivative at the origin both because there is no way to make sense of the difference quotient, and also because there is no way to draw a unique tangent line. Ask students what happens if you try to use local linearization to approximate $f(x) = |x|$ near the origin.

3.1: How do we Measure Distance Traveled?

One class.

Key points

Read this section carefully. To calculate total distance traveled, given the velocity function, you add up estimates of distance traveled over small time intervals. This leads to the idea of a Riemann sum as an approximation for the exact distance, and eventually to a precise formula in terms of a limit of Riemann sums.

Ideas for the class

Explicitly point out the parallelism between this section and 2.1. Consider only monotonic increasing distance functions (i.e. positive velocities) for now.

Go over the thought experiment in the text, but using different numbers. Better still, have the students try a problem or two for homework, before you talk about it. Start with a table of velocities—don't use any graphs at first. Have students use left and right-hand sums to give lower and upper bounds for distance traveled. Argue in an intuitive fashion, without reference to RIGHT and LEFT yet. Demonstrate that more data (intermediate velocities) will make the lower and upper bounds closer together. As much as possible, elicit the answers from the students themselves; get them to give the initial distance estimates. Spend some time leading them to the realization that the difference between the left and right sums is $(f(b) - f(a))\Delta x$; this makes it clear that the left and right sums (which bracket the true distance if the velocity function is monotonic) are converging together to a common limit.

Above all, don't rush them. Students will have trouble reading such formulae as

(Total distance traveled between A and B) $\approx f(t_0)\Delta t + f(t_1)\Delta t + f(t_2)\Delta t + \cdots + f(t_{n-1})\Delta t$

unless you are quite patient. Don't introduce $\sum$ notation yet. Make sure that the connection between whatever formalism you see fit to introduce and what was going on at the start of class is as obvious as possible: draw lots of graphs. As always, don't get bogged down in limits.

When you make a graph of velocity versus time, be alert for confusion. Students are accustomed to graphs of distance versus time and will be prone to treat the new graph as such. Even those who understand what the axes mean may be confused by the fact that an *area* on a graph is representing a *distance*. While they may be used to the idea of letting a length represent any number of quantities, they don't have much experience letting an area represent anything other than area. It helps to remind them that on such a graph vertical length represents velocity, whereas horizontal length represents time.

3.2: The Definite Integral

One class, or combine with previous class.

Key points

The definite integral as a limit of Riemann sums; practical use of the definition.

Ideas for the class

Since you'll need $\sum$ notation, it's a good idea to introduce it at the start of class. Practice it in some context other than integration (evaluate a few finite sums, for example). Once students are comfortable with the notation, return to integration.

Start off by computing a few Riemann sums by hand: compute $\int_0^1 e^{-x^2}\, dx$ by making a table of values of the function for $x = 0, 0.1, 0.2, \ldots, 1$, adding up all values but the last one, multiply by $\Delta x = 0.1$; similarly for the right sum; for a good estimate, take the average. Students should get this basic method down cold, without the need for a special integrating program. Make sure you do an example where $\Delta x \neq 0.1$, such as $\int_1^3 (\sin x)/x\, dx$. (A common mistake is to always multiply by 0.1, or to forget the Δx altogether.) Emphasize that the definite integral is a number (the above examples will help). Some students think that it is an antiderivative; many others think that $\int_a^b f(x)\, dx$ is *defined* to be $F(b) - F(a)$.

Write out the formulae you obtained during the last class for left and right-hand sums and help students figure out how to express these using the $\sum$ notation. (Make sure they understand what the subscript on the variable t means in the expression $\sum_{i=0}^{n-1} f(t_i)\Delta t$, but try not to lose sight of the forest for the trees: the goal is to understand integration, not to use the notation.)

To show the convergence of Riemann sums, you will need to use a program that computes Riemann sums with larger numbers of subdivisions. Ultimately, students should be able to give you an accurate answer for any definite integral using such a program.

If issues of convergence for non-monotonic functions arises, convince students that any definite integral can be evaluated by first breaking the domain into intervals on which f is monotonic and working on these smaller intervals.

Some students will have had calculus and will want to know why you aren't doing it 'the easy way', i.e., using the Fundamental Theorem. Neither of the examples above can be done this way, since the integrands do not have elementary antiderivatives. However, there is no need to go overboard with such examples; do a few simple ones like $\int_0^1 x^2\, dx$ also.

If you have any time left, and are using a programmable calculator, help students to key in a program on their calculator which will calculate definite integrals. In any event, refer them to the program which calculates Riemann sums, or provide them with one of your own. Tell them that using the calculator will be necessary for evaluating integrals on their homework and on tests.

3.3: Interpretations of the Definite Integral

One class.

Key points

Basic interpretations of the definite integral as total change, area, and average value. Using the notation to interpret the definite integral.

Ideas for the class

The interpretation as total change is basic. (However, do not get into the Fundamental Theorem of Calculus.) Most of the students probably still have not grasped the reasoning by which we showed that the definite integral has this interpretation, so it is important in examples to repeat the process of breaking the interval up, computing the change on each piece, and adding up the pieces. The point in this class is to carry out this process in specific examples, particularly examples in which the rate is not a velocity, like Examples 1 and 5. There is no harm in basing the class on these examples, or on some of the homework exercises, such as Page 201 #2 through Page 201 #4. But here are some other ideas.

You could start the class with a disguised repeat of the thought experiment from Section 3.1. For example, give a table of measurements of the flow rate of water through a pipe:

time(min)	rate (gallons/min)
0	50
1	31
2	19
3	12
4	8
5	7

Table 0.1: Flow rate of water through a pipe.

Ask the class how many gallons flowed past during the first minute, how many the second, etc. Then suppose that the function $R = f(t)$ gives the flow rate at any instant, and write down the integral $\int_0^5 f(t)\,dt$ for the total amount that flows past in five minutes.

A variation on the above would be to present a graph (with grid squares marked so areas can be estimated) instead of a table. Go through the same process of estimating the amount that has flowed past during each one minute interval, but do it by counting grid squares. This reinforces the visual interpretation of the Riemann sum definition.

Of course, area should also be discussed as an interpretation in its own right. Beware of the problem of area below the x-axis; when they learn that the definite integral computes such an area as a negative number, some students think they have to add a negative sign somewhere in their answers to definite integrals.

The area interpretation can be used in other interpretations. For example, draw axes, label the horizontal one as time (in seconds), mark $t = 0$ and $t = 60$ on the axis, and then draw a graph representing the acceleration of a car starting from rest (it should start out some point on the y-axis and taper off to zero; it's got children on board). Explain, or get them to explain, why area under the graph represents the velocity the car is traveling after the first minute (it is the definite integral of acceleration, and acceleration is the rate of change of velocity, so this comes from the interpretation of the definite integral as total change). Now ask what is a sensible value to mark on the y-axis as the initial acceleration. Most students probably have a rough idea what a sensible value for total area is, since they have an idea how fast a car would be traveling after a minute; on the other hand, most of them probably have no idea what a sensible value of the initial acceleration is, and this provides a nice way to estimate it.

For students who continue to resist thinking of the definite integral as a number, something like Page 200 # 1 makes an excellent on-board exercise.

3.4: The Fundamental Theorem of Calculus

One class.

Key points

Students should make a start at understanding the Fundamental Theorem of Calculus.

Ideas for the class

Note that this section comes well before the notation for the indefinite integral is introduced. Too often students end up thinking of the theorem as the definition of the definite integral; that is what we want to avoid.

Many students make the initial mistake of thinking the fundamental theorem says

$$\int_a^b f(x)\, dx = f(b) - f(a).$$

You need to drive the point home that it involves a function *and* its derivative. This is the point of Page 210 # 13 through Page 210 # 15. It is perhaps better not to ask students to find antiderivatives until you are sure they understand this point. Write down a function, give them the formula for its derivative, then compute a definite integral of the derivative using Riemann sums, then verify the fundamental theorem.

The fundamental theorem of calculus, as we have presented it, is a simple extension of the interpretation of the definite integral as total change. There is, however, an important new element. In stating the theorem, we are forced to introduce parameters a and b for the endpoints. This will later become extremely important, when we allow b to vary in order to construct antiderivatives using the definite integral. So it is a good idea now to do some examples where various different choices of a and b are considered in relation to a fixed integrand. This is the point of Page 216 # 16 and Page 215 # 15.

Help students make the connection between such graphs as Figure 3.23 and 3.24 on Pages 206 and 208. This will be very challenging for most of them.

3.5: Further Notes on the Limit

Small part of a class, or skip entirely.

Key points

Discussion of the sort of limit used to define the definite integral, and how it differs from the sort used to define the derivative.

4.1-2: Formulas for Derivative Functions, Powers and Polynomials

One class.

Key points

Don't neglect to draw graphs and use geometric arguments where possible.

Ideas for the class

This is all quite straightforward and your students will be relieved to have got onto the easy stuff (and you too, maybe!). Just remember that some of them may be seeing it for the first time. Don't spend too long on any one topic. Also, it is always worthwhile using a geometric argument if there is one; for example, to find the derivative of a linear function, or to verify the rule for the derivative of constant multiple. Whenever you compute a derivative using the definition, draw a graph first and ask what the answer ought to look like before deriving it.

You might want to give the formula for the derivative of a power function before you discuss the derivatives of sums and multiples of functions. If you do, you can use the derivative of a polynomial as an example of how to use the sum rule and the constant rule, and then say that these rules work for any functions, not just power functions.

4.3: The Exponential Function

One class.

Key points

To understand why the derivative of an exponential is a constant times itself, and to understand why this should be so. Significance of the constant e.

Ideas for the class

Start by drawing the graph of an exponential function and pointing out that its derivative should follow much the same pattern as the function: start out small and get larger and larger faster and faster.

The proof that the derivative is a constant times the original function is well worth the time and effort. Students find it quite difficult to understand that in

$$\lim_{h \to 0} \frac{a^{x+h} - a^x}{h} = \left(\lim_{h \to 0} \frac{a^h - 1}{h} \right) a^x$$

the second limit is just a constant, and only needs to be evaluated once and for all for a particular a.

You could spend the entire class running a computer lab based on computer exercises (2) and (3) from the section on Chapter 4 on page 11 of this manual.

4.4-5: The Product and Quotient Rules, The Chain Rule

One or two classes.

Key points

Making sure the students can use these rules.

Ideas for the class

A large part of these classes should be spent going over examples to make sure that the students get basic proficiency in using these rules. However, it would be nice to give them some intuitive understanding of why these rules are true. Here are a couple of ideas on how to do this through numerical examples.

For the product rule, you may want to give an intuitive or geometrical explanation (see the text) of why you'd expect the derivative to have this form. Alternatively, let $f(x) = x^2 + x + 1$, $g(x) = 3^x$ and estimate $f'(0)$ and $g'(0)$ and then $(fg)'(0)$ (from, for example, $(fg)(0.1)$ and $(fg)(0)$).

As a preliminary exercise for the chain rule, let $g(x) = x^2$, $f(x) = 3^x$, and evaluate $g(1), g(1.1)$ (to see the derivative is 2); $f(g(1)), f(g(1) + .1)$ (to see the derivative is about 3); then $f(g(1))$, $f(g(1.1))$ (to see the derivative is about 6). (Or, you can find $g'(1)$ and $f'(1)$ using formulas.)

Alternatively, think of a rod of length L. Suppose L is a function of the temperature, H, and H is a function of time, t. The we'd expect

$$\begin{pmatrix} \text{Rate of Change} \\ \text{of Length with} \\ \text{Time (cm/sec)} \end{pmatrix} = \begin{pmatrix} \text{Rate of Change} \\ \text{of Length with} \\ \text{Temp (cm/} ^\circ\text{C)} \end{pmatrix} \times \begin{pmatrix} \text{Rate of Change} \\ \text{of Temp with} \\ \text{Time (} ^\circ\text{C/sec)} \end{pmatrix}$$

$$\frac{dL}{dt} = \frac{dL}{dH} \cdot \frac{dH}{dt}.$$

Explain the chain rule using expansion factors: if $y = f(t)$, then $\frac{dy}{dt}$ is the factor by which the function f expands changes in t to give changes in y.

The notation $\dfrac{d}{dx} f(g(x)) = f'(g(x))g'(x)$ is difficult for many students. In particular, the symbol $f'(g(x))$ can be hard for them to interpret. It helps to provide an informal alternative to the notation in English, writing something like: "Take the derivative of the outside function without changing the inside, and then multiply this result by the derivative of the inside."

If you have done enough on local linearization, you may want to do the following as a preliminary exercise for the product rule. Derive the product rule in a particular case, e.g. $f(x) = \sqrt{1+x}$, $g(x) = e^x$, by writing down the local linearizations and multiplying them together:

$$e^x \approx 1 + x, \quad \sqrt{1+x} \approx 1 + (1/2)x,$$

so

$$e^x \sqrt{1+x} \approx (1+x)(1+(1/2)x) = 1 + (3/2)x + (1/2)x^2 \approx 1 + (3/2)x,$$

so the derivative of $e^x \sqrt{1+x}$ at $x = 0$ is $3/2$.

4.6: The Trigonometric Functions

One half to one class.

Key points

Understanding the derivatives of trig functions graphically; using them in the derivative rules.

Ideas for the class

Again, check that the rules make sense before stating them. Start the class by drawing a graph of $\sin x$ and asking what its derivative ought to look like; positive where $\sin x$ is increasing, negative where $\sin x$ is decreasing, repeating with the same period as $\sin x$. This sort of reasoning produces a cosine-like graph.

A more precise version of the same exercise is to graph $(\sin(x+0.01) - \sin(x))/0.01$ and then to superimpose the graph of $\cos x$.

Give the derivative of $\tan x$ using the quotient rule. Then do lots of examples involving the chain rule, as well as some with the product and quotient rules.

Remind students that these formulae are only valid when the units are in radians. They can often reset their calculators in degrees, so be sure to have them verify that their settings are correct.

4.7: Applications of the Chain Rule

One half to one class.

Key points

The chain rule is used to find derivatives of various inverse functions (for example, $\sqrt{x}$, $\ln x$, $\arctan x$).

Ideas for the class

The arguments used here are similar to those used in the next section on implicit differentiation, since in both cases the form of the derivative is implied by the chain rule.

It is worthwhile to do some of the proofs in more than one way. For example, if $f(x) = x^{\frac{1}{2}}$, $f'(x)$ can be found using the chain rule (as is done on page 258). But it can also be found using the product rule:

$$(f(x) \cdot f(x))' = x' = 1$$

$$f(x) \cdot f'(x) + f'(x) \cdot f(x) = 1$$

$$2f'(x) \cdot f(x) = 1$$

$$f'(x) = \frac{1}{2f(x)} = \frac{1}{2}x^{-\frac{1}{2}}.$$

And in the derivation of $(\arctan x)' = \frac{1}{1+x^2}$, use is made of the identity $1 + \tan^2\theta = \frac{1}{\cos^2\theta}$ to simplify the expression $\cos^2(\arctan x)$. The same expression can be simplified without using the identity by drawing a right triangle with legs 1 and x so that the hypotenuse is $\sqrt{x^2 + 1}$. By choosing θ so that $\tan\theta = x$, it follows that $\arctan x$ is θ, and from this that $\cos^2(\arctan x) = \cos^2\theta = \frac{1}{1+x^2}$. For some reason, many students think that the triangle derivation is "obvious," while the derivation using the identity is "a dirty trick."

4.8: Implicit Differentiation

A half to a whole class.

Key points

Implicit differentiation is just another application of the chain rule.

Ideas for the class

Many students do not know the difference between implicit and explicit functions. Show the class that many implicit functions cannot be solved for either variable in terms of the other.

It is worth going over at least some of the basic derivations in class; the main point to keep in mind is that we are not doing anything other than using the chain rule. Remember to draw graphs of all the functions and their derivatives; always check that the derivative rules make sense.

You can start with the circle when you introduce implicit functions, since everyone should be familiar with it, and find $\frac{dy}{dx}$ implicitly as is done in the text. Having found $\frac{dy}{dx}$, you can also find it for the upper half-circle given by $y = \sqrt{1 - x^2}$ and show that the results are the same. Be sure to work a problem like Example 1 (Page 263). If you have time, Example 2 follows Example 1 very nicely.

Point out the difference between the two formulas: $x^2 + y^2 = 1$ gives the whole circle, and is implicit; $y = \sqrt{1 - x^2}$ gives only a semicircle, and is explicit.

Having done this, you should discuss Figure 4.24, on page 263. Drawing tangent lines to the circle in all four quadrants to verify that the formula

$$\frac{dy}{dx} = -\frac{x}{y}$$

is very helpful. Organize relevant information in a table. Many students will (understandably) have trouble with the notation

$$\frac{d}{dx}(x^2) + \frac{d}{dx}(y^2) = 0.$$

Some will think $\frac{d}{dx}(y^2)$ should be zero, since y looks like a constant; others will think $\frac{d}{dx}(y^2) = 2y$. Emphasize that y depends on x, so y must change when x does.

Next, cover something like Example 1, Page 263, which considers $y^3 - xy = -6$. Convince students that they cannot solve for y (although they can solve for x!). Show them the graph (Figure 4.25), and admit that it isn't the graph of a function in the usual sense, since it fails the vertical line test. (Point out that the circle had the same problem.) Again, as you differentiate the function, keep in mind that students are confused by statements like

$$\frac{d}{dx}(xy) = y + x\frac{dy}{dx}.$$

Emphasize that you are using the product rule and the chain rule, since y is (implicitly) a function of x. It can be helpful to write $y(x)$ instead of y. Some instructors go so far as to write $y = k(x)$, telling the class that while we can't solve for k, we use it as a reminder (when applying the chain or product rule) that y depends on x. In this case, the equation

$$\frac{d}{dx}(y^3) - \frac{d}{dx}(xy) = 0$$

becomes

$$\frac{d}{dx}(k(x)^3) - \frac{d}{dx}(xk(x)) = 0,$$

an equation which shows the need for the chain and product rules.

5.1: Maxima and Minima

One class.

Key points

If the derivative is positive, the function is increasing; if negative, decreasing. Critical points; the first derivative test for local extrema; global extrema.

Ideas for the class

By now, most students should know the correspondence between the sign of the derivative and the function's behavior, but they don't necessarily know how to put it to use. Some elementary curve sketches are in order here before getting on to anything difficult. Sketch a simple cubic equation, or e^{-x^2}, or $\tan^{-1} x$; some function where you can see quickly and easily how the derivative is behaving, where there is a chance of seeing as a whole the relation between the derivative and the shape of the function.

The main point of this section is to illustrate the power of the result that if $f' > 0$ on an interval, then f is increasing there. For example, after explaining this result, write down on the board the two cubics $x^3 - x^2 + x - 1$ and $x^3 - x^2 - x + 1$. Only one of them is always increasing: which is it? (If you are using a graphing program, draw the graphs, and then ask: how could we have known which it was going to be?) The derivatives are $3x^2 - 2x + 1$ and $3x^2 - 2x - 1$, and the quadratic formula tells us that the first has no real roots, the second has two. So it is the first one, as its derivative is always positive.

Notice that a local maximum or minimum is *defined* to be at a critical point. This means that end points may be global, but not local, extrema. (The word "extrema" does not appear in the text.) Demonstrate that global extrema depend on the choice of the domain: good examples are e^x and $\sin x$.

While you should not introduce the term *inflection point* until Section 5.3, you should give an example (such as $y = x^3$) of a function with a critical point which is not a local extremum.

Rely only on the first derivative test: save the second derivative test for later.

5.2: Concavity & Points of Inflection

One class.

Key points

If the second derivative is positive, the function is concave up; if negative, concave down.

Ideas for the class

Some students have trouble with inflection points at first, because they don't jump out at you the way maxima and minima do, so you should spend some time on simple examples. Take one of the examples from the previous class, and ask them where they would expect to find an inflection point; then take the second derivative and find it. Watch out for students who think that an inflection point always occurs where the second derivative is zero.

A particularly good example is e^{-x^2}; since it has a maximum of 1 at $x = 0$ and is asymptotic to the x-axis, it must have two inflection points at least. Ask if it is possible to have a function which approaches a horizontal asymptote from above and stays concave down (answer: no, because a concave down function has to stay below its tangent line, and the tangent line at some point will be pointing down, hence it will cross the asymptote).

Do Page 297 # 19, or a variation on it, in class.

Despite all the calculation necessary, it is important to keep the discussion as focussed on graphs as possible.

5.3: Families of Curves: a Qualitative Study

One class or a computer lab.

Key points

Calculus is most useful when applied to families rather than specific functions; after all, specific functions can be analyzed individually using a graphing program, but to understand dependence on parameters you need general laws.

Ideas for the class

The best thing to do with this class is use a graphing program to analyze these curves first; preferably one like TWIDDLE (University of Arizona Software) which allows you to enter parametrized families and vary the parameters. The students find the idea of functions with parameters in them quite hard, so it is worth spending some time on this. After they get the idea from the computer graphs, you can start doing analysis using critical points, etc. as in the text.

When you begin to look at families of functions, you can point out to students that they are already familiar with several important families, including linear functions and trigonometric functions. Remind them how useful it is to study the effects that various parameters have on the graph of a general function (e.g., $f(x+a)$ represents a horizontal shift of f while $f(x)+b$ represents a vertical shift). Emphasize that with calculus, families of functions can be studied in greater detail than previously possible.

5.4: Economic Applications: Marginality

One class.

Key points

Use of differentiation in qualitative, graphical reasoning.

Ideas for the class

A good kickoff is to draw a cost function and ask the students what its slope and concavity mean. Discuss why the cost and revenue functions aren't necessarily linear, and discuss why most revenue functions are concave down. This is a good exercise in interpreting the derivative; write down a difference quotient with $h = 1$ to show that the derivative is approximately the cost of an extra item. From there you can go into more detailed analysis of cost versus revenue, etc. The beauty of this section is that the reasoning is purely graphical. Some students will feel uncomfortable with the lack of formulas here, and will try to make up formulas of their own. Others may be helped by putting (made up) units on the axes, to help them see where the derivative is increasing and where it is decreasing.

When working a problem like Example 2, Page 314, explain why a company should increase production if marginal revenue exceeds marginal cost. Keep in mind that there are several ways to attack many of these problems, all of them pedagogically worthy. In Example 4, Page 315, for example, the book gives two arguments to show that profit is maximized when marginal cost equals marginal revenue The first is graphical: when the vertical distance between cost and revenue curve is maximized, profit (or loss!) is maximized. The second is analytical. Since

$$\pi(q) = R(q) - C(q),$$

where π represents the profit, profit is maximized when $\pi'(q) = R'(q) - C'(q) = 0$, that is, when $R'(q) = C'(q)$. This solution also has a graphic interpretation (parallel tangents). In keeping with the Rule of Three, you can make a table of marginal revenue and marginal cost at different quantities. You can include marginal profit and also total profit, which is cumulative. From the table, it'll be obvious that if marginal revenue exceeds marginal cost, marginal profit is positive and total profit is therefore increasing. This exercise brings a lot of concepts together for students.

[You might want to mention that the domain of these functions are discrete (units sold, price in cents) but that it makes sense to pretend that the curves are smooth and defined for all $q > 0$.]

5.5: Optimization

One to two classes.

Key points

The derivative provides a simple criterion for optimization: look where the derivative is zero.

Ideas for the class

This is another class where you should get the students to try some examples before you talk too much; perhaps just do a couple of examples (one graphical), assign homework (not too many), and return to it a week later. The graphical examples are quite beautiful. The section on gasoline consumption (Page 323, including Example 5) is particularly challenging and very fruitful for students. It's also a lot of fun! Walk students through the units—they might not be used to relying on dimensional analysis, but it comes in very handy here.

Try not to reduce the solution of the algebraic examples to rules, and in grading homework be open to unconventional approaches. Since the emphasis is more on problem solving than on differentiation, you should work the same problem in different ways.

5.6: More Optimization: Introduction to Modeling

One class, or assign for reading and homework.

Key points

Using functions to construct models and techniques of optimization to find solutions.

Ideas for Class

This is a hard section!

Focus solely on specific examples. Return to the grapefruit example of Section 2.1, which is treated in Example 1, Page 328. Focus on optimizing height above ground. Have students give physical interpretations for everything, so they won't solve it mechanically. For example, if $y = -16t^2 + 100t + 6$ is the height above ground, then when you go through the procedure of solving $y' = 0$ to get the critical points, ask them "When does the grapefruit's velocity equal zero?" Discuss why this makes sense in context.

Example 2 on Page 329 explores how to select optimum dimensions to minimize metal for an aluminum can of given volume. Students often don't know where to begin this sort of question: it's not immediately clear what to do. Remind them that the quantity to be optimized should be given as a function of parameters they can vary. Discuss the importance of constraints here. Go over Figure 5.65, justifying the curve's shape. (Too small a radius yields a very tall can; too large a radius gives a very large top and bottom.) If you have time, bring in a real juice can. It will be taller. Ask why! (Answer: Taller containers look like they hold more and are easy to carry in one hand; moreover, the top and bottom actually have thicker walls—ask the class how that will affect their answer!)

If you work carefully through examples, you probably won't have time to do more than a couple of problems. Don't assign many homework problems. Encourage students to write down as much information as they can about their efforts, even if they can't give complete solutions.

5.7: Newton's Method

One class or skip entirely.

Key points

Description of Newton's method, with only brief mention of when it fails.

Ideas for the class

This is a computer or calculator class. Demonstrate the difference in speed between Newton's method and the bisection method.

Focusing on iteration will help connect this topic with others you may have done. If you looked at bisection, discuss how iteration was useful there. You can also connect this to the iterative process of zooming in repeatedly on solutions using a calculator or computer.

It's fun to discuss cases when Newton's Method fails, but don't spend too much time on this.

5.8: Working Backwards: Antiderivatives

One or two classes.

Key points

Concept of differential equation, parametrized family of solutions, initial conditions.

Ideas for the class

This section forms a brief introduction to differential equations, and should be treated as such. Emphasize the idea of a family of solutions, and fixing a particular solution using initial or other values.

A fun thing to do with velocity and acceleration is to ask the students to guess how fast they can throw a ball in the air. One way to get a feel for the accuracy of the guess is to see how high a ball thrown that fast would go, and ask them if they think they can really throw a ball that high.

Focus on antidifferentiation as a process of "working backwards". Emphasize that though the antiderivatives of a function form a family, when one additional condition is imposed, then there will be a unique antiderivative. Perhaps the easiest way to see a situation in which you impose additional constraints is to again look at an object thrown in the air. Starting with its initial velocity, you need one additional constraint to find its position—its initial height. Starting with its acceleration (that due to gravity) you need two initial constraints—initial velocity and position.

Don't use the notation for an indefinite integral.

5.9: Notes on Motion: Why Acceleration?

Small part of class, or skip entirely.

Key points

Historical development of ideas of motion.

6.1: The Definite Integral Revisited

One or two classes.

Key points

Review of the definite integral: left and right hand sums; interpretations as area, total change and average value; fundamental theorem of calculus.

Ideas for the class

If you are starting the semester here, you might want to make this into a class about the Two Big Ideas of Calculus, where you review the key concepts of differentiation and integration, and show the relation between differentiation and integration. Start by reviewing how to find the rate of change of a function; then introduce the inverse problem, reconstructing a function from its rate of change. Show the derivative numerically, using difference quotients, and graphically, as the slope of a curve. This should be very short—just a reminder. Then do the definite integral numerically and graphically. Recall the interpretation of the definite integral as a total distance traveled and as an area. A sample problem you could use (concerning leaking oil) is given in Example 1.

Time (hours)	0	1	2	3	4
Rate (liters/hour)	35	30	26	23	21

Table 0.2: Rate of leaking oil.

☐ **Example 1** Suppose oil is leaking out of a container at a decreasing rate. The rate is measured at hourly intervals and given in Table 0.2.

We want to estimate the total amount of oil that has leaked out of the container during the time shown. Answering these questions will show you how to set about making such an estimate.

1. What is the maximum amount of oil that could have leaked out during the first hour? The minimum?

2. What is the maximum amount of oil that could have leaked out during the second hour (i.e between $t = 1$ and $t = 2$)? The minimum? How about during the third and fourth hours?

3. During the entire four hour interval from $t = 0$ to $t = 4$, what is the maximum amount of oil that could have leaked out? The minimum? Explain where you used the assumption that the rate at which the oil was leaking was decreasing.

4. If you had to guess how much oil actually leaked in the four hour interval, what would be your guess? What is the maximum possible error in your guess? (In other words, what is the maximum possible difference between your guess and the true value?)

Suppose additional readings are obtained, and compiled in Table 0.3.

Time (hours)	0.5	1.5	2.5	3.5
Rate (liters/hour)	33	27	24	22

Table 0.3: Rate of leaking oil.

1. Is the second set of information consistent with the first? What would the rate at 0.5 hours have to be to be consistent?

2. Recalculate the upper and lower estimates in light of this new information. Make a new guess for the total amount of oil which has leaked out in the four hour interval, and estimate the maximum possible error in your guess.

3. If readings of the rate were obtained for every 1/10 hour, by how much would your upper estimate exceed your lower? What if readings were obtained for every 1/100 hour?

4. Explain why you can calculate the total amount of oil that has leaked out to any desired degree of accuracy if you have access to readings of the rate at every instant during the four hour interval.

Solution. You could do this problem first numerically; then graph the rate oil is leaking and show the sum graphically. Show students how, by expressing the total change in two different ways, you are lead to the fundamental theorem of calculus. ❑

How does one find definite integrals in practice? Numerically, using left and right hand sums, and by the Fundamental Theorem. Work out two numerical examples, one which can be done using the Fundamental Theorem and one which cannot (e.g., $\int_0^1 e^x \, dx$ and $\int_0^1 e^{x^2} \, dx$, or $\int_0^2 x^2 \, dx$ and $\int_0^2 \sin x^2 \, dx$). For each integral give its left and right hand sums with a few different choices of the number of subdivisions, to show the convergence (see Tables 0.4 and 0.5). You don't need to do all the calculations in class, but you should probably work out one or two examples on the board with a small number of subdivisions; also, you should make sure your students know how to use whatever program or calculator they will need to calculate sums with large numbers of subdivisions.

n	Lefthand sum	Righthand sum
2	1.32	2.18
10	1.63	1.81
50	1.70	1.74
250	1.71	1.72

Table 0.4: Left and right hand sums for $\int_0^1 e^x \, dx$.

n	Lefthand sum	Righthand sum
2	1.14	2.00
10	1.38	1.55
50	1.45	1.48
250	1.46	1.47

Table 0.5: Left and right hand sums for $\int_0^1 e^{x^2} \, dx$.

Draw pictures of the left and right hand sums for $\int_0^1 e^x \, dx$, showing the difference between the upper and lower estimate. Possibly get an estimate of the integral before the numerical calculations by calculating the area of the trapezoid above the graph: $(e+1)/2 \approx 1.86$. Discuss whether this is an under or overestimate; how accurate you expect it to be. Now do this integral using the fundamental theorem, and compare the answer $e - 1 = 1.71828\ldots$ with the left and right sums.

Point out that $\int_0^1 e^{x^2} \, dx$ cannot be computed in terms of elementary functions by the fundamental theorem; ask them what they think its exact value is to two decimal places. At this point you can have a discussion of the value of the fundamental theorem; it can't be applied to all definite integrals, but it is obviously so useful when it can that it is worthwhile figuring out all the cases where it can be applied; explain that that is the purpose of the next few sections, and that that is why they won't be seeing many numerical examples for a while.

One concept that gives students difficulty is the average value interpretation of the integral. It is useful to give some graphical examples to show that students' intuition about averages is actually applicable to the average value of a function – e.g. sketch $\sin x$ on the board and ask them to guess the average value of $\sin x$ for x in $[0, 2\pi]$ – clearly it has to be 0. Now look at $\sin x$ over $[0, \pi]$ – get the class to discuss whether the average should be greater than or less than 1/2.

If your students don't have access to a method of graphing $e^{-x} \sin x$ be sure to discuss its shape before assigning problem 7.

6.2: Properties of the Definite Integral

One class.

Key points

The properties in this section are mostly fairly straight-forward. However, they are fundamental for everything that follows, and you shouldn't assume that the students immediately know how to use them. This class can be quite interesting if you invite a lot of class participation in the examples.

Ideas for the class

The property

$$\int_a^b f(x) \, dx = \int_a^c f(x) \, dx + \int_c^b f(x) \, dx$$

is best explained in terms of area as in the book. Do an example like Example 1 in the text. For example, tell them that $\int_0^1 e^{x^2} \, dx = 1.46$ and $\int_0^2 e^{x^2} \, dx = 16.45$, ask them to tell you what $\int_1^2 e^{x^2} \, dx$ and $\int_{-1}^1 e^{x^2} \, dx$ are (use the symmetry of the graph for the second one). Another good example is to calculate $\int_0^3 e^{-x^2} \, dx$ and $\int_0^4 e^{-x^2} \, dx$ numerically, and ask the students why the answers are so close (they are 0.88621 and 0.88623 respectively); the answer may be seen graphically in the fact that the difference between the two is represented by a very small area.

You can get a good discussion going on the property

$$\int_b^a f(x) \, dx = -\int_a^b f(x) \, dx$$

by getting the computer or calculator to give $\int_1^0 e^{x^2} \, dx = -1.46$ and then asking why it didn't complain about the lower limit being higher than the upper limit, and why the answer is the exact negative of the answer you got before (this is assuming you are using a sensibly written program that doesn't complain). The point is that the computer quite happily computes $\Delta x = (b - a)/n$ without caring whether b or a is bigger; if a is bigger, it just gets a negative Δx, which yields the negative answer.

You don't need to spend too much time deriving the sum and constant multiple rules; it is better to start out with an example and then give a brief discussion of why they are true. Give an example that combines the two rules and uses results you got the previous class. For example, if you computed $\int_0^1 e^x \, dx$ and $\int_0^1 e^{x^2} \, dx$ last time, now do

$$\int_0^1 \left(2e^x + e^{x^2}\right) \, dx = 2 \cdot 1.72 + 1.46 = 4.90.$$

The most difficult idea in the section is the notion of using comparisons to estimate definite integrals. Students find it hard since they have trouble deciding what function they should use to compare with the given function. However, at this stage most of the bounds students will use are constant functions (e.g. $e^x \leq 9$ on [0,2] so $\int_0^2 e^x \, dx \leq 9 \times 2 = 18$). If you did $\int_0^1 e^x \, dx$ using the fundamental theorem in a previous class, you can use it to estimate $\int_0^1 e^{x^2} \, dx$ (which cannot be done using the fundamental theorem). Graph the two functions on the computer or calculator, and observe that e^{x^2} is always below e^x and always above 1 for $0 \leq x \leq 1$. Hence

$$1 \leq \int_0^1 e^{x^2} \, dx \leq \int_0^1 e^x \, dx = 1.72.$$

This agrees with the numerical value calculated earlier. The point to emphasize here is that you can estimate a hard to calculate integral by replacing it with and easier one. Later, when students have practice with evaluating integrals you should often make simple comparisons prior to working out definite integrals, so you can show a technique for judging the reasonableness of answers.

Another example is $x \geq x^2$ on [0,1], so $\int_0^1 x^2 \, dx \leq 0.5$.

6.3: Antiderivatives and the Fundamental Theorem

One class.

Key points

Introduction to systematic antidifferentiation; the 'guess and check' method. The significance of the arbitrary constant C.

Ideas for the class

When you introduce the notation for the indefinite integral, emphasize the distinction between the definite integral (a number computed by limits of sums) and the indefinite integral (the general antiderivative, which happens to be useful in computing definite integrals). You will have to do this again and again throughout this chapter; because of the similar notations, the students are likely to confuse the two concepts. One way to make the distinction real is to draw the general antiderivative as a family of functions differing by a constant. For example, draw a straight line through the origin with slope 1 and then graphically derive the shape of its antiderivative (don't draw attention to the fact that you have drawn $y = x$). Draw a few antiderivatives cutting the y-axis at different points; in this way show that you can get an antiderivative $F(x)$ with $F(0)$ equal to any given number. After doing this, find the general antiderivative of x and show how the arbitrary constant in $x^2/2 + C$ corresponds to $F(0)$. You can do the same thing with $\sin x$.

Show how you might have arrived at Table 6.2 by guessing; solicit guesses for, say, $\int x^2 \, dx$ and $\int \sin x \, dx$. Emphasize that you can always check your answer by differentiating back again ($\int \cos x \, dx$ is a good example to use here, because there is a slight temptation to put a minus sign in the answer). A good example for class participation is $\int 1/x \, dx$. However, don't spend too much time getting to Table 6.2; spend more time using it and the sum and constant multiple rules to find antiderivatives (e.g. $\int(1/x + 1/x^2)\,dx$, $\int \pi x^3\,dx$, $\int(2\cos x - 5\sin x)\,dx$). Include some examples where the constant is in the denominator, e.g.

$$\int \frac{e^x}{5}\,dx.$$

Some students may need to be reminded that the integrand is just $(1/5)e^x$.

Explain the sum and constant multiple rules as reversals of the corresponding rules for derivatives; set up the theme of reversing rules of differentiation, with the warning that it won't be so easy for the chain and product rules.

The point of all this to be able to do definite integrals using the Fundamental Theorem, e.g., $\int_2^3 (1/x^2 + 3x)\,dx$, $\int_0^{\pi/2} \cos x\,dx$. Include examples where the answer can be expressed symbolically and numerically, e.g.,

$$\int_2^3 \frac{1}{2x}\,dx = \frac{1}{2}(\ln 3 - \ln 2) = 0.2027.$$

If you have time, do an example that requires thinking about whether the answers mechanically obtained make sense; for example, ask your students to decide which is bigger, $\int_0^1 x^2\,dx$ or $\int_0^1 x^3\,dx$, just using their knowledge of the graphs of the integrands; then calculate the integrals to see if the numbers makes sense. Or, ask them to guess the order of magnitude of $\int_2^3 e^x\,dx$ and $\int_2^3 e^{-x}\,dx$, and then calculate the answer. Or, ask them to decide from the graph whether $\int_{0.5}^{1.5}(x^2 - 1)\,dx$ is positive or negative, and then calculate the answer.

Here and for the next few sections include some application problems in the homework you assign (Exercises 62 and 63).

6.4: Integration by Substitution – Part I

One class.

Key points

Simple substitutions where only a constant factor must be introduced.

Ideas for the class

Explain that the basic idea behind the substitution method is to find a way of reversing the chain rule.

Start with a very easy example such as $\int 2x \cos(x^2)\,dx$. Possibly introduce this integral by writing $\int \cos(x^2)\,dx$ first, showing how the obvious guess, $\sin(x^2)$, does not work because of the chain rule, and then point out that if the $2x$ from the chain rule had been there in the first place you could have done the integral. This gets the point across that integrands have to be in a rather special shape to be integrated using substitution, a point that you will need to come back to again and again. Then go on to do $\int t^2 e^{5t^3}\,dt$ and $\int \cos x \sqrt{\sin x + 1}\,dx$ by the guess-and-check method. If the last one is too difficult to guess, it can be replaced by a simpler example such as $\int x^3 \sqrt{2 + x^4}\,dx$ if you think it is necessary. However, working through the difficulty leads naturally to the quest for a more systematic method, namely the w-substitution (so-called to distinguish it from the u, v of integration by parts).

Once you have introduced the w-substitution, go back and do the same examples you did before using the new method. Remind them that this method grew out of looking for the end products of the chain rule; therefore, you are looking for an inside function whose derivative is somewhere outside, and when you have found it you want to put w equal to the inside function. This makes the tricky ones such as $\int \cos x \sqrt{\sin x + 1}\, dx$ easier, since once you have decided to put $w = \sin x + 1$ the rest is mechanical. Students should also see an example where 'outside function' and the 'inside function' are hard to recognize, for example $\int \frac{x}{1+x^2}\, dx$ ($w = 1 + x^2$) or $\int \frac{x}{1+x^4}\, dx$ ($u = x^2$). Be prepared for questions about what dx means or where dw came from.

Encourage your students not to rely too much on the mechanics of substitution; do examples to convince them that they really can 'guess-and-check' in simple cases, and to look for patterns. For example, $\int \cos(2x)\, dx = \frac{\sin(2x)}{2}$, $\int e^{3x}\, dx = \frac{e^{3x}}{3}$, $\int (5x - 1)^3\, dx = \frac{(5x-1)^4}{20}$ can all be done without formal substitution, if you point out the patterns to students. Always emphasize the reversal of differentiation; they are familiar with a constant coming out the front when they differentiate; so, when its not supposed to come out you have to divide by it first.

An interesting example is $\int \frac{1}{2x}\, dx$. The answer is either $\frac{1}{2} \ln x + C$ or $\frac{1}{2} \ln(2x) + C$ (using $w = 2x$).

Exercises 44 and 45 are application problems.

6.5: Integration by Substitution – Part II

A half to a whole class.

Key points

Substitutions in definite integrals; less obvious substitutions.

Ideas for the class

Calculate a definite integral, say $\int_1^2 x \sin(x^2)\, dx$ or $\int_0^1 \frac{x^2}{1+x^3}\, dx$, in two ways; by evaluating the indefinite integral first (using a substitution) and by changing the limits of integration when you make the substitution. Students will prefer the first way, even though it is often more laborious. You need to explain changing the limits of integration quite carefully; many students have trouble with it. This is partly because they have never appreciated the significance of the dx and dw in the integral (in fact many of them leave it out; this is a good place to remind them of its usefulness). Choose another example, similar to the first one you do, where a substitution does not work, and point out that it must be done numerically. For the two above, you could choose $\int_1^2 \sin(x^2)\, dx$ and $\int_0^1 \frac{x^2}{1+x^4}\, dx$ (which in fact can be done in elementary, but complicated, terms).

The text does not give a long stream of 'special substitutions', rather the suggestion that sometimes it can be helpful to substitute w for a complex part of the integrand and see what happens. The philosophy taken by the text is that students ought to be able to perform simple substitutions accurately and quickly; more complicated integrands should be antidifferentiated using tables or a computer algebra system. They should see an example like Example 4; a simpler one you can do in class is $\int x\sqrt{x-1}\,dx$ ($w = x - 1$). Problems 22–26 are good for generating class discussion. Problem 27 is an example of completing the square and trig substitution – students will find it hard.

A nice digression showing the usefulness of the substitution method in transforming integrals is to demonstrate the formula for the area of a circle by writing

$$A = 2\int_{-r}^{r} \sqrt{r^2 - x^2}\,dx,$$

and then making the substitution $u = x/r$ to get

$$A = r^2 2\int_{-1}^{1} \sqrt{1 - u^2}\,dx.$$

Then show that

$$2\int_{-1}^{1} \sqrt{1 - u^2}\,dx = \pi$$

either geometrically, numerically, or by a trig substitution (if your class is really sophisticated, point out that it could be a definition of π).

Exercise 32 is an application problem.

6.6: Integration by Parts

One class.

Key points

Integration by parts method for indefinite and definite integrals.

Ideas for the class

Continue the theme of reversing rules of differentiation with the idea of reversing the product rule.

Start with an easy example, and explain the method and the u, v notation. Do one of Examples 1 or 2, or vary them slightly by doing $\int xe^{-x}\,dx$ or $\int x\cos x\,dx$. Then do more complicated examples. You should do one example which requires integrating by parts twice, such as $\int x^2 e^x\,dx$, one which requires setting $v' = 1$, such as $\int \ln x\,dx$ or $\int \arctan x\,dx$, and one which requires the boomerang trick, such as $\int e^x \sin x\,dx$.

Exercise 50 is an application problem.

6.7: Tables of Integrals

One class.

Key points

Recognizing a given integral as a standard form in a table. Performing simple substitution to convert a given integral into a standard form.

Ideas for the class

We are replacing the standard collection of integration methods with the useful skill of using integral tables. Students find tables surprisingly hard – primarily because they have trouble identifying the form of an integral and so don't know where to look in the table. Discuss the general form of the table given in the text (here is a good place for a transparency!) and present a number of integral problems, all at once. For example, (assuming you include completing the square), put up

1. $\int \dfrac{1}{\sin x}\,dx.$

2. $\int \cos^3 4x\,dx.$

3. $\int \dfrac{1}{x^2 + 2x + 2}\,dx.$

4. $\int \dfrac{1}{x^2 + 2x - 3}\,dx.$

5. $\int \dfrac{x^3}{x^2 + 2x + 2}\,dx.$

6. $\int e^{5x}\sin(3x)\,dx.$

7. $\int (x^3 + 2x^2 - 5x + 7)\sin(3x)\,dx.$

8. $\int \dfrac{1}{\sqrt{x^2 + 2x + 2}}\,dx.$

9. $\int \dfrac{1}{\sqrt{x^2 + 2x - 3}}\,dx.$

10. $\int \dfrac{x}{\sqrt{x^2 + 2x - 3}}\,dx.$

The first step is to get the students to understand which formula in the table a given integrand resembles. Go through your list and ask students to suggest which entry in the table is the best fit. Compare examples that look similar but require different methods; e.g (3) and (4), or (8) and (9). Show how to put integrals in a form necessary for the table, e.g., by completing the square or by factoring a quadratic. Compare (5), which requires long division, with (10), which requires a substitution $u = x + 1$ and splitting up the integral. Select a few problems to work through completely. Do at least one definite integral as well.

The main point about reduction methods is to know that they are there. Do an example of deriving one if you have time; if not, it is more important to give an example of using one. For example, do $\int t^3 e^{4t}\,dt$ using the reduction formula (make sure you work it out yourself first!). Make sure students understand that when they use reduction formulas, they will *not* need to do integration by parts – that was done in the derivation of the formula.

The method of partial fractions is not treated in the body of the text, but if you like you can assign problems 66 and 67 which demonstrate the main ideas.

6.8: Approximating Definite Integrals

One class.

Key points

Comparison of the effectiveness of the Left, Right, Midpoint and Trapezoid rules.

Ideas for the class

We now turn to numerical methods for calculating integrals. In this and the next section you should draw lots of graphs to explain things. It also helps to have a programmable calculator or computer available to show how the different methods converge for increasing values of n. If the students have calculators or are in a computer classroom, you might want to consider making this and the next class into a lab where the students do their own calculations and report the results and conclusions. If you don't have any technology, produce overheads with tables of numbers.

Describe geometrically what each method is doing, and how to tell whether it is an overestimate or an underestimate by looking at whether the function is increasing or decreasing, concave up or concave down.

A good strategy for teaching this section and the following one is to choose a small set of examples and follow them through using the various approximation methods. You should do this for one problem where the exact answer is known, and another for which it is not known. The text uses $\int_1^2 (1/x)\,dx = \ln 2$ and $\int_0^{2.5} \sin(t^2)\,dt$. Other examples you might use are $\int_1^4 \sqrt{x}\,dx = 14/3$ and $\int_0^1 e^{-x^2}\,dx$. You should make it clear how you know that you have found the value to a specified degree of accuracy (e.g. 3 decimal places) – by watching the decimal places stabilize in the numerical approximations.

n	LEFT(n)	RIGHT(n)	TRAP(n)	MID(n)	SIMP(n)
2	3.8717	5.3717	4.6217	4.6885	4.6662
10	4.5148	4.8148	4.6648	4.6676	4.6667
50	4.6366	4.6966	4.6666	4.6667	4.6667
250	4.6607	4.6727	4.6667	4.6667	4.6667

Table 0.6: Different methods for $\int_1^4 \sqrt{x}\,dx$.

n	LEFT(n)	RIGHT(n)	TRAP(n)	MID(n)	SIMP(n)
2	0.8894	0.5733	0.7314	0.7546	0.7469
10	0.7778	0.7146	0.7462	0.7471	0.7468
50	0.7531	0.7405	0.7468	0.7468	0.7468
250	0.7481	0.7456	0.7468	0.7468	0.7468

Table 0.7: Different methods for $\int_0^1 e^{-x^2}\,dx$.

No attempt is made in the text to discuss any of the traditional error bounds for the various rules. You can generate discussion by drawing two curves, one gently rising the other rapidly rising and ask for which curve the left or right will give a better approximation for a given n. It should be easy to see that the errors are smaller in the gently rising curve. Similarly, you can draw two curves which have small and large second derivatives, and examine the behavior of the midpoint and trapezoidal rules. This is done in more detail in the next section, but it helps to firm up understanding of the geometry if you discuss it here.

If you assign problem 12, you might want to sketch part (a) in class. Problem 14 is excellent – part (c) has a surprise in the answer.

6.9: Approximation Errors and Simpson's Rule

A half to one class.

Key points

The idea of analyzing errors by observing their behavior for increasing n. Simpson's rule is the most accurate rule; it is defined as a weighted average of the midpoint rule and the trapezoid rule (rather than in terms of approximation by parabolas).

Ideas for the class

Students will readily observe that doubling n makes the error twice as small (or 4 or 16 times as small), but will have trouble understanding how this indicates that the error is proportional to $1/n$ (or $1/n^2$ or $1/n^4$), and how this in turn implies that increasing n by a factor of 10 gives one (or 2 or 4) extra decimal places of accuracy.

Again, it is best to teach this class using technology; otherwise you should use overheads. Be sure to emphasize that the rules presented are approximate, and won't hold exactly in any given case. For examples in this section you should continue with whatever examples you used in the previous section. A good conclusion to draw is that Simpson's rule gives reasonably approximate results in most cases for relatively small values of n.

n	Error	
	Lefthand rule	Righthand rule
2	0.7950	−0.7050
10	0.1519	−0.1481
50	0.0301	−0.0299

Table 0.8: Errors for the left and right rule Riemann sum approximation to $\int_1^4 \sqrt{x}\, dx = 14/3 = 4.6666\ldots$.

Problem 13 is important, if only to give some idea why the efficiency of the various rules has meaning in real life terms. Problems 14 and 15 are similar to each other and confusing to students. You may want to say a word of explanation if you assign them. Problems 16–19 are useful in generating class discussion.

6.10: Improper Integrals

One class.

Key points

Graphical and numerical understanding of convergence and divergence. The behavior of $\int_1^\infty 1/x^p\, dx$ for different p.

Ideas for the class

It is not a good idea to start out right away computing $\int_0^\infty f(x)\, dx$ by finding $\int_0^b f(x)\, dx$ as a function of b and then letting b tend to infinity. Many students will never get beyond the purely symbolic meaning of this. It is much better to start with a purely numerical illustration of the convergence and nonconvergence of an integral. For example compute the integrals $\int_1^{10} 1/x^2\, dx$, $\int_1^{100} 1/x^2\, dx$, and $\int_1^{1000} 1/x^2\, dx$, either with a numerical integration program, or using the fundamental theorem. Concentrate initially on the actual numerical answers, and observe that they are getting closer and closer to 1. Then do $\int_1^{\infty} 1/\sqrt{x}\, dx$ the same way, and observe that the numbers are getting larger and larger.

Having made the point numerically, examine the two functions graphically. Before doing this, remind the students of the general shape of the two functions. They probably think of them as basically the same, which makes it mysterious that they should have different convergence behavior. However, if you graph them with a graphing program on a few different scales, you can see the difference quite dramatically.

First graph them both on the same axes, with the scale going from 0 to 10 on each axis. It is quite clear from this that $1/\sqrt{x}$ is well above $1/x$. Then follow the tail out; graph them with $0 \le y \le 1$ and $10 \le x \le 100$, and then with $0 \le y \le 0.1$ and $100 \le x \le 1000$. On this last graph, $1/x^2$ is completely flat against the x-axis. If you change the scale on the y-axis to $0 \le y \le 0.01$, then $1/x^2$ becomes just visible at the beginning, but now $1/\sqrt{x}$ is completely off the top of the viewing window, even when you get to $x = 1000$. You can play around with a few other scales; the conclusion is inescapable: $1/\sqrt{x}$ has a much fatter tail than $1/x^2$. The fact that the tail is getting infinitely thin is not enough to make its area finite, because you can take long pieces of it over which the thickness does not decrease very much, and so pile up a substantial area. The same thing does not work for $1/x^2$ because if you try to take a long piece of it, you find it thins out to nothing before you have gone very far.

You can really see all this on the graphs, by combining both numerical and graphical thinking. For example, graph $1/\sqrt{x}$ on the scales $0 \le y \le 0.1$ and $100 \le x \le 1000$. At $x = 100$, the tail is 0.1 thick; if you go out to $x = 1000$, it is still about $1/3$ as thick, so you have at least $1/3$ of the area of the viewing rectangle, which is about $0.1 \times 1000 = 100$. This trick gets better the further you go out; try graphing it on a scale $0 \le y \le 0.01$ and $10,000 \le x \le 100,000$ and you will see that you get at least one third the viewing rectangle again, which now has an area of approximately $100,000 \times 0.01 = 1,000$. If you try the same thing for $1/x^2$, it doesn't work at all. Try graphing it on scales $0 \le y \le 0.01$ and $10 \le x \le 100$ (viewing rectangle has area approximately 1) and then on scales $0 \le y \le 0.0001$ and $100 \le x \le 1000$ (viewing rectangle has area approximately $1/10$).

Only after the students have grasped the numerical and graphical aspects of convergence should you give them the algebraic calculation:

$$\int_1^{\infty} \frac{1}{x^2}\, dx = \lim_{b \to \infty} \int_1^{b} \frac{1}{x^2}\, dx = \lim_{b \to \infty} \left(1 - \frac{1}{b}\right) = 1.$$

6.11: More Improper Integrals

One class or skip.

Key points

Comparison test for improper integrals.

Ideas for the class

Students find difficult the use of comparison to determine convergence or divergence. Illustrate this concept graphically; for example, take $\int_3^\infty 1/x^2 \ln x \, dx$. First compute the integral numerically with upper limit 10, 100, and 1000, as you did for $1/x^2$. Then graph the function against $1/x^2$. The graphs are quite comparable on all scales, and one is always a little below the other (more so the further out you go). Illustrate divergence with $1/\sqrt{x}$ and $\ln x/\sqrt{x}$. Before attempting to find a comparison function, make sure your students get a feel for how an integrand behaves as $x \to \infty$. If they know whether to expect convergence or divergence before making the comparison, they are much more likely to be able to choose a reasonable comparison function and to get the inequalities in the right direction. It is OK to treat this topic with a light touch.

6.12: Notes on Constructing Antiderivatives

Optional or assign for reading.

Key points

Use of a slope field to visualize antiderivatives. Use of the definite integral to define functions with no elementary antiderivatives.

Ideas for the class

This is a good opportunity to introduce slope fields, which will be used extensively in the chapter on differential equations. You can make quite a good lab out of this, using graphing calculators or computers, and since the material is not crucial right now, you can feel free to let the class go its own way without worrying that they are missing something.

For example, draw the slope field for $dy/dx = 1/x$, and follow the slope field from $(1,0)$ to $x = 2$; compare the y value obtained with $\ln 2$. The point of this is it shows how you could construct the logarithm function if you didn't already have it. You can then talk about other more exotic functions such as Si x (defined in the text) or erf x (defined in the exercises). Problems 16 to 20 are about erf x; it's a good idea to do some in class if you plan to assign them. Compare the graphical method of constructing antiderivatives with the definite integral, which gives you a way of computing their values to arbitrary accuracy. If you have a good class, you can use Euler's method on the slope field, and compare it with the lefthand sum for the definite integral; they amount to the same thing.

7.1: The Definite Integral as an Area

One class.

Key points

Using the area interpretation in understanding applications of the definite integral.

Ideas for the class

This section contains some very attractive examples of graphical reasoning. The emphasis is not on obtaining numerical answers but rather on using the area interpretation of the definite integral to analyze problems. Here are two examples you can use in class. The second one is like Exercise 15, which is a beautiful but quite difficult problem.

☐ **Example 2** Figure 1 gives the graph[1] of the rate r (in arrivals/hour) at which patrons arrive at the theater in order to get rush seats for the evening performance. The first people arrive at 8 am and the ticket windows open at 9 am. Suppose that once the windows open, people can be served at an (average) rate of 200 per hour.

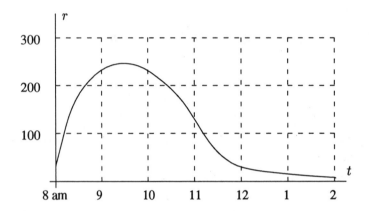

Figure 1: Rate at which theater-goers arrive.

Use Figure 1 to find or provide an estimate of:

1. The length of the line at 9 am when the windows open.

2. The length of the line at 10 am.

3. The length of the line at 11 am.

4. The rate at which the line is growing in length at 10 am.

5. The time at which the length of the line is maximum.

6. The length of time a person who arrives at 9 am has to stand in line.

7. The time at which the line disappears.

8. Suppose you were given a formula for r in terms of t. Explain how you would answer the above questions.

---

[1]From *Calculus: The Analysis of Functions*, by Peter D. Taylor (Toronto: Wall & Emerson, Inc., 1992). Reprinted with permission of the publisher.

Solution. It would be useful for students to have copies of Figure 1 if you go over this in class. Otherwise, you could start with a table, and then draw the graph on the board. ❑

❑ **Example 3** A bird[2] gathers food from a series of patches. Suppose that traveling from one patch to the next takes a fixed time T minutes, and requires c calories of energy. This cost of travel must be more than recovered from feeding in the patches. The longer the bird stays in single patch, the more food it obtains, but the rate of obtaining food decreases. The problem for the bird is to decide how long to spend in each patch to maximize its net intake of energy per unit time. Figure 2 shows a graph of the rate r at which the bird gathers food (cal/min) against the time t (min) spent in the patch. You see that r decreases with t, corresponding to the increased difficulty of finding food as the patch becomes depleted.

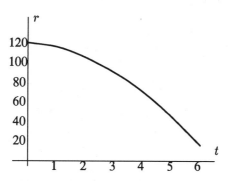

Figure 2: Feeding Rate at Patch

1. Show how to interpret on the r graph the amount of energy E obtained in t minutes of feeding in a patch.

2. Take the travel time T to be 2 minutes, and the travel cost to be

    (a) $c = 0$

    (b) $c = 60$

    Show on the r graph how to choose the optimum time t to spend in each patch.

Solution.

1. The rate r is the derivative of E :
$$r = \frac{dE}{dt}$$
   Thus the energy gained from t minutes of feeding:
$$E(t) = E(t) - E(0) \quad (\text{since } E(0) = 0)$$

---

[2]From Peter D. Taylor

can be interpreted as the area under the r graph above the interval $[0, t]$. See Figure 3

$$E(t) = \int_0^t r(t)\, dt.$$

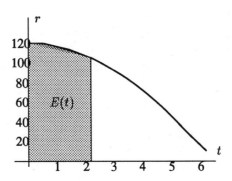

Figure 3: Energy Gain

2. The net gain of energy per minute is the net gain over one cycle divided by the cycle time, so equals

$$\frac{E(t) - c}{t + 2}.$$

This quantity will be maximized at a positive value of t, and at this point, its derivative will be zero. Calculating the derivative, recalling that c is a constant:

$$\frac{E'(t)(t+2) - (E(t) - c)}{(t+2)^2} = 0.$$

Since $r(t) = E'(t)$, this can be written

$$r(t)(t+2) - E(t) + c = 0.$$

The first two terms can be interpreted in terms of the areas in Figure 4 as follows:

$$\begin{aligned} r(t)(t+2) &= A + C \\ E(t) &= B + C \end{aligned}$$

And so their difference is $A - B$. The condition becomes:

$$\boxed{A - B + c = 0.}$$

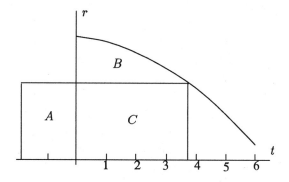

Figure 4: Energy Gain

(a) $c = 0$. The condition is $A = B$. Observe that if t is small, then A will be greater than B, and if t is large, then A will be less than B. Somewhere between, there will be a point where A is equal to B. This gives the optimal value of t which appears to be approximately

$$t \approx 3.8 \text{ min.}$$

(b) $c = 60$. The condition is $A = B - 60$. This requires a smaller value of A and a larger value of B than above. This is obtained by increasing t slightly. It's hard to get a very good estimate of just where this happens without doing some careful measurements, but the idea is clear enough. A reasonable estimate of the new optimal value of t is

$$t \approx 4.5 \text{ min.}$$

❏

7.2: Setting Up Riemann Sums

One or two classes.

Key points

How to 'divide and conquer'; how to know which way to divide up a region; how it depends on density rather than the shape of the region.

Ideas for the class

This section is fundamental for the entire chapter. You will need to come back again and again to the ideas that you set out in this class, so you should choose carefully your examples and how you are going to explain them.

The concept of density is important. You may want to start with an example of density along a line, such as Example 1 in the text. It is important that the students understand that the Δx in a Riemann sum and the dx in a definite integral are important elements that can have physical meaning, and not just pieces of notation that can be dispensed with. You can bring this out by being careful to specify units; if you have a piece of highway of length Δx miles and the population density in the vicinity is $f(x)$ people per mile, then the population in the piece is $f(x)\Delta x$ people. You can vary this example by choosing a highway in your state, and by giving a specific function that approximates the density along this highway.

Don't try to cover all the examples in this section; it is better to cover one or two examples carefully. Here are some other examples you can use.

Squaresville is a city in the shape of a square 5 miles on a side, with a highway running along one side of it. The population density d miles from the highway is $20 - 4d$ thousand people per square mile. What is the approximate population of Squaresville? You can work this one out in detail, then compare it with Ringsburg (Example 5 in the text). In particular, bring out the different ways of slicing (parallel to the highway in Squaresville, in concentric circles in Ringsburg). The key point to get across is that you want to slice the problem in such a way that the density is approximately constant along the slices.

A problem that forces them to think carefully about how to slice is the following, taken from one of the past exams (you could also use this problem in Section 7.4, below, on Applications to Physics).

□ **Example 4** A compressible liquid has density which varies with height. At the level of h meters above the bottom, the density is $40 \times (5 - h)\frac{\text{kg}}{\text{m}^3}$.

1. The liquid is put in the container depicted in the picture. The cross sections of the container are isosceles triangles. It has straight sides, and looks like a triangular prism. How many kg will it hold when placed as shown in Figure 5, resting on the triangular side?

2. How many kg will it hold if it is placed (with some support, of course) as shown in Figure 6?

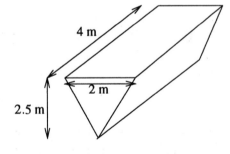

Figure 6: Resting on side.

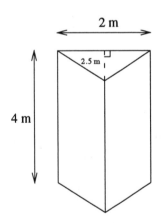

Figure 5: Resting on end.

A reasonably difficult example, suitable if you plan to spend more than one class on this section, is to use the function for the density of the earth's atmosphere given in Example 3 to calculate the entire mass of the earth's atmosphere. This requires slicing by spherical shells, which is probably best explained in a manner analogous with the Ringsburg example; the volume of a thin shell of thickness Δr and radius r is approximately its surface area times its thickness, $4\pi r^2 \Delta r$.

7.3: Geometric Applications

One to one and a half classes.

Key points

Volumes by slicing; arclength.

Ideas for the class

Avoid the temptation to slide back into tradition and teach methods such as 'volumes by washers' and 'volumes by shells'. By all means give examples that use these techniques, but do each example by slicing, finding the volume of that slice, and summing.

It is a good idea to cover Example 1 in class (the volume of the Great Pyramid of Egypt) since it is revisited in the next section where the total work required to build it is computed. In addition, it is easy to think of the Great Pyramid as being laid down in layers of square cross sections.

Problem 19 is lovely (and hard); assign it with the expectation of going over in class. As with all 'table of values' problems, if you are going to do this in class, it might be a good idea to hand out a copy of the table rather than writing it on the board. A simpler version of the same idea is problem 17. You might want to ask your students why it is natural to have circumference measures for the tree rather than radius measures.

Derive the general formula for the volume of a right circular cone, and discuss a few variations; a skewed cone, a pyramid (cone with square cross-sections). Without going through the derivation, you might want to mention the general formula; all of these figures have volume equal to 1/3 the area of their base times their height; this is the generalization to three dimensions of the formula for the area of a triangle. Problem 15 is relevant here.

If you cover arclength, avoid examples that have been artificially constructed so that the integral can be easily calculated using the fundamental theorem. A lot of Chapter 6 is devoted to getting across the point that there are naturally occurring integrals that cannot be evaluated in elementary terms, or not easily, and that for such integrals one may and sometimes must fall back on numerical methods; it would be a pity to waste all that preparation. So pick any interesting curve you like, such as a piece of a parabola or a cubic, or an arch of the sine function.

Although we don't cover surface area, you can make quite a good project out of it, namely the following project on viewing the earth from a spacecraft orbiting the earth and from the moon.

☐ **Example 5**   On Christmas Day, 1968, the Apollo 8 crew orbited the moon. In April, 1983, two members of the space shuttle Challenger performed an activity outside the Challenger at an altitude of 280 km above the surface of the earth.

What percentage of the Earth's surface could the Apollo 8 team see? What percentage could the Challenger team see? How far above the surface of the earth would you have to be to see 10% of the earth's surface?

Here are some useful facts: the earth is approximately a sphere of radius 6,380 km, the moon is approximately 376,000 km from the center of the earth.

This requires the student to know the formula for the area of a segment of a sphere. Most of them won't be able to derive it correctly, but there is a lot to be learned from the effort. Most of them will make the standard mistake of trying to calculate the surface area using cylinders rather than frustra (sloped cylinders). It is good to let them make this mistake for two reasons; first, it yields absurd answers, and thus provides a good test of how much they are using their common sense (only about 40% of the earth is visible from the moon: if they don't think that's absurd, ask them how much of the moon can be seen from the earth). Second, the correct way of calculating surface area is much better appreciated once the obvious approach has been seen to be wrong. By the way, a few students will look the formula up in a book; by all means give them full marks for this, as long as they can give the reference. The ability to find an answer by research will stand them in good stead and should not be discouraged. The point of this project is not to teach the students the method for calculating areas of solids of revolution, but to train them in solving real world problems where the method is not laid out before them.

7.4: Applications to Physics

One to two classes.

Key points

Definition of Work. Getting total force using known pressure.

Ideas for the class

Use your judgement and interests to choose which applications you wish to cover from this section. The concept of work is often puzzling to students, so make it clear that work is force exerted during motion in a direction parallel to the force. Show in class, by holding a heavy object stationary and walking across the room that you are doing no work, since the force is perpendicular to the direction of motion. By all means do Example 2 in class.

The escape velocity examples are good if you have a class that has some background in physics – otherwise it is just mystifying. It does give an example of a typical improper integral that is often seen in physics.

The examples on force and pressure are good for a wider audience – most everybody has experienced water pressure.

Here is a pair of examples that can generate some good discussion of the physical concepts of work and force. (Of course, this is a calculus course, not a physics course, but it seems pointless to discuss applications to physics without getting some intuition for the concepts of physics). Consider a large aquarium tank (say, in the New England Aquarium). You are facing the front glass panel of this tank, which is 10 feet high and 20 feet long. The distance to the back of the tank is 5 feet wide. First find the force exerted on the front glass panel of this tank, then find the work required to pump all the water out of it. You will find that the work required is equal to force on the front panel times the distance to the back of the aquarium. This is true no matter what dimensions you choose. Is there another way of seeing this? Answer: you could pump all the water out of the tank by pushing the front glass panel to the back of the tank (assuming the seal with the side walls and floor did not leak). This brings out a number of physical concepts: first, that the work done is independent of the method used, and secondly that the force on the front panel does not depend on the distance to the back of the aquarium. This latter point is implicit in the way the force is calculated, but may not have been appreciated by the students. If they have an intuitive notion that the force *should* depend on the distance to the back of the aquarium, ask them to imagine that the glass is holding back an ocean; does it have to be twice as strong for an ocean twice as big?

Problem 18 is hard – watch out!

7.5: Economic Applications

One or two classes.

Key points

Definitions of present and future value. Income streams. Consumer and producer surplus.

Ideas for the class

Students of different ages react very differently to the material of present and future values. Adult students who have paid off mortgages or sent children to college understand the time value of money readily; for regular-age undergraduates or high school students the idea is much harder. If you cover this section be prepared to go slowly. Before you talk about any integrals at all, make sure you have clearly established the point that $100 now is not the same as $100 a year from now. Some students will understand this intuitively, others will have a great deal of trouble with it, particularly when you try to quantify the difference. After explaining this point, do an example like Example 1, where you are given a choice between a lump sum payment now, or smaller payments in the future. How do you decide which is more favorable? (The text ignores inflation – you might want to ask students to show how inflation affects the decision.) Then do an example where you assume the income stream is continuous and evaluate an integral. Here are a couple of possibilities.

Suppose you are a writer working on a best seller. Publisher X offers you an advance of $50,000, and 5% royalties on sales, which, starting two years from now, are expected to increase exponentially for five years according to the function $S(t) = 1000000 \cdot e^{0.1t}$ dollars/year, and then abruptly die away. Publisher Y offers you no advance but 6% royalties, with the same expectations for sales. Which deal is better, assuming an interest of 10% for the next 7 years? (Answer: both deals have the same present value.)

Here is another problem: the typical high school graduate will get a job starting at $20,000 a year, and the typical college graduate will get a job starting at $30,000 a year. Both can expect 5% annual pay raises. College tuition runs at about $10,000 a year. Does it pay to go to college? Assume an annual interest rate of 10%. This problem can be made more complicated and realistic, which would be suitable if you wanted to make it into a project. You can have different rates for the pay raises, have ceilings on the salaries, and take into account the shorter working life of the college graduate.

One point that persistently confuses students is the following; if you have a constant income stream of $1000 per year, at an interest rate of 10%, is the present value equal to $\int_0^\infty 1000e^{-0.1t}\,dt$, or is it $\int_0^\infty 1000te^{-0.1t}\,dt$? (Answer: the first.) They have a tendency to want to multiply the rate money is coming in by the time before integrating. This is a sign that they are not thinking of the dt in the correct way; it *is* the time by which you multiply the rate. This is a chance to repeat this point.

Problem 9, on the Siberian pipeline, is quite hard but a very good test of the students' modeling ability; the hard part is not evaluating the integral, but figuring what integral to evaluate. You may want to assign it as a project rather than a normal homework problem; if so, you can supplement it as follows.

Suppose that the Soviet Union follows the deal outlined in Problem 9, and delivers gas at the rate you have found until 1992. By this time, neither West Germany nor the Soviet Union exists; the newly unified Germany urgently needs cash, and is willing to accept a reduced return of 6% (compounded continuously); and the Commonwealth of Independent States wishes to discharge some of the contracts which its predecessor, the Soviet Union, negotiated. So it starts increasing the rate of gas delivery by 2 billion m^3 each year. When will the loan be paid off and at what rate will the Commonwealth be delivering gas in that year?

You can choose not to cover Consumer/Producer surplus, but it is a lovely application of integration. It probably takes about a half class to set up, since you have to explain supply and demand curves as well as the notion of equilibrium price.

7.6: Distributions and Probability

One or two classes.

Key points

The notion of a continuous distribution as being a smoothed out histogram. General density functions. Definitions of mean and median for any density function. Interpretation of cumulative distribution. Normal distributions.

Ideas for the class

There is a lot here, and almost all of it will be new to students. Probability is an important application of the definite integral, so it is worthwhile spending class time presenting this material carefully. The main hope is to introduce the students to the basic terms and what they mean. Students have some familiarity with 'grading on a curve' so you can use this to motivate a discussion of the normal distribution. Bear in mind, however, that this is not intended to be a mini course in probability.

One of the things that students find hard is the idea of displaying data according to percentages. It's also not such an easy thing to smooth out a histogram. They are dying to assign an interpretation to the value of the density function itself rather than be content with an interpretation of its integral over an interval. In other words, many students believe that $p(20) = 0.18$ is telling them that 18% of the population has $x = 20$.

When you talk about the normal distribution you should mention the connection between the standard deviation and the inflection point of the curve. This is a good opportunity to remind them of their earlier work on families of curves back in Chapter 5. (Varying the shape of the standard distribution curve was one of the examples in that section.)

A good class exercise is to hand out a worksheet with a probability density function for the grades in a hypothetical calculus class. Make the curve skewed in some way, and graph it on paper with grid squares so that areas can be estimated. Then ask various questions about the class: how many students are getting a B or better? how many are failing? what are the median and mean grades? (Note that the mean is harder to estimate from the graph.)

Another possibility is to take a survey (say of heights) of the students in your class and use this to generate the histogram and probability density function. These ideas are done in more detail in the appendix on page 86 (an alternative class outline).

Problem 12 is difficult but worthwhile; assign in one class and discuss in the next.

8.1: What is a Differential Equation?

A half to one class.

Key points

What a differential equation looks like and what it means for a function to be a solution. The significance of initial conditions and arbitrary constants in solutions.

Ideas for the class

This class can be combined with the next one if you want to get straight into the visualization of differential equations using slope fields.

One way to introduce differential equations is by analogy with algebraic equations. Differential equations have functions as solutions rather than numbers. Algebraic equations model simple problems where the solution is a number; differential equations model more complex problems where the solution is described by a function.

Start with a simple example that illustrates this modeling procedure, such as the following. A yam is placed inside a $200°C$ oven. The yam gets hotter at a rate proportional to the difference between its temperature and the oven's temperature. When the yam is at 120°C, it is getting hotter at a rate of 2° per minute. Write a differential equation that models the temperature, T, of the yam as a function of time, t. (Answer: $dT/dt = 0.025(200 - T)$.) Show that

$$T = 200 - Ce^{-0.025t}$$

is a solution to this differential equation for any constant C. Discuss the significance of the constant C (it's the initial temperature difference between the yam and the oven). Solve for C in the particular case when the initial temperature of the yam is 20°. You do not need to explain how to get this solution now, but you should mention that part of this chapter will be devoted to methods of finding such solutions. Discuss from an intuitive point of view why you would expect an arbitrary constant in the solution (the differential equation describes many different situations, with different initial temperature differences) and how you calculate the specific value of the constant given a specific initial value.

Point out that antidifferentiation is a particular case of solving a differential equation, namely $dy/dx = f(x)$, and that there the arbitrary constant appears added to the solution, not multiplied.

Repeat that the solution to a differential equation is a *function*, and that unless specific conditions are given there are usually many solutions to a given differential equation. It's a good idea to do a few examples where you verify that a certain function solves a certain equation, i.e., make sure they know what it means to 'plug in' a function to a differential equation.

For example, verify that $y = 2x - 4$ is a solution to $dy/dx = x - (1/2)y$, and that $y = \sin 2t$ is a solution to $d^2y/dt^2 + 4y = 0$. At this stage you should also mention the concept of the order of a differential equation, and its relation to the number of arbitrary constants to expect in the solution. Solve a simple second order differential equation such as $d^2y/dx^2 = x$ to show that you get two arbitrary constants in that case. Do not at this stage go too deeply into the question of determining these constants; for the next few sections the book concentrates on first order differential equations.

8.2: Slope Fields

A half to one class.

Key points

Solving first order differential equations graphically.

Ideas for the class

It's best for this section (and others that follow) if you have available a computer program that draws slope fields and can project them on a screen, such as the University of Arizona program SLOPES. Slope field programs for the graphing calculator are included in this manual. If no technology is available, you can photocopy some of the prepared slope fields later in this manual, or make overhead transparencies of various slope fields and trace the solutions in pen. In any event, you may want to do an example by hand, just to make sure that the students get the point; in particular, make sure that they remember what various slopes look like: a large positive slope, a small positive slope, a large negative slope, a slope of 1/2, 1 or 2. (You might want to begin by revisiting the problem of constructing antiderivatives as in Section 6.12, as a special case of a first order differential equation.) You can explain slope fields as a set of sign posts. There's one at each point, and wherever you are, it tells you in what direction to move. You move a little, and there's the next sign post, etc., etc. Students are often uncomfortable with eyeballing slope fields at first. It is surprising how accurate you can be with careful drawing of slope fields; try drawing the solution to $dy/dx = 1/x$ from $x = 1$, $y = 0$ to $x = 2$, and see how close to $\ln 2 = 0.7$ you get (or get the students to do this on work sheets). If you are projecting slope fields onto a white board, get students to come and draw solutions directly on the board, over the projected slope field, and then ask them to criticize each other's efforts. Make sure that they understand that the solutions they draw on the slope field are the same as the solutions given in the previous class. For example, if you gave the example $dy/dx = x - (1/2)y$ with solution $y = 2x - 4$ in the previous class, show in this class how the graph of $y = 2x - 4$ fits into the slope field of that equation.

One good exercise, that can be done either in the way described above, or on worksheets that you hand out, is to give students the slope field of the yam equation from the previous class (or, if you gave them another example, give the slope field from that example). You can see a lot more about the general behavior of solutions from the slope field than from the specific solution. Illustrate how the general behavior of the solution depends on the initial conditions by getting the students to draw three solutions, one starting above the equilibrium solution ($T = 200$), one starting on it, and one starting below it. It is a good test of their understanding whether they will cross the equilibrium solution, or whether, starting on it, they will stay on it. Ask them why a solution can never cross the equilibrium solution. (Once you are on the line $T = 200$ you can't leave it because the signposts don't let you.) Also, point out how to read the arbitrary constant in the previously derived analytic solution from the graph of the solution on the slope field (it is the difference between 200 and the point where the solution crosses the y-axis).

For the homework exercises you might want to hand out worksheets which are photocopies of the problems in the book. Students can hand these in instead of ripping out pages from their books.

8.3: Euler's Method

One class.

Key points

Solving differential equations numerically.

Ideas for the class

Having treated first order differential equations graphically, we now treat them numerically. You can teach this class as a computer lab rather than a conventional lecture. But be sure that the students realize just exactly what it is they are computing; what is the data they supply, what is the output. Again, it is important that they realize that the solutions they produce numerically are the same as the ones of the previous two lectures. Make the connection with the graphical point of view by illustrating Euler's method on a slope field; show how to see graphically whether approximate values are greater than or smaller than the true value.

For example, give them $dy/dx = 1/x$, and ask them to compute the value at $x = 2$ of the solution that goes through the point $(1, 0)$, using 2 steps first, and then 10. This is of course the natural logarithm, so they can compare their answers with $\ln 2$. The first time they do Euler's method, they should do it by hand (i.e., using a calculator for the actual calculations, but not a program). However, don't give the impression that they need to be able to do it by hand all the time; in practice they will use a calculator or computer. The point of the exercise is to understand the algorithm by going through it step by step. If you are using a slope field program that draws in solutions as well, you can introduce Euler's method by asking the students how they think the program draws the solution curves.

Another possibility is to take the yam equation, start at $T = 20°$ when $t = 0$, and follow its temperature for the first 5 minutes. These sorts of calculations are best set up as a table of values, with t, T, and dT/dt in three columns (see Table 0.9). This way they can see how to calculate each piece of data from the previous one. Compare this solution with the exact one obtained two classes ago, to show that the numerical solution is an approximation to that solution.

Mention that there are more efficient methods than Euler's method, and that in real life differential equations are often solved numerically. Just as it's an exception to be able to find a simple

t	T	$dT/dt = 0.025(200 - T)$	Exact solution: $200 - 180e^{-.025t}$
0	20	4.50	20.00
1	24.5	4.39	24.44
2	28.89	4.28	28.78
3	33.17	4.17	33.01
4	37.34	4.07	37.13
5	41.41	3.96	41.15

Table 0.9: The yam in the oven.

antiderivative for a given function, it's an exception to be able to find a simple formula for the solution to a differential equation.

8.4: Separation of Variables

One class.

Key points

Solving certain special first order differential equations analytically. Equilibrium solutions, stable and unstable equilibria.

Ideas for the class

This is the only analytic technique students will be shown for solving first order differential equations. Success with the method depends on being able to antidifferentiate both sides after the variables have been separated.

It is very important to retain the graphical point of view while doing these exercises; students often fail to make the connection between the analytic solutions and the ones pictured in the slope fields. Take the yam equation (or whatever other running example you have been using) and solve it using separation of variables; then graph the solutions for various different values of the constant, and show that they look the same as the ones obtained from the slope field. Explain also how to read the equilibrium solution from the analytical form of the differential equation (look for a y value that makes the right hand side zero), and point out that this is the same as looking for horizontal lines on the slope field where all the slopes are zero.

Choose a few examples from the long list of problems at the end of the section. Make sure you do some initial value problems as well as those with general solutions.

8.5: Growth and Decay

One class.

Key points

Solutions of the growth equation. Applications to compound interest, radioactive decay, Newton's Law of Cooling.

Ideas for the class

While this section covers some material that has been seen earlier, there is a shift in emphasis towards modeling which is a good preparation for the following section. Emphasize how to go from a verbal statement to a differential equation. Do a simple population or bank balance example; for example, consider a population of rabbits that starts at 100 and grows at a continuous rate of 3%; how many rabbits are there after 10 years? Some students will know immediately that the answer is $100e^{0.3}$, but they may not know how to translate the percentage growth rate into a statement about derivatives; that is the point of going over this exercise in detail. Explain how the continuous growth rate of 3% a year translates into the equation

$$\frac{dP}{dt} = 0.03P,$$

where P is the population after t years. Something like the following will do: since the growth rate is 3%, the percentage growth during a time interval of dt years is $0.03\,dt$, so the actual change in population is $0.03P\,dt$, i.e., $dP = 0.03P\,dt$. You need to be careful about the distinction between an annual growth rate and a continuous growth rate. The students should have seen this distinction before, but you might want to ask them to read the paragraphs at the end of this section, where it is explained again. Emphasize that it is not necessary to know what P is to write down the differential equation for it; in fact, that's the whole point. Then solve the differential equation by separation of variables ($P = P_0 e^{0.03t}$), and show how to go back and look at the problem to find the initial value ($P = 100$ when $t = 0$); then use the initial value to find the arbitrary constant ($P_0 = 100$). Finally, use the solution to answer the question: $P(10) = 135$, so there are 135 rabbits after 10 years. Since we are interested in modeling the real world here, it is worthwhile discussing why it does not make sense to quote $P(10)$ to more decimal places ($100e^{0.3} = 134.98588$). It is also worthwhile asking whether the answer makes sense (yes, the population grew in 10 years by 35%, which is close to but more than 10 times the annual percentage rate of 3%, as it should be). In this and the next few sections you should continually remind the students to check their answers against common sense.

Also do a more complicated example, such as Example 3, where the differential equation itself contains an arbitrary constant (the constant of proportionality) whose numerical value is not given, or must be gleaned from the word problem. You can get an interesting class discussion by asking whether Newton's Law makes any sense. If you have been doing the yam equation (or even if not), assign 8, or do it in class.

Students may need to be reminded of the meaning of continuous compounding; some, remembering that it has something to do with the exponential function, will want to say that if B is a bank balance compounded continuously at a rate of 10% then $dB/dt = e^{0.1}B$ or some such error. Don't bring this up if they don't; just be prepared for it.

8.6: Applications and Modeling

One to two classes.

Key points

Translating a verbal description into a differential equation.

Ideas for the class

In this section we go into more detailed examples of how to model a real-world application with a differential equation. It is better to do a couple of examples carefully than to do many perfunctorily. The examples in the text provide models for how the analysis should proceed. Some of your students will feel they should be able to write down the differential equation all at once, without breaking the problem up into pieces. A compartmental analysis problem, such as Example 3 in this section, is a good example to counteract this tendency, because although it is too complex to solve in one blow, it is susceptible to a simple logical analysis. To help students set up differential equations, write the equations in words first. Show how to recognize stable and unstable equilibria.

Here is another example you can use in class. A person is in an unventilated room, which is 3m long, 2m wide, and 2.5m high. The person's rate of breathing depends linearly on the amount of carbon dioxide in the air; when the air has its usual amount of carbon dioxide, 0.04%, the person breathes at a rate of 15 cubic decimeters per minute; but when the carbon dioxide increases to 3.0%, the rate of breathing doubles (a decimeter is 1/10 of a meter). Expired air contains about 4.0 percentage points more carbon dioxide than the air breathed in. Write a differential equation for the concentration of carbon dioxide in the air at time t. Answer: let c be the concentration at time t. The rate of breathing r depends on c linearly; we have $r = 15$ when $c = 0.04$, and $r = 30$ when $c = 3.0$, so

$$r = 5.07c + 14.8.$$

The concentration of carbon dioxide in expired air is $c + 0.04$, so carbon dioxide is being added to the air at a rate of $(c + 0.04)r$ decimeters per minute. The volume of the room is 15,000 cubic decimeters, so to get the rate of change of the concentration you need to divide the above rate by 15,000. Thus

$$\frac{dc}{dt} = \frac{(c+0.04)r}{15,000} = \frac{(c+0.04)(5.07c+14.8)}{15,000} = \frac{5.07c^2 + 15c + 0.59}{15,000}.$$

At this point it might be best to solve the equation using slope fields, although it can be solved by separation of variables. It is also worth pointing out that neither of the equilibrium solutions make any physical sense in this problem.

Problem 2, which has to do with weight gain and loss, can generate lively class discussion.

In working any examples, make sure that you pause to ask whether the numbers given make sense; for example, in the respiration problem above, ask whether a breathing rate of 15 dc^3/min makes sense; get the students to give rough estimates of the amount of air they expel with each breath and the number of breaths per minute. In the body weight problem, ask the students how many calories there are in a typical bowl of cereal, and convert the given caloric intake in part (c) into bowls of cereal to see if it makes sense.

8.7: Models of Population Growth

One to one and a half classes.

Key points

Exponential and logistic models of population growth. Analyzing the logistic equation using slope fields.

Ideas for the class

It is sufficient to cover the logistic model qualitatively – you needn't derive the exact solution. If you do, you will need to explain the partial fractions or use the table of integrals. Explain how to recognize the general form of the logistic equation, as distinct from the exponential growth or Newton's law type. The logistic equation is very good for teaching students to read differential equations (without solving them); one can easily see the equilibrium solutions are $P = 0$ and $P = L$, and this in turn gives an interpretation of the constant L. One can also see that when P is small relative to L, the equation is approximately the same as the exponential growth equation, with exponential growth rate kL. This means that kL is roughly the initial growth rate of the population. It is well worth pointing out that the inflection point in the logistic curve occurs when the population reaches half the carrying capacity; you can see this analytically, as in the book, or you can simply observe it from the solution curves on the slope field. It also makes sense that the growth rate should be at its maximum when you are half way to the maximum population.

As a variation on exercise 6 you can try to fit a logistic curve to U.S. population data (given in that exercise) in the following way. First, determine the initial exponential growth rate, either numerically by taking successive ratios of the initial data, or graphically on a computer by experimentally finding an exponential function which fits the data initially (the University of Arizona program TWIDDLE would be useful for this). Then plot all the data and estimate where the inflection point is (there is a lot of room for disagreement here). This enables one to estimate the carrying capacity L, and since kL is equal to the initial growth rate, one can then estimate the constant k. As a followup you can assign exercise 6 to see if it works any better. No matter how you do it, you can't get a really satisfying fit with the logistic curve; this can lead to a discussion of models vs. real world data, how good a fit one should expect, and what constitutes a good fit.

Problem 5 is a lovely one for generating discussion. Ask the class to justify (or dispute) the two models proposed for the spread of information.

8.8: Two Interacting Populations

One class.

Key points

Systems of differential equations. Phase planes, trajectories. Equilibrium points.

Ideas for the class

The example in the book is a good one and you can base your classes on it, perhaps changing the robins and worms to lynxes and hares. You need to be extra careful here in explaining what the solution curves on the slope field mean; emphasize that the curves being drawn on the slope field are not the solutions to the system of differential equations, but trajectories of solutions; time is not shown on either axis. Also be sure to explain how to see in what direction each closed trajectory is traversed, both from the signs in the differential equation, and from common sense (it makes sense that the maximum in the predator population should be closely followed by the minimum in the prey population, but not the other way around).

It is also a good idea to assign or to discuss the models for competing and symbiotic populations. The pictures of slope fields are a great help here. See, for example, exercises 15 and 16. Put some equations like the ones in these exercises on the board and ask the students what sort of situations they represent; predator-prey, symbiosis, competition. Problem 7 is also very good for discussion.

If you want to say more, an excellent reference for additional material is M. Braun's book 'Differential Equations and Their Applications', published by Springer. In Chapter 4, he has a discussion of the history of Volterra's involvement with these problems, the basic phenomenon being populations of predator fish and prey fish in the Mediterranean. An interesting thing to do, which isn't too hard, is to prove the result that the average values of each population over a period are their equilibrium values. This allows one to take into account the effects of fishing, for example. This was part of Volterra's original problem, according to Braun.

8.9: Second Order Differential Equations: Oscillations

One or two classes.

Key points

Deriving the differential equations from the laws of motion; two parameter families of solutions need two initial conditions or boundary conditions; physical interpretation of coefficients and initial conditions.

Ideas for the class

Concentrate on interpretation and understanding in this section, rather than algebraic manipulation. Make sure, however, that you do a few routine examples showing how to find the constants using the initial conditions. Start with an example (perhaps a sideways spring so you don't have to mention gravity); guess the solutions; then substitute and check.

Show graphically that the two ways of parametrizing the solutions of the undamped spring equation ($C_1 \cos t + C_2 \sin t$ and $A \sin(t + \phi)$) yield the same set of solutions (the University of Arizona program FORTUNE is useful for this). You can make quite a good class exercise using computers out of this; write down both forms of the solution, and ask if this means there are four arbitrary constants in the solutions; then get the students to investigate both families on the computer. Do not, however, emphasize the mechanics of going from one form to the other.

In doing examples of initial value problems, continually ask what the solution means in practical terms, and whether it makes sense; for example, if the initial position is zero and the initial velocity is non-zero, it makes sense to get a sine curve, whereas if it's the other way around it makes sense to get a cosine curve. Also discuss the physical significance of the spring constant; a large constant means a stiff spring and a small constant means a weak spring. Relate this to the fact that the frequency is $\sqrt{k/m}$; a stiff spring oscillates rapidly and a weak spring oscillates slowly. Also discuss the effect of the mass on the frequency from the point of view of both the differential equation and common sense.

Questions 10 and 11 are very much in the right spirit, and may be used for class discussion.

Remember that the students do not know any linear algebra, so you can't talk about linear combinations.

8.10: Damped Oscillations and Numerical Methods

One class.

Key points

Equations for damped simple harmonic motion. Expressing a second order linear differential equation with constant coefficients as a pair of first order differential equations; numerical and graphical investigation of these.

Ideas for the class

Explain the idea of damping and the differential equation for damped simple harmonic motion. If you derive the equation, explain carefully the sign of the coefficients by going through a whole cycle and showing that at each stage the damping force is in the opposite direction to the velocity and the spring force is in the opposite direction to displacement; since the velocity and displacement themselves go through all possible sign combinations, this means that sometimes the spring and damping force are in the same direction and sometimes in the opposite direction; point out that the differential equation is automatically taking care of this. After explaining the forces, explain why you expect the solution to look the way it does (oscillations with damped amplitude). Resist explaining to much about how to derive solutions at this stage, since it will be covered later.

Optional: Discuss using Euler's Method for systems of differential equations, using examples from the text or ones of your own.

8.11: Solving Second Order Differential Equations

One class.

Key points

Superposition. The Characteristic Equation; under- and overdamped cases. Solutions using complex numbers.

Ideas for the class

Explain the qualitative difference between the underdamped and overdamped cases, both algebraically and from the point of view of common sense (ask them to compare in their minds a spring oscillating in air and one trying to oscillate in molasses). Do not spend much time on the critically damped case, where the characteristic equation has repeated roots. However, it is worth mentioning that the critically damped solution is often the one with most practical value, since it represents the case where the object returns to its equilibrium as fast as possible without overshooting. This is useful in electronic circuits; for example, the circuit governing your speedometer should be critically damped, so that the needle will react to changes in speed quickly but without overshooting the mark (you used to be able to see examples of both over and underdamped speedometers in old cars).

Work plenty of examples, introducing complex numbers as necessary. It might be a good idea to have students read the appendix on complex numbers before you give this class.

8.12: Appendix: Complex Numbers

As needed.

Key points

Complex numbers. Polar representation. Euler's Formula.

Ideas for the class

Introduce these topics only to expedite the development of other material. You can assign this section for reading, and give a few homework problems on the algebra of complex numbers, but there's no need to go into any of this in great detail.

9.1: Taylor Polynomials

One class.

Key points

Approximating functions by polynomials; making a local approximation around a point by matching values and derivatives at that point.

Ideas for the class

Note that there is no discussion of infinite processes or convergence in this class; all that can wait until later. This class is greatly improved if you have graphing calculators or computer graphing programs in the classroom; otherwise you will want to prepare lots of overheads. It makes an enormous difference to be able to show the students the graphs of the Taylor approximations.

This section is as extension of the ideas in Section 4.9 (Notes on Local Linearity). There we made linear approximations to a curve; here we make polynomial approximations.

Start by reviewing the tangent line approximation, say for e^x at $x = 0$. Compare the value $e^{0.1} = 1.1051709$, obtained on a calculator, with the value of the linear approximation $P_1(x) = 1+x$ ($P_1(0.1) = 1.1$). Draw the graph of e^x and its linear approximation, and point out that the linear approximation has the same value and the same slope as e^x at $x = 0$; then explain that you would expect a better approximation if you could make it have the same rate of bending at $x = 0$. Then go through the derivation of the quadratic approximation by matching the values of the second derivatives. Add the graph of the quadratic approximation to your picture, then calculate

$$P_2(0.1) = 1 + 0.1 + \frac{(0.1)^2}{2} = 1 + 0.1 + 0.005 = 1.105.$$

Then do the general case; add the graphs of P_3 and P_4 and calculate

$$P_3(0.1) = 1 + 0.1 + \frac{(0.1)^2}{2} + \frac{(0.1)^3}{6} = 1 + 0.1 + 0.005 + 0.000167 = 1.105167$$

$$P_4(0.1) = 1 + 0.1 + \frac{(0.1)^2}{2} + \frac{(0.1)^3}{6} + \frac{(0.1)^4}{24}$$
$$= 1 + 0.1 + 0.005 + 0.000167 + 0.000004 = 1.105171.$$

Explain that the calculator could be using a Taylor approximation to calculate its value.

Give the general formula for a Taylor polynomial around $x = 0$, and calculate a few more examples, e.g., the Taylor polynomial of degree 7 for $\sin x$, the Taylor polynomial of degree 3 for $1/(1 + x)$.

Also do an example of an expansion around a point other than $x = 0$, for example $\sqrt{x}$ around $x = 1$.

Each time you do an example, draw the graph of the function and its approximation, and perhaps calculate a value of the approximation and compare it with the function value.

Make sure that students understand the coefficients in the Taylor polynomials are *numbers* that must be obtained by *evaluating* derivatives at a specific point; they are likely to hand in homework answers where the coefficients are functions of x.

You may want to do a couple of examples like Exercises 27 to 29 in class, and assign some others for homework.

9.2: Taylor Series

One class.

Key points

Carrying the Taylor polynomial to infinity; intervals of convergence.

Ideas for the class

This is another class where a graphing calculator or computer graphing program is enormously helpful; the notion of an interval of convergence is very easy to see graphically.

Start the class by pointing out that the approximations for e^x from the previous class (or whatever example you used) all agree for the first few terms, and that each successive approximation is obtained by adding a higher degree term, but leaving the earlier terms the same. This means that to evaluate the next approximation at a point, you simply need to add or subtract a number from the previous one. This quite naturally introduces the idea of thinking of all the terms at once as packaged into a single power series, that you evaluate as many terms of as you want. You should also remind the student of the analogy with decimal expansions at this stage. Draw the graphs of many approximations to e^x to show that they seem to get closer and closer to the graph; calculate e^2 using the Taylor series and compare the rather slow rate of convergence with the rapid rate for $e^{0.1}$; point out that it does converge nonetheless.

Do some similar graphs and calculations for $\sin x$; ask the students how to compute $\sin 100$ using the Taylor series (answer: in principle you could just plug 100 into the series, but in practice it makes sense to first use the periodicity to get close to 0).

Next do an example which has a finite interval of convergence, for example

$$\sqrt{x} = 1 + (1/2)(x - 1) - (1/8)(x - 1)^2 + (1/16)(x - 1)^3 - (5/128)(x - 1)^4$$

around $x = 1$ or $1/x$ around $x = -1$. Show the contrast between what happens at a point inside the interval of convergence and outside, both graphically and numerically. Graphically, successive approximations bunch closer to the graph of the function inside the interval, and diverge more and more sharply outside. Numerically, try calculating $\sqrt{1/4}$ and $\sqrt{4}$ using the Taylor approximation for $\sqrt{x}$ around $x = 1$. Compare the convergence for $\sqrt{1/4}$ with the convergence for $\sqrt{0.9}$.

9.3: Finding and Using Taylor Series

One or two classes.

Key points

Shortcuts for finding Taylor series; applications of Taylor series.

Ideas for the class

Make the point that the Taylor series is not much use as an approximation if you can't find the derivatives of f at $x = a$ relatively easily, or come up with some other way of calculating the Taylor series. Then do some examples similar to those in the text. Here are some other examples: find the Taylor series for e^{-x^2} by substitution; find the Taylor series for

$$\text{Si } x = \int_0^x \frac{\sin t}{t}\, dt$$

by dividing out t from the Taylor series for $\sin t$ then integrating term by term. Check the accuracy of this by comparing its value at $x = 1$ with the value obtained numerically. Or, instead of Si x, do

$$\text{erf } x = \frac{1}{\sqrt{2\pi}} \int_0^x e^{-\frac{t^2}{2}}\, dt.$$

Exercises 19 to 22 are like Example 5; go over one of them in class if you plan to assign them. These examples are good examples of how scientists use Taylor series in practice.

To get students comfortable with applications may take some time as the variables tend to be different (they're not x). However, this time is well spent for students going into science and engineering.

9.4: The Error in a Taylor Polynomial Approximation

One class.

Key points

How to use Taylor's error formula and why you would want to.

Ideas for the class

Many students are not clear on the point of error estimates. One way to motivate this class is to ask them to imagine that they are making a scientific calculator that is supposed to give $\sin x$ accurate to 12 places. The calculator is programmed to subtract multiple of 2π from x to get a number in the range $-\pi \leq x \leq \pi$, and then use a Taylor series. You need to know how many terms of the Taylor series to take to guarantee this accuracy. Emphasize that the point of the error term is to estimate the maximum possible error on an interval; to use it you will need to know some sort of upper bound for the higher derivatives on the interval.

9.5: Fourier Series

One class.

Key points

Global approximations over an interval as opposed to local approximations near a point.

Ideas for the class

This is intended to be a non-technical introduction to Fourier approximations. You don't need to give the justification for the formula for the coefficients. Use a graphing calculator or computer graphing program to show the successive approximations to a function. Do a few examples showing how to calculate Fourier coefficients. The measles example is an example where Fourier polynomials are used not to approximate a function, but to analyze it. Another point to make is that the Fourier series for a periodic function is way of breaking down a complex wave into its simple components; that this is possible is illustrated by the fact that when you listen to a recording of a symphony you can hear all the different instruments individually; your ear (or brain) is performing a Fourier analysis on the sound it hears.

IV Sample Syllabi

Syllabus for Calculus I (Chapters 1-5): University of Arizona

Monday	Wednesday	Friday	Homework
		1.1, 1.2	
1.3, 1.4	1.5 (lab)	1.6-8	Page 6 #1, Page 8 #12; Page 15 #7, Page 15 #10, Page 16 #12, Page 17 #17, and Page 18 #19; Page 29 #16 and Page 29 #18; Page 39 #14.
Holiday	1.10, 1.11	1.9, 1.12 or 1.12 (lab)	Page 47 #8 and Page 49 #17; Page 67 #16; Page 84 #24, Page 86 #36 and Page 87 #42; Page 95 #14.
Homework review	Test 1	Post mortem	
2.1	2.2	2.3	Page 126 #8 and Page 127 #9; Page 145 #3, Page 145 #8; Page 179 #20.
2.4	2.5	2.6	Page 153 #7, Page 153 #8; Page 159 #2, Page 160 #6 and Page 161 #10; Page 165 #4, Page 167 #9 and Page 167 #10
Homework review	3.1	3.2	Page 189 #6 and Page 189 #9; Page 195 #6 and Page 195 #8.
3.3	3.4	4.1, 4.2	Page 201 #2, Page 201 #3, Page 202 #9, Page 209 #6, Page 213 #9, Page 214 #11; and Page 216 #16; Page 223 #3; Page 223 #4; Page 230 #6, Page 230 #7, Page 230 #8, Page 231 #28, Page 231 #29, Page 231 #31, Page 231 #33, Page 231 #36 and Page 232 #41.
Homework review	Test 2	Post mortem	

4.3	4.4	4.5	Page 237 #2, Page 237 #3, Page 237 #7, Page 237 #8, Page 238 #27, Page 238 #28 and Page 239 #30; Page 243 #1, Page 243 #3, Page 243 #7, Page 243 #13 and Page 245 #31; Page 249 #1, Page 249 #6, Page 249 #15, Page 249 #17 and Page 249 #20.
4.6	4.7	Lab on implicit differentiation	Page 255 #3, Page 255 #7, Page 255 #11 and Page 256 #27; Page 261 #2, Page 261 #4, Page 261 #7, Page 261 #8; + Lab reports.
5.1	5.2	5.3	Page 286 #10, Page 287 #18, Page 287 #20, Page 289 #29; Page 297 #18, Page 297 #20, Page 298 #22 to Page 298 #27, Page 356 #21.
Holiday	5.3	5.4	Page 308 #3, Page 309 #6, and Page 310 #13; Page 317 #2.
5.5	5.5, 5.6	Holiday	Page 327 #14, Page 335 #1, Page 335 #3, Page 336 #9.
5.7	5.8	Spare	Page 341 #12 and Page 341 #13; Page 350 #5, Page 350 #6, Page 350 #17 and Page 350 #29-Page 350 #31; Page 351 #34 and Page 351 #38.
Homework review	Test 3	Post mortem	
Review			

Syllabus for Calculus I (Chapters 1-5): Southern Mississippi

Note: Since the number of class days will vary from institution to institution, dates have been omitted from this syllabus. Class periods are assumed to be approximately 50 minutes long. The suggested problems have been selected to give an overview of the types of problems in each section, but there are many excellent problems in the text that are not on the suggested list. Individual instructors may want to add more problems or replace listed problems with others that require less or more use of technology. Do keep in mind that the solution manual is to be viewed with skepticism at this point (i.e., some answers may not be correct), and many of the problems do not have "unique" answers, so be prepared to be flexible. It will be especially helpful if each of you will make note of problems which you liked (or disliked) and any answers that need to be changed. Not all of us have attempted to teach through the entire Chapter 5 in the first semester. You may want to end the semester after 5.3 or 5.4 and adjust the exams.

Section	Approximate Number of Classes	Suggested Problems
1.1	1/2	1, 2, 5, 12, 13, 16
1.2	1	6, 7, 10, 12, 14, 15, 16, 17, 20
1.3	1	1, 2, 5, 7, 8, 17, 18, 19
1.4	1/2	1, 4, 13, 14
1.5	1/2	8, 9, 11, 15, 17
1.7	1/2	4 through 19 (as needed), 20, 21, 25, 27
1.8	1/2	5, 8, 9, 13
1.6	1/2	13, 14, 15, 16
1.11	1/2 to 1	23, 24, 25, 28, 31, 33, 35, 42
1.9	1/2 to 1	1, 2, 3, 6, 11, 14, 15
1.10	1/2 or opt.	1, 2, 14, 15, 35, 37
1.12	1/2 or opt.	5, 8, 11, 13, 20,
Misc. Exercises as needed and then Exam 1		
2.1	1/2 to 1	1, 2, 5, 6, 8, 9
2.2	1	3, 5, 6, 8, 11, 13, 14, 19, 20
2.3	1/2 to 1	3, 4, 8, 14, 17, 20, 31
2.4	1/2 to 1	1, 3, 4, 5, 7, 10, 12
2.5	1	2, 4, 6, 9, 10, 11
2.6	1	2, 4, 9, 10, 11
2.7	opt.	1, 5, 6
2.8	opt.	1, 2, 3
3.1	1	1, 4, 6, 9, 10
3.2	1	4, 6, 8, 11, 14
3.3	1	1, 2, 3, 7, 10
3.4	1	6, 7, 9, 16, 17
3.5	opt.	(none)
Misc. Exercises as needed, then Exam 2		

4.1	1/2	1, 2, 3, 4
4.2	1/2	6, 7, 8, 9, 15, 22, 23, 26, 27, 28, 31, 33, 36, 41
4.3	1	2, 3, 7, 8, 20, 22, 23, 26, 28, 30
4.4	1	1, 3, 7, 11, 13, 18, 22, 24, 31
4.5	1	1, 3, 6, 14, 15, 17, 20, 25, 26
4.6	1/2 to 1	2, 3, 6, 7, 9, 11, 14, 15, 19, 27, 28, 29
4.7	1/2 to 1	2, 4, 7, 9, 13, 15, 17, 18, 20
5.1	1	10, 12, 14, 16, 18, 19, 24, 26
5.2	1	6, 7, 9, 12, 18, 19, 20, 22, 23, 24, 27, 28
Misc. Exercises as needed, then Exam 3		
5.3	1	1, 3, 6, 9, 13
5.4	1	1, 2, 4
5.5	1 to 2	1, 2, 3, 5, 9, 14
5.7	1 or opt.	1, 8, 9, 12, 13
5.8	1	5, 6, 15, 17, 19, 21, 31, 41
Misc. Exercises from Ch 4 and 5 as needed, then Exam 4		

Syllabus for Calculus I (Chapters 1-5): Harvard University

Monday	Wednesday	Friday
1.1, 1.2, 1.3	1.4, 1.5	1.6, 1.7, 1.8
1.10	1.11	1.9
Holiday	2.1	2.2
2.3	2.4	2.5
Review for Exam 1	2.6	3.1
3.2	3.3	3.4
4.1, 4.2, 4.3	4.3, 4.4	4.4 (Lost Day!)
Break	Break	Break
4.5	4.6	4,7, 4.8
Review for Exam 2	5.1, 5.2	5.3
5.3	5.4	5.5
5.6	5.8	5.8
Review	Review	Review

Some of the following problems were used by instructors for in-class examples; others were used for homework. Keep in mind that many new problems were added to the text after this syllabus was written.

Section	Problems
1.1	1, 5, 8, 9, 16
1.2	7, 10, 13
1.3	1 through 6, 8, 10 through 13, 17 through 20
1.4	1, 2, 13
1.5	8, 9, 11, 13, 14, 17
1.6	13, 14
1.7	4, 5, 8, 12, 14, 18, 20, 21
1.8	5, 8, 9, 10, 12
1.9	1, 2, 3, 12 through 15, 16, 17, 18, 19, 19, 20, 26 through 28, 35
1.10	19 through 26, 28, 33 through 36, 42, 44
1.11	1, 2, 11 through 18, 22
2.1	1 through 6, 8 through 10
2.2	3 or 4, 5, 9 through 13
2.3	3 through 6, 8, 10 or 11, 14, 16, 18, 21
2.4	1, 2, 4, 7, 8, 10 through 12
2.5	1 through 7, 10, 11
Misc.	5 through 11, 16 through 19, 22

Section	Problems
3.1	1 or 3, 4, 6, 9
3.2	1, 3, 4, 6, 10, 15, 16
3.3	1, 2, 4, 7, 8, 10
3.4	5, 6, 7 or 8, 9 through 15
Misc.	8, 9, 10, 14, 15, 16
4.1	1, 2, 3, 5
4.2	any of 1 through 16, 17 through 19, 21, 23, 26 through 30, 33, 41, 42
4.3	1, 2, 3, 5, 7, 14, 19 through 22, 26, 27, 30
4.4	1, 2, any of 3 through 16, 19 through 21, 24, 26, 27, 31
4.5	any of 1 through 23, 25, 26
4.6	any of 1 through 20, 24 or 25, 28, 29
4.7	any of 1 through 15, 16 or 17
4.8	11, 12, 14 through 17
Misc.	33, 39
5.1	10, 11 or 12 or 13, 14, 16, 17, 19, 24, 26, 27, 29
5.2	any of 4 through 7, 8, 9 or 10, 11, 12, 15, 19, 21, any of 22 through 27
5.3	1 or 2, 3, 6 or 7, 9, 10, 11, 13
5.4	any of 1 through 5
5.5	1 or 2 or 3, any of 4 through 7
5.6	1, 3, 5 or 6 or 7, 8, 9, 10
5.8	any of 1 through 28, any of 29 through 32, 35 through 38, 40, 41
Misc.	39

Syllabus for Calculus II (Chapters 6-9): Harvard University

(For students who had taken a traditional first semester calculus course from another text)

Monday	Wednesday	Friday
Review: 2.2, 2.3; 3.1, 3.2	3.3, 6.1, 6.3	6.4, 6.5
6.6	6.7	6.8
6.10	6.11	Holiday
6.12	7.1	Review for Exam 1
7.2	7.3	7.3
1.4, 7.4	7.4	7.5
7.5	8.1, 8.2	8.3
Holiday	8.4	8.5, 8.6
8.6	Review for Exam 2	8.7
8.8	Holiday	Holiday
8.9	(8.10), 8.11	8.13
8.12	9.1	9.3
Review	Review	Review
Review	Review	Review

Some of the following problems were used by instructors for in-class examples; others were used for homework. Keep in mind that many new problems were added to the text after this syllabus was written.

Section	Problems
2.2	5, 6, 7, 8
2.3	8
2.4	5, 6
3.1	9
3.3	1, 10
3.4	9, 10, 11, 12, 16
6.3	11, 12, 13, 14, 15, 17, 18, 44, 60, 62
6.4	20, 21, 22, 23, 24, 25, 30, 31, 32, 39, 40
6.5	17, 19
6.6	3, 4, 7, 10, 13, 14, 24, 29, 31, 25
6.7	2, 17, 20, 22, 23, 32, 33, 37, 38, 65
6.8	9, 11, 12, 14, 15, 16, 17, 18, 19
6.10	2, 4, 5
6.12	2

Section	Problems
7.1	2, 5, 9, 11, 15
7.2	1, 2, 5, 6, 10, 12
7.3	2, 3, 5, 6, 8, 12, 14, 17, 18, 20, 21, 22, 25
7.5	4, 5, 7, 8, 9
7.6	1, 2, 8, 9, 12, 15
8.1	2, 5, 6
8.2	1, 2, 3, 9, 10, 11, 12, 13, 14, 15
8.3	1, 2, 6, 7
8.4	9, 10, 11, 12, 13, 14
8.5	4, 6, 7, 8, 9, 10
8.6	1, 2, 5, 7, 9, 10, 11
8.7	2, 3, 5, 6
8.8	4, 5, 6, 7, 11, 15
8.9	7, 8, 9, 10, 11, 13, 14, 21, 22, 27, 29, 31, 41, 42
8.11	1, 2, 3, 9, 11, 14, 15, 24, 25
9.1	1, 2, 3, 4, 7, 10, 12, 22, 32, 34

V   Appendix: Additional Class Material

Probability

Probability Density

Suppose we measure the heights of all the students at a certain college and make a bar graph, or histogram. We mark the horizontal axis in inches, and over each interval we draw a rectangle representing the proportion of the students with heights in that interval, as in Figure 7. For example, the rectangle between 70 and 71 has height 0.07, meaning that 7% of the students have heights between 70 and 71 inches. Notice that the graph is very low at the extremes because few people are

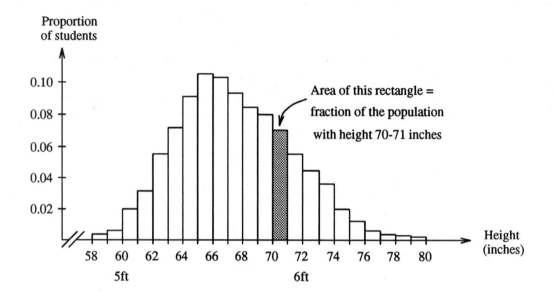

Figure 7: Heights of College Students

very short or very tall. It has a hump in the middle where most people's heights are.

How would we calculate the proportion of students with heights between 5 and 6 feet (that is, between 60 and 72 inches)? We would add the heights of the rectangles corresponding to the intervals 60–61, 61–62, ..., 71–72. Since each rectangle is one unit wide, the height of each rectangle is equal to its area, and we are in fact adding up the areas of these rectangles. Thus the proportion of the student population between 5 and 6 feet tall is the area of the part of the graph between 60 and 72 inches.

Now we will use this histogram to visualize probabilities. Suppose we select a student randomly by writing each student's name on a slip of paper, mixing up the papers and picking one. The *probability* that such a randomly selected student has height between 70 and 71 inches is 0.07, or the area of that rectangle. The probability that the student is between 5 feet and 6 feet tall is the area of the part of the graph between 60 and 72 inches.

Next we will define the *probability density* function, *P*, whose graph will represent probabilities in the same way as the histogram. The tops of the rectangles in Figure 7 form a rough curve. We often idealize by forgetting the rectangles and thinking of the curve as the graph of a smooth function, P, as in Figure 8. This is what you would expect from a large sample and a histogram with very narrow rectangles. The exact details of how such a histogram is constructed are rather complicated and so are not included. However P is defined in such a way that the area under its graph represents probabilities.

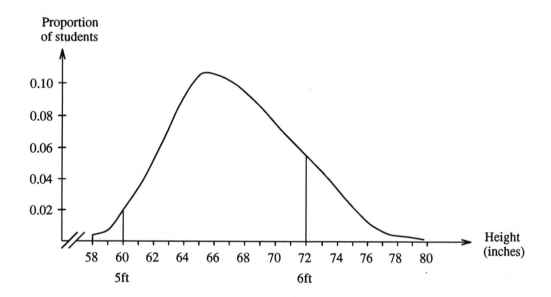

Figure 8: Heights of College Students

Using the histogram, we added up the areas of rectangles to find the probability of picking a student with height between 60 and 72 inches. What we were really doing was computing a Riemann sum for P between these two values. For the idealized function P, the sum of areas of rectangles gets replaced by the area under the curve, or the definite integral:

$$\int_{60}^{72} P(x)\, dx = \text{probability student's height is between 60 and 72 inches}$$

Thus the probability of a student being between 70 and 71 inches tall is the area under the graph between 70 and 71, which is approximately a rectangle of height $P(70)$. See Figure 9. Assuming, as we did earlier, that the proportion of the population with heights in this interval is 0.07, then $P(70) \approx 0.07$.

We are thinking of the heights of the students observed as determined by a random process. In probability theory, a variable whose value is determined by a random process is called a *random variable*. The most important thing to know about a random variable is the probability that it will fall in any particular interval, and this is specified in terms of the areas under the graph of the probability density function. If P is the probability density for the random variable height, then, for $a < b$,

$$\int_{a}^{b} P(x)\, dx = \text{probability that a student's height is between } a \text{ and } b$$

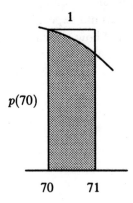

$p(70)$

70   71

Figure 9: Area representing probability a student's height is between $70''$ and $71''$.

Not every function can serve as a probability density function. *If P is a probability density*:

- P must not take on negative values, because probabilities are never negative.

- The total area under the graph of P must be 1, since the total probability of all possibilities is equal to 1.

The probability density

$$P(x) = \frac{1}{\sqrt{2\pi}}e^{-\frac{x^2}{2}}$$

is called the *normal distribution* and represents a distribution which is clustered symmetrically around $x = 0$. See Figure 10. This is one of the most frequently encountered distributions in statistics.

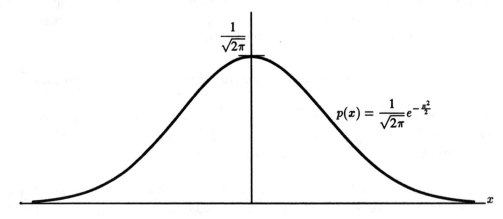

Figure 10: The Normal Distribution

☐ **Example 1**   A random variable is distributed normally. What is the probability that its value falls between

(a) $x = -1$ and $x = 1$

(b) $x = -2$ and $x = 2$

Solution.

(a) Probability that $-1 \leq x \leq 1 = \int_{-1}^{1} \frac{1}{\sqrt{2\pi}} e^{-\frac{x^2}{2}} \, dx$. Since $e^{-\frac{x^2}{2}}$ has no elementary antiderivative, this integral must be found numerically; its value is about 0.68. So

$$(\text{Probability that } -1 \leq x \leq 1) \approx 0.68.$$

(b) Finding the integral numerically again,

$$(\text{Probability that } -2 \leq x \leq 2) = \int_{-2}^{2} \frac{1}{\sqrt{2\pi}} e^{-\frac{x^2}{2}} \, dx \approx 0.95.$$

Notice that $0.68 \approx \frac{2}{3}$ and $0.95 = 95\%$, so we have a rule of thumb that is often used in statistics:

For a normal distribution, $\frac{2}{3}$ of the observations are within 1 of the centerpoint and 95% of the observations are within 2 of the centerpoint.

❑

❑ **Example 2**   There is considerable concern at the moment about the fraction of elderly people in the U.S. population. If this fraction becomes large, the current wage-earners may be unable to support the elderly through Social Security. Figure 11 gives the probability density of ages in the U.S. population in 1988[3]. Use it to estimate the probability that a randomly selected person is
(1) over 65   (2) between 25 and 26.

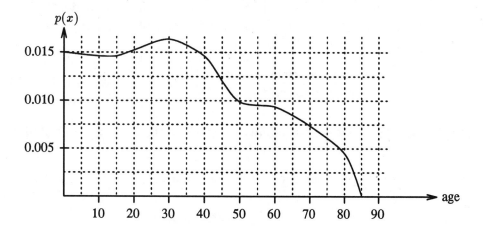

Figure 11: Age Distribution of US Population in 1988

---

[3]Data from "Census and You" (April 1990)

Solution.

1. We want the area under the curve to the right of 65, which is somewhere between 0.10 and 0.15–let's say 0.12. Therefore

   Probability of someone being 65 or over ≈ 0.12.

2. The area under the graph between 25 and 65 is about 0.5, so

   Probability of a person being between 25 and 65 $= \int_{25}^{65} P(x)\,dx \approx 0.5$

❏

Cumulative Probability Distribution

Another way of representing the distribution of a random variable like height is using a *cumulative probability distribution*. For any height h, $C(h)$ is the proportion of the population who are that height or shorter. In other words:

$$C(h) = \text{probability that a randomly selected person has height} \leq h$$

Figure 12 shows the cumulative probability distribution of the heights of the college students whose probability density is in Figure 8. The graph of C starts at zero, and increases slowly because there aren't many very short people. As h passes through the typical range of heights, the graph rises more rapidly. For very large heights, the graph rises slowly again. Eventually, $C(h) = 1$ because h will eventually be larger than the heights of all the students.

How can we use C to find the probability that a randomly selected student is between 5'6'' and 6' (66'' and 72'')? We can read from the graph that $C(66) \approx 0.4$, so the probability of a person being 66'' or less is 0.4, meaning that 40% of the population is 66'' or less. Similarly, $C(72) \approx 0.9$ tells us that 90% of the population is 72'' or less. Thus the proportion of the population between 66'' and 72'' is $0.9 - 0.4 = 0.5$. Therefore

$$\left(\begin{matrix} \text{Probability that a randomly selected} \\ \text{person has height between 66'' and 72''} \end{matrix} \right) = C(72) - C(66) \approx 0.5.$$

What is the Relationship between Probability Density and the Cumulative Probability Distribution?

Since $C(h)$ is the probability that someone has height h or less,

$$C(h) = \int_0^h P(x)\,dx$$

You can confirm this by looking at the area under the graph of P. For small h, the area under the graph of P is small, and so is C. As h increases, we reach the part of P where most of the heights are and begin to pick up area rapidly; this corresponds to the steeply increasing part of C. As we

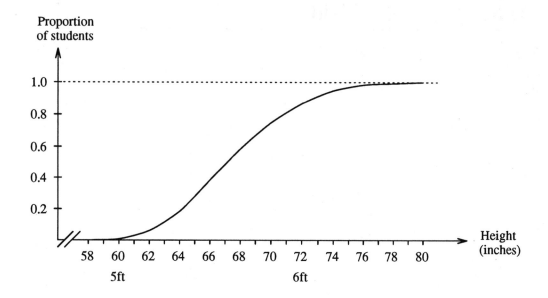

Figure 12: Cumulative Probability Distribution

reach unusually tall heights, the area grows more slowly and the rate at which C is increasing slows down. As $h \to \infty$, $C(h) \to 1$, since the area under the graph of P approaches 1.

Since C is the integral of P, it follows from the Fundamental Theorem of Calculus that

$$C'(h) = P(h)$$

This also fits with the fact that the graph of C is nearly flat at the extremes, where P is nearly zero, and that C is steepest where P is largest. P is largest at about $h \approx 65''$, and at this point C has an inflection.

In summary,

Probability that a person has height between a and $b = \displaystyle\int_a^b P(x)\,dx = C(b) - C(a)$

VI   Appendix: Slope Fields

Masters for overhead transparencies.

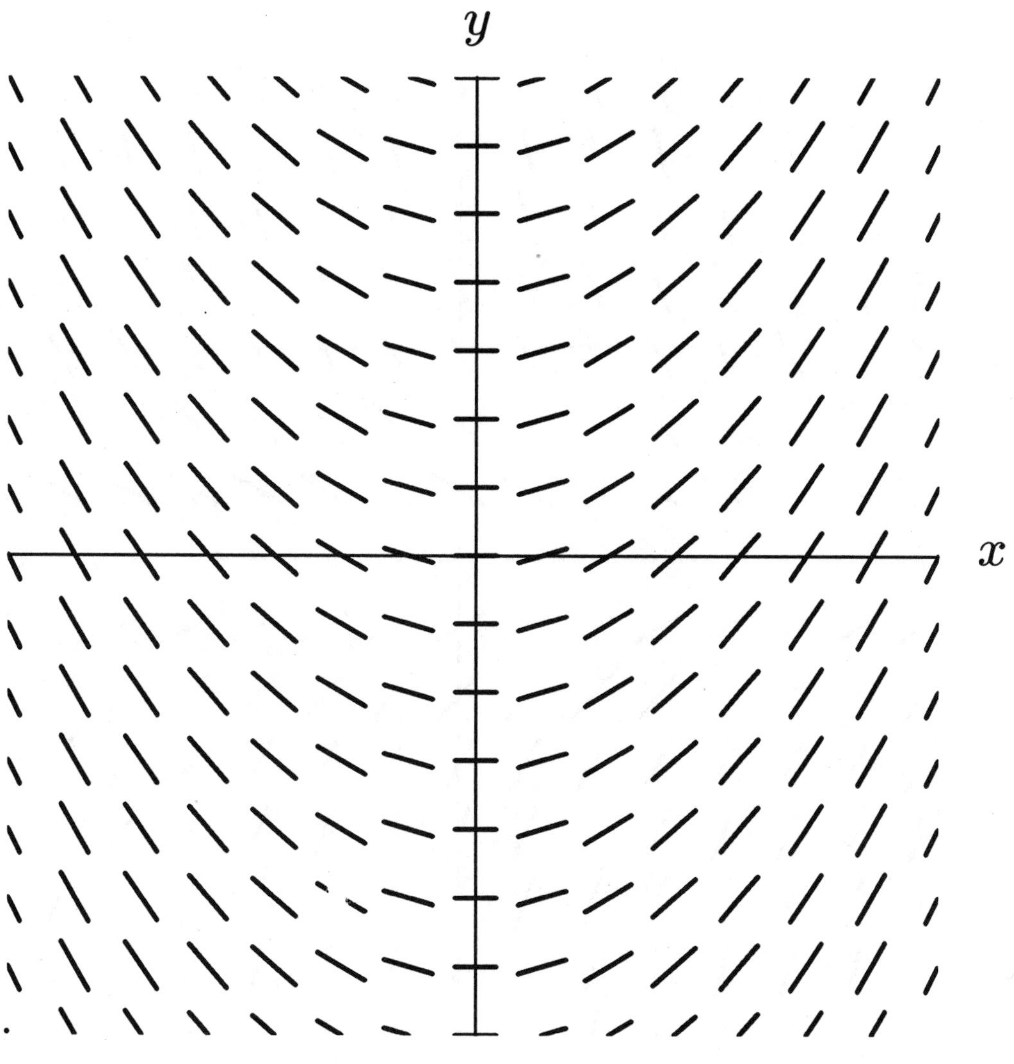

$$\frac{dy}{dx} = x$$

$$-2 \leq x \leq 2 \qquad -2 \leq y \leq 2$$

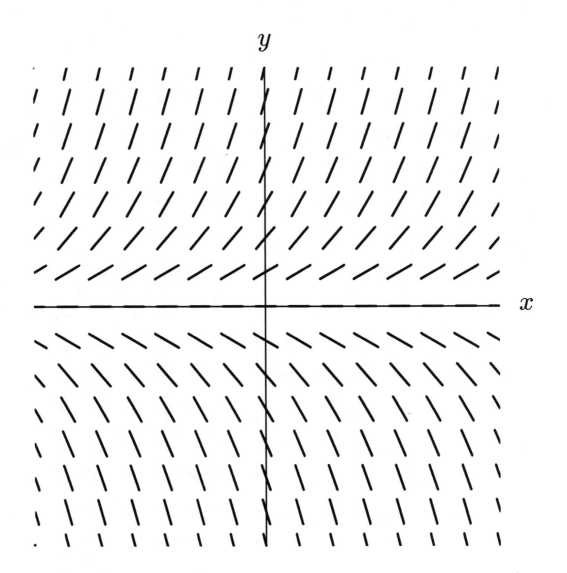

$$\frac{dy}{dx} = y$$

$$-4 \le x \le 4, \qquad -4 \le y \le 4$$

$$\frac{dy}{dx} = x - y$$

$$-4 \le x \le 4, \qquad -4 \le y \le 4$$

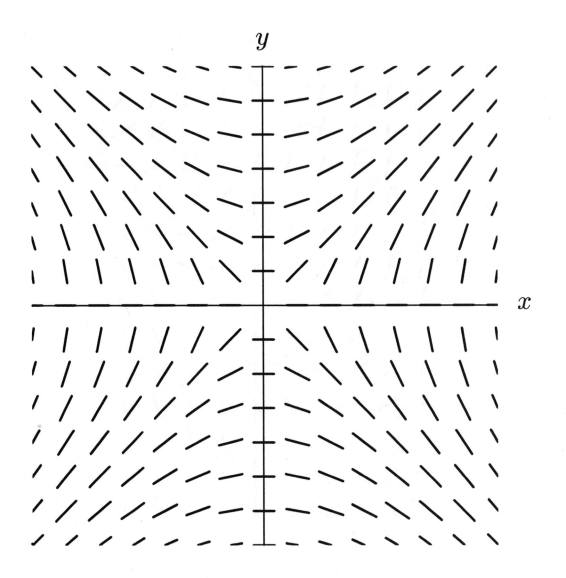

$$\frac{dy}{dx} = \frac{x}{y}$$

$$-4 \leq x \leq 4, \qquad -4 \leq y \leq 4$$

$$\frac{dy}{dx} = x^2 - y^2$$

$$-4 \leq x \leq 4, \qquad -4 \leq y \leq 4$$

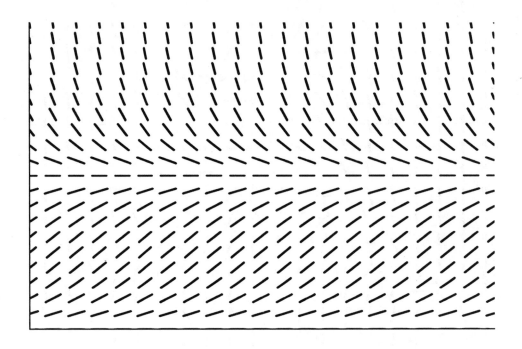

$$\frac{dy}{dx} = 2y - y^2$$

$$-4 \leq x \leq 4, \qquad -4 \leq y \leq 4$$

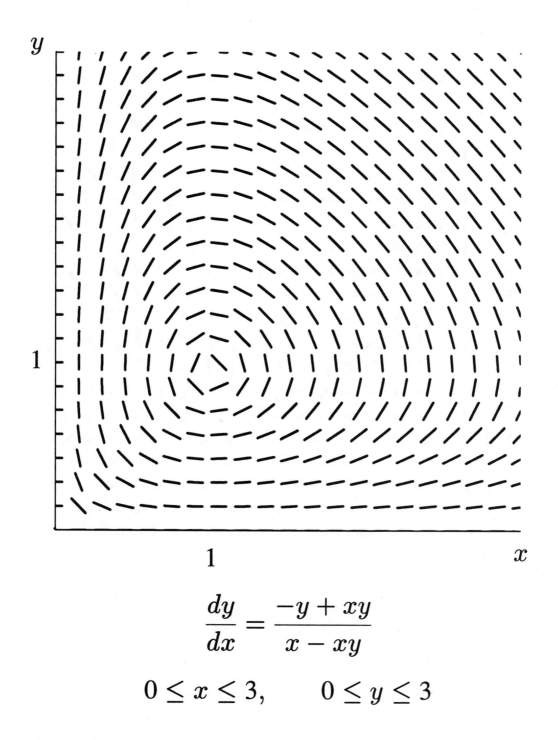

$$\frac{dy}{dx} = \frac{-y + xy}{x - xy}$$

$$0 \le x \le 3, \qquad 0 \le y \le 3$$

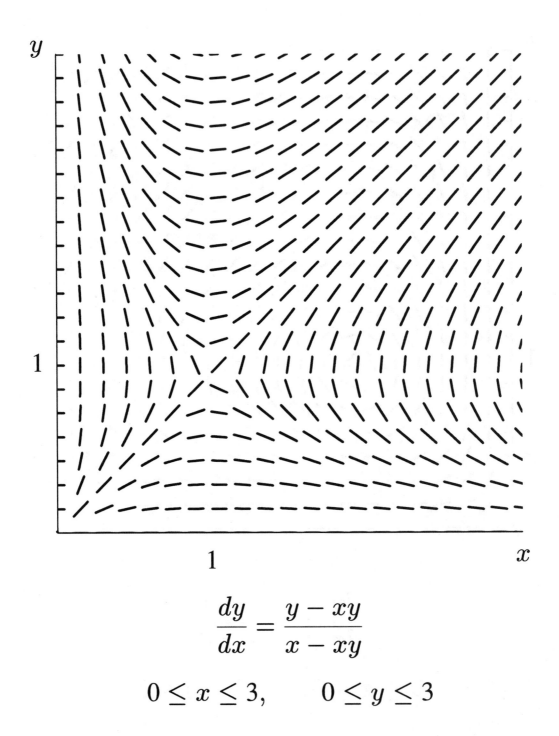

$$\frac{dy}{dx} = \frac{y - xy}{x - xy}$$

$$0 \le x \le 3, \qquad 0 \le y \le 3$$

CALCULATOR PROGRAMS

for the

TI-81

Program to Calculate Riemann Sums to Evaluate a Definite Integral

Select 'PRGM' to get the program menu, move to 'EDIT' to enter a program. When you select a program number, you must first give it a name (for example, 'RSUMS') to the right of the program number.

Program	Notes
:Disp "L-LIM"	Disp and Input are accessed via PRGM, I/O, pressed while in the middle of
:Input A	a program. The " " are on the + key when you have pressed the ALPHA key.
:Disp "U-LIM"	
:Input B	
:Disp "NO.STEPS"	
:Input N	
:$A \to X$	$\to$ is on the 'Sto' key.
:$0 \to S$	
:$1 \to J$	
:$(B - A)/N \to H$	
:Lbl 1	Lbl is accessed via PRGM,CTL.
:$S + Y_1 * H \to S$	Y_1 is accessed via Y-VARS (=2nd VARS).
:$X + H \to X$	
:$IS > (J, N)$	$IS > ($ and GoTo are accessed via PRGM,CTL.
:GoTo 1	
:Disp "LHSUM IS"	
:Disp S	
:$S + Y_1 * H \to S$	
:$A \to X$	
:$S - Y_1 * H \to S$	
:Disp "RHSUM IS"	
:Disp S	

Bug: If the lower limit is greater than the upper, the right hand sum is reported as the left hand and vice versa.

103

This program calculates left and right Riemann sums, and the trapezoidal and midpoint approximations. Since there is not room on the calculator screen for a separate labelling of each approximation, the label LEFT/RT indicates that the next two numbers are the left and right Riemann sums, respectively.

A pair of square brackets indicates a single command. For example, $[IS > (]$ means that the PRGM buttom nust be pushed and then $IS > ($ selected, not that I, S, $>$, and $($ are to be entered separately. [Disp] and [Input] are found under PRGM, I/O pushed while entering a program.

The function to be integrated must be entered as Y_1 (accessed by the "$Y=$" button). When Y_1 occurs in the program, it is evaluated at the current value of X.

To enter a program, hit PRGM and select EDIT and a program number. To finish a line, hit ENTER; to finish entering a program, hit 2nd QUIT.

To run a program, select PRGM,EXEC. To stop a program while it is running, hit ON.

Prgm 1: INTEGRAL	The title.
:[Disp] "LOWER"	
:[Input] A	Enter lower limit of integration.
:[Disp] "UPPER"	
:[Input] B	Enter upper limit of integration.
:[Disp] "N"	
:[Input] N	Enter number subdivisions.
:$(B - A)/N \to H$	Stores size of one subdivision in H ($\to$ means hit STO button).
:$A \to X$	Start X off at beginning of interval.
:$0 \to L$	Initialize L, which will keep track of left sums, to zero.
:$0 \to M$	Initialize M, which will keep track of midpoint sums, to zero.
:$1 \to J$	Initialize J, the counter for the loop.
:[Lbl] 1	Label for top of loop.
:$L + Y_1 H \to L$	Increment L by $Y_1 H$, the area of one more rectangle (Y_1 is accessed via Y-VARS, or 2nd VARS).
:$X + H/2 \to X$	More X to middle of interval.
:$M + Y_1 H \to M$	Evaluate Y_1 at middle of interval and increment M by rectangle of this height.
:$X + H/2 \to X$	Move X to start of next interval.
:$[IS > (]J, N)$	The most difficult step in the program: adds 1 to J and does the next step if $J \leq N$ (i.e., if haven't gone through loop enough times); otherwise, skips next step. Thus, if $J \leq N$, goes back to Lbl 1 and loops through again. If $J > N$, loop is finished and goes on to print out results.
:[Goto] 1	Jumps back to Lbl 1 if $J \leq N$.
:[Disp] "LEFT/RT"	Continues here if $J > N$, in which case the value of X is now B.
:[Disp] L	L now equals the left sum, so diplay it.
:$L + Y_1 H \to R$	Add on area of right-most rectangle, store in R.
:$A \to X$	Reset X to A.
:$R - Y_1 H \to R$	Subtract off area of left-most rectangle.
:[Disp] R	R now equals right sum, so display it.
:[Disp] "TRAP/MID"	
:$(L + R)/2 \to T$	Trap appproximation is average of L and R.
:[Disp] T	Display trap approximation.
:[Disp] M	Display midpoint approximation.

SLOPE FIELD PROGRAM

<u>Where To Find The Command</u>

:ClrDraw	2nd Draw
:All-Off	2nd Y-Vars/OFF
:7$(X_{max} - X_{min})/83 \rightarrow H$	Vars/RNG
:7$(Y_{max} - Y_{min})/55 \rightarrow K$	
:1$/(0.4H) \wedge 2 \rightarrow A$	
:1$/(0.4K) \wedge 2 \rightarrow B$	
:$X_{min} + 0.5H \rightarrow X$	
:$Y_{min} + 0.5K \rightarrow Z$	
:1 $\rightarrow I$	
:Lbl 1	Prgm
:1 $\rightarrow J$	
:$Z \rightarrow Y$	
:Lbl 2	
:$Y_1 \rightarrow T$	
:1$/\sqrt{(A + BT \wedge 2)} \rightarrow C$	
:$TC \rightarrow S$	
:Line$(X - C, Y - S, X + C, Y + S)$	2nd Draw
:$Y + K \rightarrow Y$	
:$IS > (J, 8)$	
:Goto 2	Prgm
:$X + H \rightarrow X$	
:$IS > (I, 12)$	Prgm
:Goto 1	Prgm

This program for the TI-81 obtains and graphs an approximate solution for the differential equation $y' = f(x,y)$ using Euler's method.

The function f is entered as $Y_1 = f(X,Y)$. When called, the program asks for the coordinates of the starting point, the final value of X, and the number of steps to use. The graph is then drawn. The program does not clear the screen to start with, so solutions with different starting points can be graphed consecutively, or solutions with the same starting point but different numbers of steps, or solution curves can be super - imposed on a direction field. When the program is finished, the final Y-value remains in cell Y.

```
:Disp "X START"              *1
:Input X
:Disp "Y START"
:Input Y
:Disp "FINAL X"
:Input B
:Disp "STEPS"
:Input N
:(B − X)/N → H               *2
:All-Off                     *3
:1 → J
:Lbl 1                       *4
:X + H → U
:Y + Y₁H → V                 *5
:Line(X,Y,U,V)               *6
:U → X
:V → Y
:Is > (J,N)                  *7
:Goto 1
```

*1 Disp and Input are single symbols from the PRGM I/O menu.

* 2 The character → stands for the STO key.

* 3 All-Off is a single symbol from the 2nd VARS OFF menu.

* 4 Lbl and Goto are single symbols from the PRGM CTL menu.

* 5 Y_1 is a single symbol from the 2nd VARS menu.

* 6 Line(is a single symbol from the DRAW (= 2nd PRGM) menu.

* 7 Is>(is a single syumbol from the PRGM CTL menu.

Summary

To analyze the trajectories of a system

$$\frac{dx}{dt} = f(x,y), \quad \frac{dy}{dt} = g(x,y),$$

we proceed as follows:

- Qualitative Phase Plane Analysis

  (a) Find the *null-clines*, i.e., the curves where $\frac{dx}{dt} = 0$ *or* $\frac{dy}{dt} = 0$.

  (b) Find the *equilibrium solutions*, i.e., the points where $\frac{dx}{dt} = 0$ *and* $\frac{dy}{dt} = 0$ (the intersections of the null-clines, $\frac{dx}{dt} = 0$ and $\frac{dy}{dt} = 0$).

  (c) Determine the "*general direction*" of the trajectories in the various "sections" between the null-clines and on the various "segments" of the null-clines (choose sample points).

  (d) Sketch possible trajectories, realizing that a limit point of a trajectory must be an equilibrium point.

- To get more detailed *numerical* information, we can use the *Euler Method*, either to approximate the trajectory (Program TRAJECT), or to approximate the solutions $x(t)$ and $y(t)$ (program TIMESER).

- We can find the *slope of the trajectory* at a point (x,y) as

$$\frac{dy}{dx} = \frac{dy/dt}{dx/dt} = \frac{g(x,y)}{f(x,y)},$$

if $\frac{dx}{dt} \neq 0$. In some simple cases, this allows us to find an equation for the trajectories.

Program for Trajectories

Numerical approximation for the *trajectory* (in the phase plane) of the system

$$\frac{dx}{dt} = f(x,y) , \quad x(0) = x_0$$

$$\frac{dy}{dt} = g(x,y) , \quad y(0) = y_0$$

Prgm:TRAJECT
:All-Off
:Disp "X(0)"
:Input X
:Disp "Y(0)"
:Input Y
:Disp "STEP SIZE H"
:Input H
:Lbl 1
:Line(X, Y, X + HY_1, Y + HY_2)
:X + HY_1 \to X
:Y + HY_2 \to Y
:Goto 1

Command	Menu	Mode
All-Off	Y-VARS	OFF,1
Disp	PRGM	I/0,1
Input	PRGM	I/0,2
Lbl	PRGM	CTL,1
Line	DRAW	2
Goto	PRGM	CTL,2
Y_1, Y_2	Y-VARS	Y,1,2

To run this program:

- Enter the differential equations, as $Y_1 = \frac{dx}{dt} = f(X,Y)$, $Y_2 = \frac{dy}{dt} = g(X,Y)$.

- Choose an appropriate RANGE.

- Run the program; if you have seen enough of the trajectory, press "ON" and "2". Then press "ENTER" to continue with other initial values, or another step size.

- To get rid of previously drawn trajectories, press "ClrDraw" (from the DRAW menu), or change the RANGE.

- If you get an edgy, disconnected, or otherwise weird trajectory, choose a smaller step size H.

Program for Time Series

Numerical approximation for the *solutions* $x(t)$ and $y(t)$ of the system

$$\frac{dx}{dt} = f(x,y) , \quad x(0) = x_0$$

$$\frac{dy}{dt} = g(x,y) , \quad y(0) = y_0$$

Prgm:TIMESER
:All-Off
:Disp "$X(0)$"
:Input X
:Disp "$Y(0)$"
:Input Y
:Disp "STEP SIZE H"
:Input H
:$0 \to T$
:Lbl 1
:Line($T, X, T + H, X + HY_1$)
:Line($T, Y, T + H, Y + HY_2$)
:$X + HY_1 \to X$
:$Y + HY_2 \to Y$
:$T + H \to T$
:If $((X_{max} - T)(T - X_{min})) > 0$
:Goto 1

Command	Menu	Mode
All-Off	Y-VARS	OFF,1
Disp	PRGM	I/0,1
Input	PRGM	I/0,2
Lbl	PRGM	CLT,1
Line	DRAW	2
Y_1, Y_2	Y-VARS	Y,1,2
If	PRGM	CTL,3
X_{min}	VARS	RNG,1
X_{max}	VARS	RNG,2
>	TEST	3
Goto	PRGM	CTL,2

To run this program:

- Enter the differential equations, as $Y_1 = \frac{dx}{dt} = f(X,Y)$, $Y_2 = \frac{dy}{dt} = g(X,Y)$.

- Choose an appropriate RANGE (note that X_{min} and X_{max} refer to the horizontal axis of the window, which is time in our case; Y_{min} and Y_{max} refer to the vertical axis: x and y in our case).

- Run the program. To continue with other initial values, press "CLEAR" and "ENTER". To quit, press "CLEAR" twice.

CALCULATOR PROGRAMS

for the

CASIO fx

THE CASIO PROGRAMS COVER LETTER

•All the Casio integration programs call on the function you put in Program 0. The Casio does not have a way to evaluate functions on the fly that the TI does (i.e. Y_1), so the formula that you wish to integrate must be put into Program 0. That is, hit MODE 2, EXE, type $4X^2+11$ or whatever it is you're trying to evaluate (nothing but the unintegrated function itself), and hit MODE 1. Then go for PROG whatever.

•You can put either a colon (:) or a carriage return (EXE) after each instruction (to separate them), except after display signs: ◢ . Those provide their own carriage return.

•If you run out of program steps ("__ Bytes Free") type MODE . 0 which will free up all 422 available steps.

SMALLER CASIO Numerical Integration Program

This is a **Casio fx series** calculator program for the Simpson's Rule numerical integral approximation only. It is derived from a program provided in the Casio documentation, but it is streamlined and condensed

```
"A"→A
"B"→B
"N"→N
A→X
Prog 1
Ans→S
(B−A)÷2N→H
Lbl 1
X+H→X
Prog 1
S+2Ans→S
Dsz N
Goto 1
B→X
Prog 1
S−Ans→S
SxH÷3
```

CASIO Numerical Integration Program

This is a **Casio fx series** calculator program for various numerical integrals. It will display the Left and Right Riemann Sums and the Trapezoid Rule, Midpoint Rule, and Simpson's Rule approximations all at once. The way this program evaluates integrals is by keeping a running total of function values on n subintervals, and then multiplying by the width of the rectangles to obtain the area at the very end. At the end of the program, hitting **EXE** will let you reevaluate the integral with a different number of subdivisions, and hitting **AC** will let you out of the program.

"A="?→A	Integrate from X=a...
"B="?→B	to X=b...
"N="?→N	over N subdivisions.
(B–A)÷2N→H	calculates half the width of a subdivision.
0→L	initialize L, which will keep track of the left sums.
0→M	initialize M, the midpoint sum.
A→X	place X at a, the beginning of the interval.
Lbl 1	top of loop:
Prog 0	evaluate the function at the left edge of the interval.
Ans+L→L	add the result to the left-hand sum running total.
X+H→X	move X to the middle of the interval.
Prog 0	evaluate the function at the middle of the interval.
Ans+M→M	add the result to the midpoint running total.
X+H→X	move X to the beginning of the next interval.
Dsz N	decrease N by 1; if N=0, skip the next step and go on.
Goto 1	bottom of loop.
"L,R,T="	
2HL→L	multiply the sum of left-hand function values by width 2H.
L	display the left-hand sum.
Prog 0	evaluate the function at X=b: the rightmost function value.
L+2HAns→T	add the area of the rightmost rectangle with the left-hand sum
A→X	put X back at a.
Prog 0	evaluate the function at the leftmost edge of the interval.
T–2HAns→T	take the area of the leftmost rectangle out of T.
T	display what is now the right-hand sum.
(L+T)÷2→T	average the left- and right-hand sums.
T	display the trapezoid approximation.
"M,S="	
2HM→M	multiply the midpoint values sum by the interval width.
M	display the midpoint approximation.
(2M+T)÷3→M	calculate Simpson's Rule by weighted averaging.
M	display the Simpson's Rule approximation.

CASIO Slope Field Program

This is a **Casio fx series** calculator program that will generate slope fields

      Unlike the TI program, this doesn't adjust to the preset range. It automatically graphs on X = -4.7 to 4.7 and Y = -3.1 to 3.1. This means that a line of slope 1 will always *look* like a line of slope 1. You can also use multiples of the range ratio, for example from X = -94 to 94 and Y = -62 to 62. The program will work, however, with whatever range you give it; change the 1ˢᵗ 2 lines of this program when you need to.

4.7→D	half the width of the screen area
3.1→E	half the height of the screen area
Range -D,D, ,-E,E	clears the screen and sets the range as just defined
7x2D÷83→H	calculates widths for 11 scaled horizontal divisions
7x2E÷55→K	calculates heights for 7 scaled vertical divisions
K÷H→B	factor needed to calculate segment components
-D+.8H→X	left edge margin
-E+.8K→Z	bottom margin
11→I	do this eleven times:
Lbl 1	top of outer loop (moves across rows)
Z→Y	start down by the bottom of the screen
7→J	do this seven times:
Lbl 2	top of inner loop (moves up columns)
Prog 0	evaluate the function in Program 0
Ans÷B→S	slope of segment
H÷2√(1+S²)→C	cosine, or x-component of segment
BCS→S	sine, or y-component (don't need slope now)
Plot X–C,Y–S	mark end of slope segment from center at X,Y
Plot X+2C,Y+2S	backtrack and mark other end
Line	connect-the-dots
X–C→X	put X back to where it was
Y–S+K→Y	put Y back, then move up ¹/₇ the way
Dsz J	have I done this seven times?
Goto 2	if not, go to the top of the inner loop
X+H→X	if so, move right ¹/₁₁ the way across
Dsz I	have I done this eleven times?
Goto 1	if not, go to the top of the outer loop + start all over
	[if so, the program ends.]

CASIO Euler's Method Program

This is a **Casio fx series** calculator program that will demonstrate graphical solutions for differential equations using Euler's Method.

The fuction to be evaluated is entered as some function of X or Y or both. So instead of typing in something like ln X^2 the way you always do, you can type weird and crazy stuff like $X^2 - Y^2$. When you run the program, it will ask for a starting X and Y value, and an end X value. (When the program ends, the final Y value will be in the Y register.) Unlike the TI, it does not ask you for the number of steps to take—it figures out the best number for itself. However, it counts on the range being X from -4.7 to 4.7 and Y from -3.1 to 3.1. (remember the slope field program?) You may fiddle with this number (the value given to H) if you'd like to. This program does not clear the screen before graphing, so that you can superimpose solutions on slope fields or see solutions in more than 1 place at once, etc.

"X I"?→X	trace the solution passing through (X,...
"Y I"?→Y	Y), and follow it to the point...
"X F"?→B	(X,???).
.15→H	length of a horizontal step.
Lbl 1	top of loop
X+H→U	move horizontally 1 step
Prog 0	figure out how much to...
Y+HAns→V	move vertically
Plot X,Y	plot the old point
Plot U,V	plot the new point (changing (X,Y))
Line	connect-the-dots
X<B⇒Goto 1	If not all the way there, keep going.

CALCULATOR PROGRAMS

for the

HP 48SX

CALCULUS PROGRAMS FOR
THE HEWLETT-PACKARD

PRELIMINARIES

- For Riemann Sums, type: '*expression*', ENTER , 'FUNC', STO

- For Slope Fields, type '*expression*', ENTER , 'EQ', STO

- For Euler's Method, type '*expression*', ENTER , 'DYDX' STO
  For instance, to use Euler's Method on $\frac{dy}{dx} = y(1-y)$, type: 'Y*(1-Y)', ENTER , 'DYDX', STO

- For Trajectories, type '*expression*', ENTER , 'DXDT', STO
  '*expression*', ENTER , 'DYDT', STO

EXECUTING PROGRAMS

- Type RIEM (no quotes this time) to execute the Riemann Sum program

- Type SFIELD to execute the Slope Field program

- Type EULER to execute the Euler's Method program

- Type TRAJ to execute the Trajectory program

NOTES

- It is very important to type the code EXACTLY as it appears on the page.

- To get □ (as appears in TRAJ), you must type ⌐ ·

- To get :: you must type ⌐ +

- Use the △ and ▽ keys to go between answers in Riemann Sums and between X and Y coordinates during input.

RIEMANN SUM PROGRAM

```
        ≪    "INTERVAL
LENGTH?"
":N:" INPUT OBJ→ 'K' STO
"LOWER LIMIT?"
":A:" INPUT OBJ→ 'A' STO
"UPPER LIMIT?"
":B:" INPUT OBJ→ 'B' STO
0 'SUM' B A - K / 'DELTA'
STO
A 'X' STO SUMM SUM 'I'
STO
0 'SUM' STO
A DELTA + 'X' STO SUMM
SUM 'J'
STO 0 'SUM' STO
A  DELTA  2 / + 'X' STO
SUMM
SUM 'H' STO
I DELTA * 'I' STO
J DELTA * 'J' STO
H DELTA * 'H' STO
I J + 2 / 'C' STO
2 3 / H * C 3 / + 'S' STO
S "SIMPSON" →TAG
H "MIDPT" →TAG
C "TRAP" →TAG
J "RHAND" →TAG
I "LHAND" →TAG
{ K A B J I C X Y SUM H S
DELTA
TOTAL} PURGE ≫ ENTER
'RIEM' STO
```

```
       ≪ 1 K FOR C FUNC
EVAL SUM + 'SUM' STO X
DELTA + →NUM 'X'
STO NEXT ≫ ENTER
'SUMM' STO
```

SLOPE FIELD PROGRAM

```
        ≪ RCLF 'flags'
STO -19 SF -2 SF
ERASE { # 0d # 0d }
PVIEW DRAX PPAR
EVAL 4 DROPN OBJ→
'Ymax' STO 'Xmax'
STO OBJ→ 'Ymin' STO
'Xmin' STO '7*(Xmax
-Xmin)/131' →NUM
'H' STO '7*(Ymax-
Ymin)/64' →NUM 'K'
STO .4 H * 'A' STO
K H / 'B' STO 'Xmin
+.5*H' →NUM 'X' STO
'Ymin+.5*K' → NUM
'Z' STO 1 'I' STO
SUB1 {C S Y J I Z
X B A K H Xmin Ymin
Xmax Ymax } PURGE
flags STOF 'flags'
PURGE
        ≫
    'SFIELD' STO
```

```
        ≪ 1 'J' STO Z
'Y' STO SUB2 X H +
'X' STO 'I' INCR
        IF 20 <
        THEN SUB1
        END
    ≫
  'SUB1' STO
```

```
        ≪ EQ →NUM 'S'
STO 'A/√ (1+SQ(S))'
→NUM 'C' STO B C*
S * 'S' STO X C - Y
S - →V2 X C + Y S +
→V2 LINE Y K + 'Y'
STO 'J' INCR
        IF 10 <
        THEN SUB2
        END
    ≫
  'SUB2' STO
```

EULER'S METHOD PROGRAM

```
           ≪ RCLF 'flags'
STO -19
SF -2 SF
"INITIAL COORDS?"
":X:□:Y:" INPUT OBJ→
'X' STO 'Y' STO
"X INCREMENT?"
":x:" INPUT OBJ→
'DELTA' STO
"# ITERATIONS?"
":N:" INPUT OBJ→
'TOTAL' STO
{ # 0d # 0d }
PVIEW DRAX SUB3
{ X Y K C S TOTAL DELTA }
PURGE
flags STOF 'flags' PURGE ≫
ENTER
'EULER' STO
```

```
           ≪ 1 TOTAL FOR
B DYDX →NUM 'K'
STO 'X + DELTA'
→NUM 'C' STO
'Y + DELTA * K' →NUM
'S' STO X Y →V2
C S →V2 LINE
C 'X' STO S 'Y' STO
NEXT ≫ ENTER
'SUB3' STO
```

TRAJECTORY PROGRAM

```
           ≪ RCLF 'flags'
STO
-19 SF -2 SF
"INITIAL COORDS?"
":X:□:Y:" INPUT OBJ→
'X' STO 'Y' STO
"TIME INCREMENT?"
":T:" INPUT OBJ→
'DELTA' STO
"# ITERATIONS?"
":N:" INPUT OBJ→
'TOTAL' STO { # 0d # 0d }
PVIEW DRAX
SUB4 {X Y I K C S TOTAL
DELTA}
PURGE flags STOF
'flags' PURGE ≫ ENTER
'TRAJ' STO
```

```
           ≪ 1 TOTAL FOR
B DXDT →NUM
'K' STO DYDT →NUM
'I' STO 'X + DELTA * K'
→NUM 'C' STO
'Y + DELTA * I' →NUM
'S' STO X Y →V2
C S →V2 LINE
C 'X' STO S 'Y'
STO NEXT ≫
ENTER
'SUB4' STO
```

SAMPLE EXAMS

1. Estimate the value of $f'(x)$ for the function $f(x) = 10^x$.

2. Given $f(x) = x^3 - 6x^2 + 9x - 5$,

   a) Find the slope of the tangent line to the curve at $x = -2$.

   b) What is the equation of this tangent line?

   c) Find all points where the curve has a horizontal tangent.

3. A particle moves in such a way that $x(t) = 4t^2 + 7\sin t$.

   a) What is the instantaneous rate of change at $t = 0$?

   b) What is the instantaneous rate of change at $t > \frac{\pi}{2}$?

   c) What is the average rate of change between $t = 0$ and $t = \frac{\pi}{2}$?

4. Given the following function:

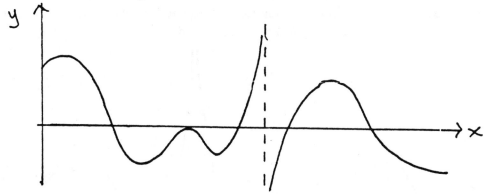

   a) Indicate intervals where it is increasing, decreasing, concave up and concave down.

   b) Sketch the graph of the derivative function.

5. Suppose the Long Island Rail Road's first train out of Easthampton leaves at 4:30 am and takes two hours to reach Manhattan before returning. Draw a graph representing the distance the train is from the Farmingdale station as a function of time from 4:30 pm to 10:30 pm.

1. Differentiate each of the following:

(a) $f(x) = x^{\frac{3}{4}} - x^{\frac{4}{3}} + x^{-\frac{4}{3}}$ (b) $f(x) = xe^{-x}$

(c) $f(w) = \sqrt{(w^2 + 5)}$ (d) $f(\theta) = \sin(2\theta^3 + 1)$

(e) $f(z) = e^{z^2}/(z^2 - 3)$ (f) $f(x) = (x + \sin x)^\pi$.

2. <u>Estimate</u> the value of $f'(1)$ for the function $f(x) = \log_{10} x$.

3. (a) What is the instantaneous rate of change of the function $f(x) = e^{-x^2}$ at $x = 0$? at $x = 1$? at $x = 2$?

(b) Use the information from part (a) to sketch the graph of the function for $x \geq 0$.

4. Find the equation of the tangent line to the curve given by $f(x) = x \sin x$ at the point where $x = \pi/4$.

5. Given the following graph, label all points where the function has a maximum, a minimum, a horizontal tangent, a vertical tangent, a point of inflection or a point where f is not defined.

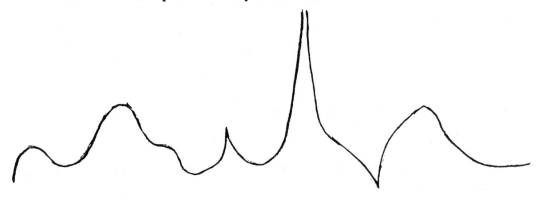

6. (Extra credit.) Consider a ten story building with a single elevator. From the point of view of a person on the sixth floor, sketch a graph indicating the height of the elevator as a function of time as it travels. Remember to indicate when it stops. Try to take into account all <u>types</u> of cases that can happen, but don't worry about <u>every</u> possible situation. (There are many different possible graphs that could be drawn for this.)

1. Given $f(x) = x^4 - 4x^3 - 8x^2 + 1$ on the interval $[-5, 5]$. Find all the maxima and minima and points of inflection. Use this information to sketch the curve.

2. Sketch the graphs of $g(x) = x$ and $h(x) = e^{-x}$ for $x \geq 0$. Use Newton's method to estimate the location of the point of intersection of the two curves correct to four decimal places.

3.   (a) Use the formula for the Taylor polynomial approximation to the function $g(x) = e^x$ about $x_0 = 0$ to construct a polynomial approximation of degree 6 to $f(x) = e^{x^2}$.

   (b) Use the approximation you constructed in (a) to estimate the value of $e^{(.2)^2}$.

   (c) What is the error in this approximation?

4. Find two positive numbers whose sum is 8 such that the sum of the cube of the first and the square of the second is a minimum.

5. A rectangular building is to cover 20,000 square feet. Zoning regulations require 20 foot frontages at the front and the rear and 10 feet of space on either side. Find the dimensions of the smallest piece of property on which the building can be legally constructed.

6. Extra Credit: A water tank is constructed in the shape of a sphere seated atop a circular cylinder. If water is being pumped into the tank at a *constant* rate, sketch the graph of the height of the water as a function of time. Be sure to indicate the location of all "interesting" points, including any critical points where the function has horizontal slope or is not differentiable, and points of inflection.

129

Part A:

1. Differentiate each of the following:

    (a) $f(x) = (x + \sin x)^e$

    (b) $g(x) = e^{(x+\sin x)}$

    (c) $F(z) = \dfrac{\tan z}{\ln z}$

    (d) $P(w) = 5^w w^{-\frac{5}{2}}$

    (e) $R(\theta) = \sqrt{\theta} \cos(\theta^2)$.

2.   (a) Find the equation of the tangent line to $f(x) = e^{-3x}$ at $x = 2$.

    (b) Use it to approximate the value of $f(2.2)$.

    (c) Find the point where the tangent line crosses the x-axis.

3. Given the following table of values for a Bessel function, what is your best estimate for the derivative at $x = .5$?

x	0	.1	.2	.3	.4	.5	.6	.7	.8	.9	1.0
$J_0(x)$	1.0	.9975	.9900	.9776	.9604	.9385	.9120	.8812	.8463	.8075	.7652

4. What is the instantaneous rate of change of the function $f(x) = x \ln x$ at $x = 1$? at $x = 2$? What do these values suggest about the concavity of the function between 1 and 2?

5. Given the function $f(x) = x^2 e^{-2x}$, find all maxima, minima and points of inflection and use this information to sketch the graph.

6. Construct the Taylor polynomial approximation of degree 3 to the function $f(x) = \arctan x$ about the point $x = 0$. Use it to approximate the value of $f(.25)$. How does the approximation compare to the actual value?

7. Sketch the graph of the derivative of the function whose graph is shown:

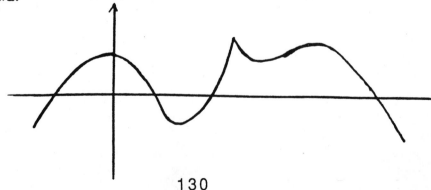

Part B:

1. Evaluate **each** of the following:

    (a) $\int (x^2 + e^{3x})(x^3 + e^{3x})^{\frac{4}{5}} dx$

    (b) $\int \dfrac{\cos(\ln x)dx}{x}$

    (c) $\int \dfrac{8e^{-2w}}{6 - 5e^{-2w}} dw$

    (d) $\dfrac{d}{dx} \displaystyle\int_e^x \log_5 t^{21} \sin(\sqrt{t}) dt.$

2. (a) Estimate the value of $\displaystyle\int_0^1 e^{-2x} dx$ using Riemann sums for both left and right sums with $n = 5$ subdivisions.

    (b) Approximate the function $f(x) = e^{-x^2}$ with a Taylor polynomial of degree 6.

    (c) Estimate the integral in (a) by integrating the Taylor polynomial approximation from (b).

    (d) Indicate briefly how you could improve the results in both cases.

3. Find the total area bounded between the curve $f(x) = x^3 - 5x^2 + 4x$ and the x-axis.

4. A ball is thrown vertically upwards from the top of a 320 foot cliff with initial velocity of 128 feet per second. Find:

    (a) how long it takes to reach its peak;

    (b) its maximum height;

    (c) how long it takes until impact;

    (d) the velocity on impact.

5. A landscape architect plans to enclose a 3000 square foot rectangular region in a botanical garden. She will use shrubs costing \$25 per foot along three sides and fencing costing \$20 per foot along the fourth side. Find the dimensions that minimize the total cost.

6. Sketch the graph of the area function associated with the following function:

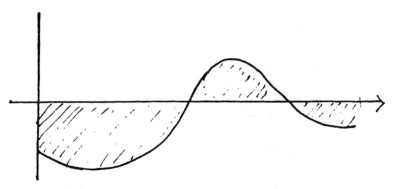

7. Consider the following ski trail down the side of a mountain and sketch graphs showing:

    (a) the speed of the skier as a function of time;

    (b) the total distance covered by the skier as a function of time.

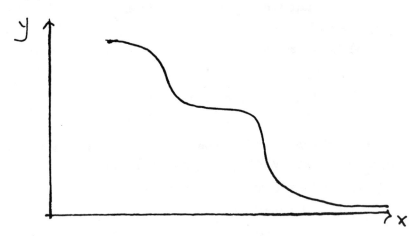

1. Evaluate each of the following and show **all** work:

a) $\int \sin^2 x \cos^3 x \, dx$

b) $\int x \, e^{-x} \, dx$

c) $\int \dfrac{x^2}{x^2 + 1} \, dx$

d) $\int \dfrac{t^2}{\sqrt{9 - t^2}} \, dt$

2. Use the results of problem 1a to evaluate

$$\int_0^{\pi/2} \sin^2 x \cos^3 x \, dx$$

3. a) Use the trapezoid rule with n = 4 to approximate

$$\int_0^1 \sqrt{1 + e^{-x}} \, dx$$

   b) Do the same using Simpson's rule with n = 4.

   c) Indicate how much more accurate you would expect the results to be if you used n = 40 in each case.

4. The following are some of the values for a function known as the Gudermannian function G(x).

x:	0	.1	.2	.3	.4	.5	.6	.7	.8	.9	1
G:	0	.998	.098	.296	.390	.480	.567	.649	.726	.798	.866

Use these values to approximate the value of

$$\int_0^1 G(x) \, dx$$

5. Use the table of antiderivatives to evaluate each of the following:

a) $\int \dfrac{dx}{x^2 - 6x + 10}$

b) $\int \dfrac{dx}{\sqrt{x^2 - 6x + 10}}$

c) $\int \dfrac{x^2}{x^2 + 5} \, dx$

d) $\int \dfrac{dt}{\sqrt{9 - 5t^2}}$

e) $\int e^{4x} \cos 3x \, dx$

1. Given the following data about a function, f,

x	3	3.5	4	4.5	5	5.5	6
$f(x)$	10	8	7	4	2	0	-1

   (a) Estimate $f'(4.25)$ and $f'(4.75)$.

   (b) Estimate the rate of change of f' at $x = 4.5$.

   (c) Find, approximately, an equation of the tangent line at $x = 4.5$.

   (d) Use the tangent line to estimate $f(4.75)$.

   (e) Estimate the derivative of $f^{-1}(x)$ at $x = 2$.

2.   (a) Explain how the average rate of change of a function f can be used to find the instantaneous rate of change of f at a point x_0.

   (b) Give a geometric interpretation of the instantaneous rate of change.

3.   (a) If $x(V) = V^{\frac{1}{3}}$ is the length of the side of a cube in terms of its volume, V, then calculate the average rate of change of x with respect to V over the intervals $0 < V < 1$ and $1 < V < 2$.

   (b) What might we conclude about this rate as the volume V increases? Is it increasing? Decreasing?

4.   (a) Estimate $f'(0)$ when $f(x) = 2^{-x}$.

   (b) Will your estimate be larger or smaller than $f'(0)$? Explain.

5. Consider an accelerating sports car which goes from 0 ft/sec to 88 ft/sec in 5 seconds [88 ft/sec=60 mph]. The car's velocity is given in the table below.

t	0	1	2	3	4	5
$V(t)$	0	30	52	68	80	88

134

(a) Find upper and lower bounds for the distance the car travels in 5 seconds.

(b) In which time interval is the average acceleration greatest? Smallest?

6. The graph shown below is that of the velocity of an object (in meters/second).

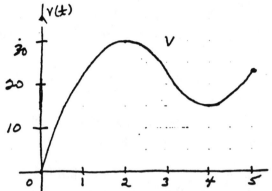

(a) Find an upper and a lower estimate of the total distance traveled from $t = 0$ to $t = 5$ seconds.

(b) At what times is the acceleration zero?

7.   (a) The acceleration of an object is given by the graph shown below. Make a graph of the velocity function v, of this object if $v(0) = 0$.

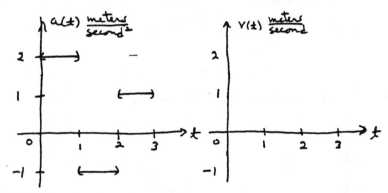

(b) What is the relationship between the total change in $v(t)$ over the interval $0 \leq t \leq 3$ and $a(t)$?

1. You need to rent a Lear jet for a day. Knowing that Air Swiss rents a Lear jet, with pilot and crew, for $2,000 a day and $1.75 per mile, while Air France rents a Lear jet for $1,500 a day and $2.00 per mile, complete the following:

   (a) For each company, write a formula giving the cost of renting a Lear jet for a day as a function of distance traveled. Let x be distance traveled.

   (b) Sketch graphs of both functions, labeling intercepts and points of intersection.

   (c) If cost were the main factor, when would you rent from Air Swiss and when from Air France?

2. A population is growing exponentially at 3.5% a year. Given that this population in 1980 was 10 million, do the following:

   (a) write a formula that gives population as a function of t in years.

   (b) Find the doubling period for this population.

   (c) Find the size of this population in the year 2000.

3. Match the stories with the graphs and write a story for the remaining graph. Between home and school, there are three traffic lights.

   (a) While driving to school I had to stop at only the first traffic light.

   (b) I had to stop only at the third traffic light.

   (c) I had to stop at the first and second traffic lights.

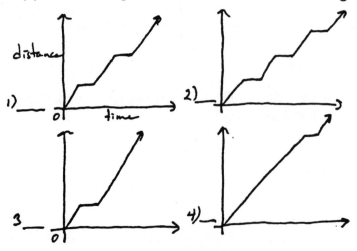

4. Match the formulas with the graphs in the figure below which represent the same functions.

(a) $1 + \sin(x)$,   (b) $\arctan(x + \frac{\pi}{4})$,   (c) $\ln(1-x)$,

(d) $2^{-x}\cos(x)$,   (e) $(x-1)^2 - 2$,   (f) $2^{-x} - 1$,   (g) $(x-1)^2(x+1)$.

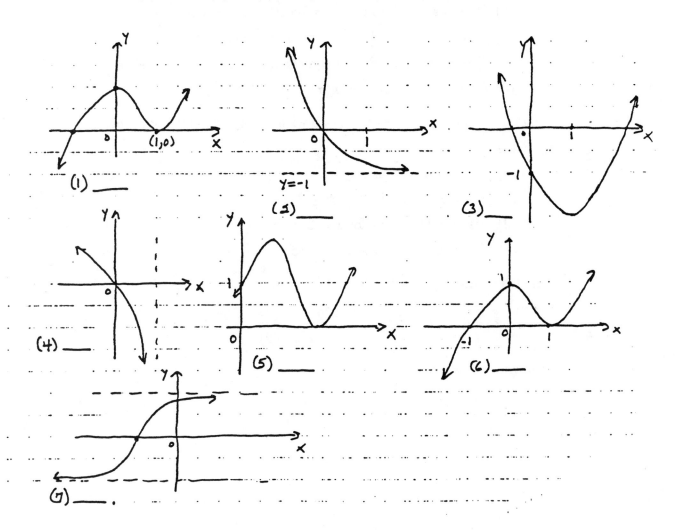

5. On the same graph, graph the function f given by $f(x) = \dfrac{1}{x-1}$, $x \neq 1$, and its inverse function, f^{-1}. Show all asymptotes.

6. Graph each of the following functions:

    (a) $f(x) = \sin(2x)$ and $g(x) = 2\cos(2x)$, $0 \leq x \leq 2\pi$.

    (b) $f(x) = \sin(x)$ and $g(x) = \sin(x)\sin(20\pi x)$, $0 \leq x \leq 2\pi$.

    (c) $f(x) = \tan(x)$ and $g(x) = \arctan(x)$. (Just one period of tan.)

    (d) $f(x) = e^x$ and $g(x) = \ln(x)$.

7. Sketch a function defined for $x \leq 0$ with all of the following properties:

    (a) $f(0) = 1$

    (b) f is increasing for $x \geq 0$

    (c) f is concave up for $0 \leq x \leq 2$

    (d) f is concave down for $x \geq 2$

    (e) $f(x)$ approaches 4 as $x \to +\infty$.

8. Sketch a rough graph of

$$f(x) = \frac{(x+2)(x-3)(x-4)}{x(x-2)}$$

showing all asymptotes.

Math 42 **Final Exam** **March 18, 1991**

1. (20 pts.) Evaluate the following integrals symbolically.(i.e. don't use numerical integration programs.)

   a.) $\displaystyle\int_{\frac{\pi}{6}}^{\frac{\pi}{2}} \frac{d\theta}{\tan\theta}$ b.) $\displaystyle\int_{-\pi}^{\pi} e^{2x}\cos 2x\,dx$ c.) $\displaystyle\int u^{-1}\ln u\,du$

   d.) $\displaystyle\int \frac{x^2}{(1+x^2)}\,dx$

   HINT: Recall that $1+\tan^2\theta = \dfrac{1}{\cos^2\theta}$ and use integral tables.

2. (15 pts.) a) The average value of a function g on $0 \le x \le 1$ is a constant $\bar{g}$ given by

   $$\bar{g} = \frac{1}{1-0}\int_0^1 g(x)dx = \int_0^1 g(x)dx.$$

   Show that

   $$\int_0^1 \bar{g}\,g(x)dx = \bar{g}^2$$

   b.) Since $(g(x)-\bar{g})^2$ is ≥ 0 (being a square) we have

   $$0 \le \int_0^1 (g(x)-\bar{g})^2 dx.$$

   Use this and part a) to show that

   $$\left(\int_0^1 g(x)dx\right)^2 \le \int_0^1 g(x)^2 dx$$

3. (15 pts.) Consider the region bounded by $y = e^x$, the x-axis and the lines $x = 0$ and $x = 1$. Find the volume of the solid whose base is the given region and whose cross sections perpendicular to the x-axis are isosceles right triangles with hypotenuse lying in the region.

4. (35 pts.) Below is the graph of $y = \arctan x$

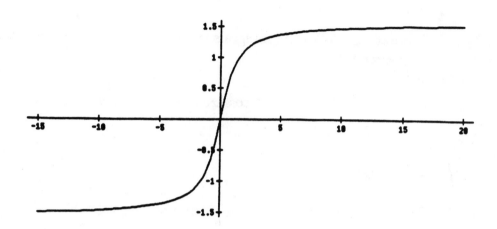

(Note that arctan is the $\tan^{-1}$ button on your calculator).

a.) For any number of subdivisions N write an inequality between RIGHT(N), LEFT(N) and $\int_{-10}^{16} \arctan x\, dx$ Explain.

b. In computing $\int_{-10}^{16} \arctan x\, dx$ using left and right hard sums we record the following table.

N	LEFT	RIGHT
2	-2.877	35.8465
3	-8.2473	17.474
4	-0.3163	19.0505

Why do you think there are such wide variations in this table? You might want to illustrate your reasoning using the graphs below. Be sure to distinguish between the variation for different N and the difference between right and left for a particular N.

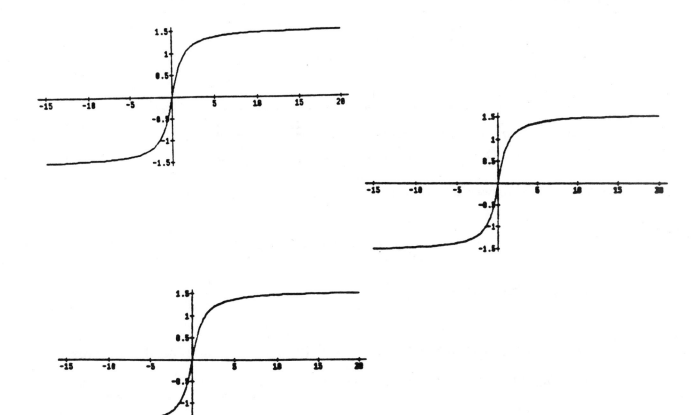

c.) The point $x = 0$ is an inflection point for $y = \arctan x$. If we write

$$\int_{-10}^{16} \arctan x \, dx = \int_{-10}^{0} \arctan x \, dx + \int_{0}^{16} \arctan x \, dx$$

then we can get over estimates and under-estimates for the integrals on the right via the midpoint and trapezoidal rules. Explain.

d. We have the following data

$$\int_{-10}^{0} \text{arctan } x \, dx:$$

N	Midpoint	Trapezoid
50	-12.40537	-12.40041

.

$$\int_{0}^{16} \text{arctan } x \, dx:$$

N	Midpoint	Trapezoid
50	21.363787	21.35097

Based on your answer to part c.) Find numbers A and B such that

$$A \leq \int_{-10}^{16} \text{arctan } x \, dx \leq B$$

Explain. How big is $B - A$?

e. Evaluate $\int_{-10}^{16} \text{arctan } x \, dx$ "symbolically" (plug in the limits but don't evaluate).
(**Hint:** Integrate by parts using $\dfrac{d}{dx} \text{arctan } x = \dfrac{1}{1 + x^2}$.)

5. (15 pts.) A 5 gram drop of thick red paint is added to a large can of white paint. A red disk forms and spreads outward, growing lighter at the edges. Since the amount of red paint stays constant through time, the density of the red paint in the disk must vary with time. Suppose that its density p in gm/cm^2 is of the form

$$p(r,t) = k(t)f(r)$$

for some functions $k(t)$ of time and $f(r)$ of the distance to the center of the disk.

a. (10 pts.) Let $R(t)$ be the radius of the disk at time t. Write an integral that expresses the fact that there are 5 grams of red paint in the disk. Explain.

(**Hint:** Divide the disk into thin concentric rings and ask yourself how much paint there is in each ring.)

b.) (5 pts.) For fixed r write down an integral for the average density of red paint at a distance r from the center of the disk from 0 to T seconds.

6. (15 pts.) a.) You love the function $y = \frac{2}{3}x^{\frac{3}{2}}$ and you also love the number 4. What is the arclength of this curve from $x = 0$ to $x = 4$

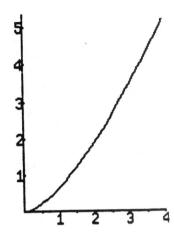

b.) (10 pts.) You have a gold chain which is exactly 4 feet long. As a tribute to your favorite function you want to mount your chain in the shape of $y = \frac{2}{3}x^{\frac{3}{2}}$ from $x = 0$ to $x = 4$ on a beautiful rectangular piece of rosewood. If the lower left corner is labeled with the coordinate $(0,0)$ and the upper right corner is labeled with the coordinate $(4, \frac{16}{3})$ and a unit on the x-axis and a unit on the y-axis represent the same number of feet, what are the dimensions of the piece of wood in feet?

7. (30 pts.) In a hydrogen atom in the unexcited state, the probability of finding the sole electron within x meters of the nucleus is given by

$$F(x) = \frac{4}{(a_0)^3} \int_0^x r^2 e^{\frac{-2r}{a_0}}\, dr, \quad x \ge 0$$

where $a_0 \approx 5.29 \times 10^{-11}$ meters.

a.) $F(x)$, as given above, is a cumulative probability distribution function. What is its corresponding probability density function $f(x)$? Sketch a graph of $y = f(x)$. What happens to $f(x)$ as $x \to \infty$ and what is $f(0)$?

Hint: Find $f'(x)$ to locate any local maxima or minima.

b.) Carry out the integration given in the definition of $F(x)$ to find a more likable formula for $F(x)$. Simplify your formula. (Remember to evaluate the integral between 0 and x.)

c. What is the probability that the electron will be found within a spherical shell of radius a_0?

d. What is the probability that the electron will be found with $\frac{3}{2}a_0$ meters of the nucleus?

8. (15 pts.) A diligent student has a slow leak in her bike tire, but has been too busy studying for exams to fix it. Assume that the pressure in the tire decreases at a rate proportional to the difference between the atmospheric pressure (15 lbs.) and the tire pressure. Monday at 6:00 pm she pumped up the pressure to 85 lbs. By 6:00 pm Tuesday it was down to 75lbs. How much longer can she wait to pump up the tire if she wants to keep the pressure at a minimum of 40 lbs.? (You may keep your answer in number of days from Monday at 6:00 pm if you like.)

9. (15 pts.) Match the direction fields to the equations. Explain.

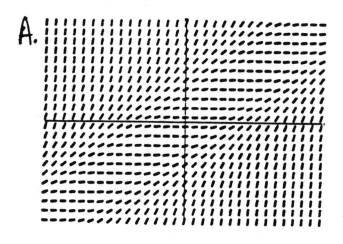

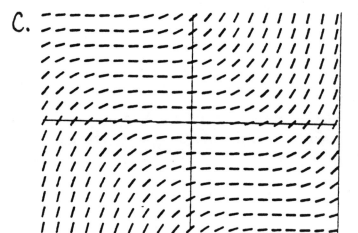

I.) $\frac{dy}{dx} = (x - y)^2$ II.) $\frac{dy}{dx} = (x + y)^2$ III.) $\frac{dy}{dx} = x^2 - y^2$

144

10. (25 pts.) This problem concerns the differential equation

$$\frac{dy}{dx} = x - \frac{1}{2}y$$

a.) Show that $y = 2x - 4$ is the unique solution of the equation that is a straight line. (Write $y = ax + b$ and show that a must $= 2$ and b must $= -4$.)

b.) Give a reasonable sketch of the direction field for the equation. Take account of your answer to part a.) (If you use the direction field program, try $-6 \leq x < 6$, $-6 \leq y \leq 6$ with x scale and y scale both 1).

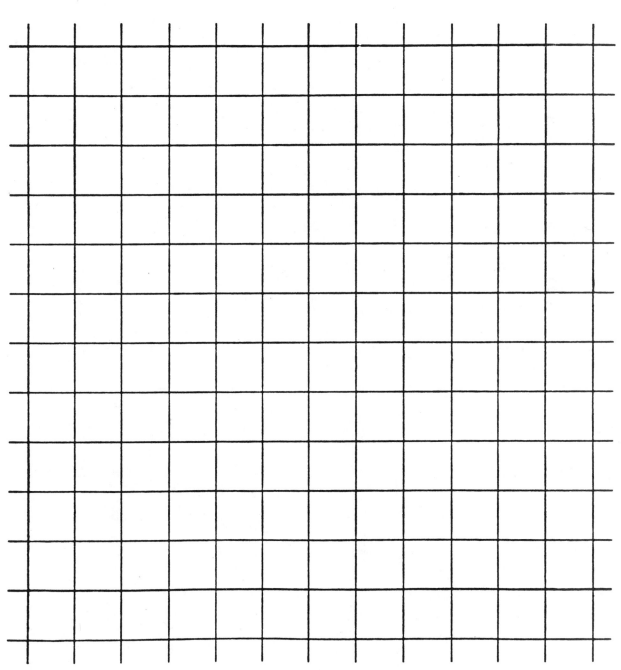

c.) Take a point (x_0, y_0) in the first quadrant which does not lie on the line in part a). Can a solution curve through (x_0, y_0) cross the line? Why or why not?

d.) Show that
$$y = 2x - 4 + Ce^{-\frac{x}{2}}$$
is a solution for *any* constant C.

e.) Find the solution passing through the point $(0, -2)$ and describe its qualitative behavior as $x \to \pm\infty$.

Math 42   First Midterm   January 31, 1991

For credit show all work.

A copy of the three page table of anti-derivatives in the book is attached at the end of the exam.

1. (8 points ea.) Integrate

   a.) $\int x^2(2x-1)dx$ b.) $\int \dfrac{\cos^3 x}{\sin x}dx$ c.) $\int \dfrac{x}{\cos^2 x}dx$ d.) $\int_2^4 \dfrac{e^{2x}}{\sqrt{e^x-1}}dx$

   e.) Derive the reduction formula

   $$\int (\ln x)^n dx = x(\ln x)^n - n\int (\ln x)^{n-1}dx$$

2. (15 points) Find the area of the dumbbell shaped region bounded by the curve $y^2 = x^6(1-x^2)$

Hint 1: Sketch the graphs of $y = x^3\sqrt{1-x^2}$ and $y = -x^3\sqrt{1-x^2}$ (using your calculator) and use symmetry to decide what integral to evaluate.

Hint 2: You may find that the substitiution $x = \sin\theta$ is helpful in evaluating your integral, as well as Formula IV .22 in the table of integrals.

3. (35 points) Below is the graph of $y = \arctan x$

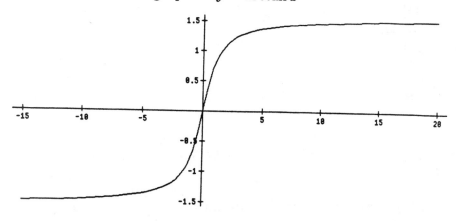

(Note that arctan is the $\tan^{-1}$ button on your calculator).

   a.) For any number of subdivisions N write an inequality between RIGHT(N), LEFT(N) and $\int_{-10}^{16} \arctan x\, dx$ Explain.

b. In computing $\int_{-10}^{16} \arctan x \, dx$ using left and right hard sums we record the following table.

N	LEFT	RIGHT
2	-2.877	35.8465
3	-8.2473	17.474
4	-0.3163	19.0505

Why do you think there are such wide variations in this table? You might want to illustrate your reasoning using the graphs below:

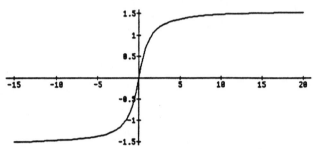

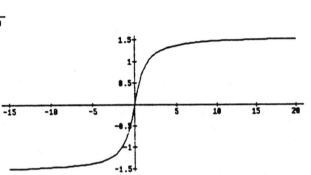

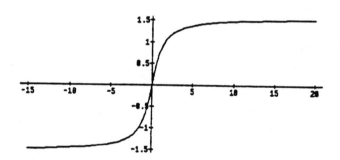

c. The point $x = 0$ is an inflection point for $y = \arctan x$. If we write

$$\int_{-10}^{16} \arctan x \, dx = \int_{-10}^{0} \arctan x \, dx + \int_{0}^{16} \arctan x \, dx$$

then we can get over-estimates and under-estimates for the integrals on the right via the midpoint and trapezoidal rules. Explain.

d.   We have the following data

$$\int_{-10}^{0} \arctan x\,dx:$$

N	Midpoint	Trapezoid
50	-12.40537	-12.40041

$$\int_{0}^{16} \arctan x\,dx:$$

N	Midpoint	Trapezoid
50	21.363787	21.35097

Based on your answer to part c.) find numbers A and B such that

$$A \leq \int_{-10}^{16} \arctan x\,dx \leq B$$

Explain. How big is $B - A$?

e.   Evaluate $\int_{-10}^{16} \arctan x\,dx$ "symbolically" (plug in the limits but don't evaluate). (**Hint:** Integrate by parts using $\dfrac{d}{dx}\arctan x = \dfrac{1}{1+x^2}$.)

4. (20 points) The table below contains numerical data for a definite integral approximated by the left end point, midpoint, trapezoid, and Simpson's rule methods. Which column is which? Why?

N	?	?	?	?
1	2.4737	-44.1930	0.4737	-67.5263
3	-39.6662	-45.5098	-40.3329	-48.4316
9	-44.8687	-45.5261	-45.0909	-45.8548
27	-45.45315	-45.52630	-45.62722	-45.5629
81	-45.518171	-45.526300	-45.572862	-45.530364

5. (30 points)

Focus On Engineering

It's time for the School of Engineering class picture and you are the photographer! You stand at the origin with your camera and your classmates are strung out along the curve $y = e^{-x}$ from $(0,1)$ to $(2, e^{-2})$.

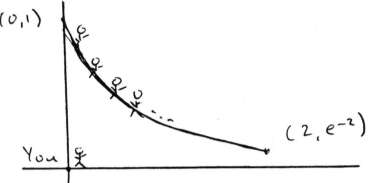

a. As a function of x, what is your distance to to your classmate at a point (x, y) on the curve.

b. Write down an integral that gives the average value of the function in a).

c. Use your calculator to evalute the integral in b). to one decimal place. Say what you are doing.

d. You focus your camera according to your answer to part c.). Who is more in focus, the person at $(0,1)$ or the person at $(2, e^{-2})$?

e. Approximately where on the curve should you tell your best friend to stand so that she will be in focus. (Use your calculator to solve graphically for her x-coordinate).

150

Stanford University
Mathematics Department
Math 41
B. Osgood and Friends
December 10, 1990
Final Exam

1. (16 points)   Each of the quantities below can be represented in the picture. For each quantity, state whether it is represented by a length, a slope or an area. Then using the letters on the picture, make clear exactly which length, slope or area represents it. [Note: The letters P, Q, R, etc., represents points.]

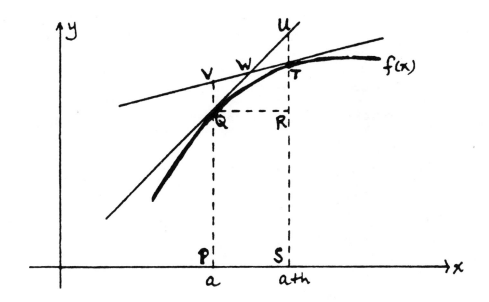

a) $f(a + h) - f(a)$

b) $f'(a + h)$

c) $f'(a)h$

d) $f(a)h$

2. (15 points) Given below are the graphs of two functions $f(x)$ and $g(x)$.

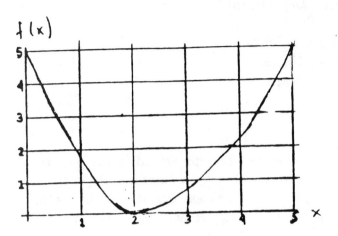

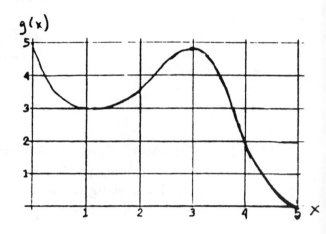

Graph of $f(x)$ Graph of $g(x)$

Let $h(x) = f(g(x))$. Use the graphs to answer the following questions about h.

a) Find (approximately) the critical points of h and classify them.

b) Where is h increasing? decreasing?

c) On the axes below sketch a graph of h.

3. a) (25 points) Differentiate the following functions

    i) $f(x) = \sqrt{x} + \dfrac{1}{\sqrt[3]{x}}$.

    ii) $g(t) = 2^{2(t-1)}$.

    iii) $h(\theta) = \theta \sin(\theta^2)$.

    iv) $f(y) = \ln \dfrac{1+y}{1-y}$.

b) (5 points) If P dollars is invested at an annual interest rate of $r\%$, then at t years this investment grows to F dollars, where

$$F = P\left(1 + \frac{r}{100}\right)^t$$

Find $\dfrac{dF}{dr}$. (Assuming P and t are constant). In terms of money, what does this derivative tell you?

152

4. (4 points each) Assume that f and g are differentiable functions defined on all of the real line. Mark the following TRUE or FALSE.

____ It is possible that $f > 0$ everywhere $f' > 0$, and $f'' < 0$ everywhere.

____ f can satisfy $f'' > 0$ everwhere, $f' < 0$ everywhere and $f > 0$ everywhere.

____ f and g can satisfy $f'(x) > g'(x)$ for all x and $f(x) < g(x)$ for all x.

____ If $f'(x) = g'(x)$ for all x and if $f(x_0) = g(x_0)$ for some x_0 Then $f(x) = g(x)$ for all x.

____ If $f'' < 0$ everwhere and $f' < 0$ everwhere then $\lim\limits_{x \to \infty} f(x) = -\infty$

____ If $f'(x) > 0$ for all x and $f(x) > 0$ for all x then $\lim\limits_{x \to \infty} f(x) = +\infty$

5. (25 points) Suppose that the function $P(t)$ satisfies the differential equation

(∗) $$P'(t) = P(t)(4 - P(t)) \quad .$$

with the initial condition $P(0) = 1$.
Even without knowing an explicit formula for $P(t)$ we can find many of its properties. For example, note first that

$$P'(0) = P(0)(4 - P(0)) = 1(4 - 1) = 3$$

a) Find $P''(t)$ in terms of $P(t)$. Find $P''(0)$.

b) Which of the following is a possible   graph for $P(t)$ for small $t > 0$? Explain.

a)

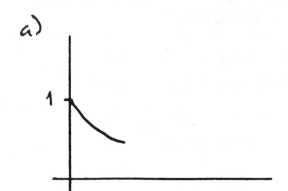

b)

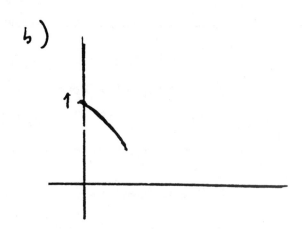

c)

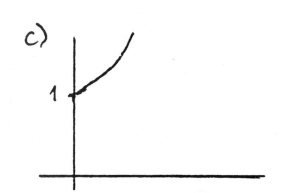

d)

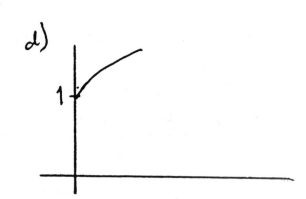

c) Since $P(0) = 1$ the function $P(t)$ starts out less than 4. If it reaches 4, that is, if there is a first time t_o where $P(t_0) = 4$ then

$$P'(t_0) = P(t_0)(4 - P(t_0)) = 0.$$

So near t_0 the graph of P would look like either

a)

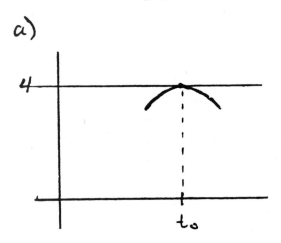

or

b)

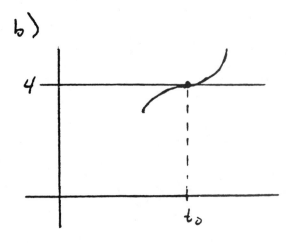

Are either of these consistent with $P(t)$ satisfying the equation $P'(t) = P(t)(4 - P(t))$? Explain.

154

d) Sketch the complete graph of the function $P(t)$, $t > 0$. Explain any critical points, inflection points, concavity, and the behavior of $P(t)$ as $t \to \infty$.

6. (20 points)   Every day the Office of Undergraduate Admissions receives inquiries from eager high school students (e.g. **Please,.please** send me an application, etc.) They keep a running account of the number of inquiries received each day, along with the total number to that point. Below is a table of *weekly* figures from about the end of August 1989 to about the end of October 1989.

Week of	Inquiries That Week	Total tor Year
8/28 - 9/01	1085	11,928
9/04 - 9/08	1193	13,121
9/11 - 9/15	1312	14,433
9/18 - 9/22	1443	15,876
9/25 - 9/29	1588	17,464
10/02 - 10/06	1746	19,210
10/09 - 10/13	1921	21,131
10/16 - 10/20	2113	23,244
10/23 - 10/27	2325	25,569

a) One of these columns can be interpreted as a rate of change. Which one? Of what? Explain.

b) Based on the table write a formula that gives approximately the total number of inquiries received by a given week? Explain.

c) Using your answer in part b), roughly how many inquiries will the admissions office receive in 1989?

d) The actual number of inquiries in 1989 was about 34,000. Discuss this, using your knowledge of how people apply to college.

(30 points)   **Unimodal Functions**

7. Consider the 1-parameter family of functions

$$f(x) = ax(1 - x), \ a > 0,$$

for $0 \le x \le 1$.

As simple as this family is, it exhibits many remarkable properties which have been studied intensively over the last several years.

a) On the axes below sketch several members of the family for a in the range $0 < a < 5$. Also sketch the line $y = x$. Label your choices of a. (Remember, take $0 \le x \le 1$).

155

b) Find the local and global maxima and minima of $f(x)$ in terms of a.

c) What is the largest value of a such that we have $f(x) \leq 1$ for all $0 \leq x \leq 1$?

d) In terms of a, find all points x in $0 \leq x \leq 1$ where $f(x) = x$. These are called the "fixed points" of the function. How can you spot the fixed points from you sketches in part a)?

e) If x_0 is a fixed point of $f(x) = ax(1-x)$ and $x_0 \neq 0$, show that $f(x) < x$ for $x > x_0$. Prove this using calculus and also relate it to your sketches in part a).

8. (30 points)   One fine day you take a hike up a mountain path. Using your trusty map you have determined that the path is approximately in the shape of the curve

$$y = 4(x^3 - 12x^2 + 48x + 36)$$

Here y is the elevation in feet above sea level and x is the horizontal distance in miles you have travelled, but your map only shows the path for 7 miles, horizontal distance.

a) How high above sea level do you start your hike.

b) How high above sea level are you at the beginning of the 7th mile.

c) Use your calculator to draw an informative graph of the path (i.e. one that looks like a cubic.) and sketch your answer on the axes below. Show the scale you use. (Take your answers in parts (a.) and (b.) into account!).

d) Where on the path is a nice flat place to stop for a picnic. Explain.

e) Estimate the elevation after 7.5 horizontal miles. (you do not know the shape of the path explicitely after 7 miles!)

f) If your friend, who is *not* in "good shape" followed this path for 15 miles total horizontal distance the day before, does it make sense for the equation for the elevation continue to hold much beyond the 7 mile mark? Explain.

9. (20 points)   Consider the region A that is bounded above by the graph of $f(x) = e^{-x^2}$, bounded below by the graph of $g(x) = e^{x^2} - 1$, and bounded on the left by the y-axis.

a) Sketch and label the curves $f(x)$ and $g(x)$ and shade the region A. Find (approximately if necessary) and label the coordinates of the three corner points of A.

b) By just looking at your sketch in (a), decide whether the area of A is more or less than 0.7. Is it more or less than 0.3? Give a graphical justification for your answers.

c) Express the area of the region A as integral, or as a sum or difference of integrals. Approximate the value(s) of the integral(s) with an accuracy that allows you to decide whether the area of A is more or less than 0.5. Explain what you are doing.

10. (15 Points) A submarine can travel 30 mi/hr submerged and 60 mi/hr on the surface. The submarine must stay submerged if within 200 miles of the coast. Suppose that this submarine wants to meet a surface ship 200 miles off shore. The submarine leaves from a port 300 miles along the coast from the surface ship. The submarine leaves from a port 300 miles along the coast from the surface ship. What route of the type sketched below should the sub take to minimize its time to rendezvous.

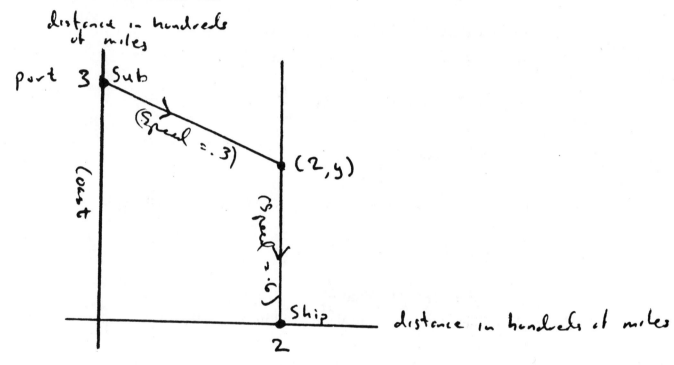

1. (15 points) Consider the graph of $y = e^x$.

   a.) Find the equation of the tangent line to the graph at (a, e^a).

   b.) Find the x and y intercepts of the line in part (a).

   c.) Show that the highest y-intercept of *any* tangent line is $y = 1$. (You may give a geometric argument as long as you say clearly what properties of the graph you are using.)

2. (5 points each) Find the indicated derivatives.

   a.) $f(x) = 4x^3 - 3x^2 + 2x - 8$. Find $f'(x)$.

   b.) $y = u\sqrt{u+1}$, $u = 2x^2 + 3$. Find $\dfrac{dy}{du}$, and $\dfrac{dy}{dx}$.

   c.) $y = e^{\cos^2 \theta}$ Find $\dfrac{dy}{d\theta}$.

   d.) $p(x) = \ln((x - a)(x - b)(x - c))$ a, b, c constants. Find $p'(x)$.

   e.) $x = \dfrac{\sin t}{1 + \cos t}$. Find $\dfrac{dx}{dt}$.

   f.) $(x + y)^2 = (2x + 1)^3$. Find $\dfrac{dy}{dx}$.

   (Use implicit differentiation. Your answer will involve both x and y.)

3. (10 points) The table below gives values for functions f and g, and for their derivatives.

x	-1	0	1	2	3
f	3	3	1	0	1
g	1	2	2.5	3	4
f'	-3	-2	-1.5	-1	1
g'	2	3	2	2.5	3

   a.) Find $\dfrac{d}{dx}(f(x)g(x))$ and $\dfrac{d}{dx}\left(\dfrac{f(x)}{g(x)}\right)$ at $x = -1$.

   b.) Find $\frac{d}{dx}f(g(x))$ and $\frac{d}{dx}g(f(x))$ at $x = 0$.

   158

5. (15 points) In computing his tables of logarithms, Napier needed certain inequalities for the purpose of interpolation. He showed that if $a > b$ then

$$\frac{1}{a} \leq \frac{\ln a - \ln b}{a - b} \leq \frac{1}{b}$$

In this problem we will prove Napier's estimates.

(10) a.) Using calculus (not a calculator) prove that for $x \geq 1$ we have the inequalities

$$\frac{x-1}{x} \leq \ln x \text{ and } \ln x \leq x - 1.$$

(5) b.) From part a.) we have $\dfrac{x-1}{x} \leq \ln x \leq x - 1$. For $a > b$ let $x = \dfrac{a}{b}$ and deduce Napier's estimates.

6. (40 points) Consider the 2-parameter family of curves.

$$y = ax + \frac{b}{x}$$

Assume that $a > 0, \ b > 0$.

a.) For three (reasonable) choices of a and b with $a < b, a = b, a > b$, respectively, sketch the three curves on the axes below. (You may use your calculator. Label your choices of a and b.)

b.) For the family

$$y = ax + \frac{b}{x}$$

determine the critical points, critical values, local and global maxima or minima and concavity in terms of the parameters a and b. (In the general case, not just for your curves in part (a)).

c.) In words and in sketches explain how the sizes of a and b influence the shape of $y = ax + \dfrac{b}{x}$.

d.) From part b.) deduce the famous inequality between the arithmetic and the geometric mean:

If a and b are positive numbers then:

$$\sqrt{ab} \leq \frac{a+b}{2}$$

159

7. (30 points)   Lunch at Wilbur.

Below is the graph of the *rate r* at which people arrive for lunch at Wilbur.

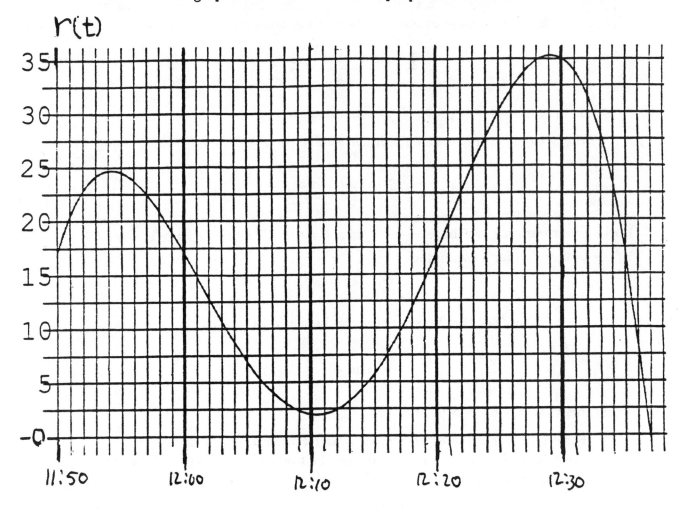

r(t)

Checkers start at 12:00 noon and can pass people through at a constant rate of 5 people/minute.

Let $f(t)$ be the length of the line (i.e. number of people) at time t. Remember from the first exam that at 11:50 there are already 150 people lined up from breakfast.

Using the graph together with the information above, answer the following. Explain your answers. (6 points each)

a.) Find and classify all critical points of f.

b.) When is f increasing? decreasing?

c.) When is f concave up? concave down?

d. When is the line longest? shortest?

e.) Sketch the graph of f. Label the important points.

160

Math 125a, Section 1 - Final Exam
Show all your work. The answer alone is not good enough.
There are 6 questions, each worth 17 points.
The computer programs Fortune, Rootfind, and Slopes, might be useful during this test.

Question 1. Two politicians, named A and B, carefully inspect a table of values, x versus y. A claims that the table is linear, while B claims it is exponential.
(a) You look at the table and agree with A. Explain what you saw in the table.
(b) You look at the table and agree with B. Explain what you saw in the table.
(c) You look at the table and realize that neither is exactly right, but both of them are approximately correct. Explain why this can be so. Reference to the derivative might be appropriate.

Question 2. (a) Find the best linear approximation to $f(x) = (1 + x)^{1/2}$ at $x = 0$.
(b) Use the computer to plot $f(x)$ and your linear approximation. Describe what program you used, what you did, and how this confirms that your linear approximation is reasonable.

Question 3. The purpose of this problem is to find all the roots of $f(x) = 3x^3 + 2x^2 - 4x + 1$ exactly.
(a) Use the computer to obtain all the roots of $f(x)$ to 5 decimal places. Do this using both the bisection method and Newton's method. Explain what program you used, and what you did, paying particular attention to the number of iterations, bracketing and initial values. How do you know you have found all the roots?
(b) If you have done part (a) correctly, then one of the approximate roots you have obtained should suggest an exact root. Which one, and how did you confirm that the root was exact?
(c) Based on the information you have obtained in part (b), find exact expressions for all the roots.

Question 4. The purpose of this problem is to explain the graph of $f(x) = \dfrac{1}{(1 + ae^{-x})}$ for $a > 0$.

(a) Use the computer. Graph the function $f(x)$ for $a > 0$. Do this for various values of a. Based on what you see, write down what you think happens to the graph of $f(x)$ as a increases. Pay particular attention to what happens to any asymptotes, maxima, minima, and points of inflection.
(b) It is claimed that if x represents time, then $f(x)$ is related to the number of people on Earth. Briefly explain why this might be reasonable.
(c) Forget what you did in parts (a) and (b). Calculate df/dx and d^2f/dx^2.
(d) Using the results you obtained in part (c) confirm that the statements you made in part (a) are accurate.

Question 5. The purpose of this problem is to find the x value which produces the shortest distance from the point $(0, 0)$ to the curve $y = e^x$.
(a) Use the computer. Plot the curve $y = e^x$ and a circle of radius a centered at $(0, 0)$. By varying a, estimate the value of x which gives the shortest distance form $(0, 0)$ to the curve. What is your estimate? Explain what you did.
(b) Using calculus, confirm that the statement you made in part (a) is accurate. (You may need to use the computer to find roots.) What is your estimate for x, accurate to 10 decimal places? Explain what method you used to get this accuracy.

Question 6. The purpose of this problem is to sketch the implicit function $x^3 + y^3 = -8$.
(a) Find all the y values for which $x = 0$.
(b) Calculate dy/dx.
(c) Use parts (a) and (b), and the computer, to sketch this implicit function. Explain what program you used, and what you did, and copy the sketch of the implicit function from the computer screen to your paper.

Stanford University
Mathematics Department
Math 41
B. Osgood et al
October 22, 1990

1. (12 points) Find an equation for the line L shown below. Your answer will contain the positive constant b. Simplify as much as possible.

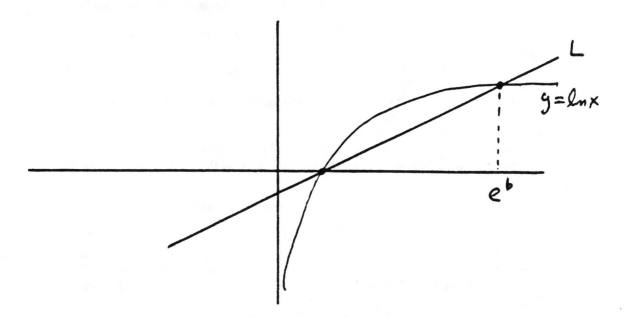

2. (20 points)
(10) a) Using the standard viewing rectangle $(-10 \leq x \leq 10, -10 \leq y \leq 10)$, I graph a cubic polynomial and see two more or less vertical lines.

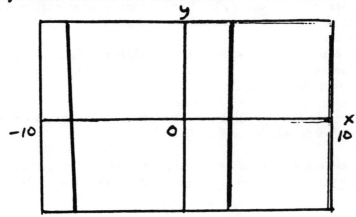

Need there be another root? Explain. Sketch some possibilities for the complete graph. Explain.

(10 points) b) Once again, using the standard viewing rectangle, I graph $y = x^2 - e^{0.1x}$ and I see a parabola.

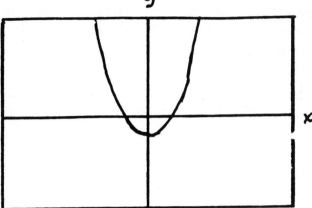

Is this all there is to the graph? Sketch what you think the complete picture should be. Explain.

3. (35 points) Consider the function.

$$c(x) = \cos x + .5 \cos 2x$$

(5 points) a) Is $c(x)$ a periodic function? If so, what is its smallest period.

(10 points) b) Using your calculator, draw the graph of $c(x)$. Adjust the scales so you can see the patterns and symmetries clearly. Sketch your final version on the axes below, showing the scale you use, and describe what you see.

(5 points) c) At what points x is $c(x)$ a maximum. Explain.

(5 points) d) Let x_0 be the first positive number where $c(x_0) = 0$. Find an interval containing x_0 whose length is $< \frac{1}{10}$. Explain briefly how you did this.

(5 points) e) Looking again at the symmetries in your graph in part b), argue that the next positive number where $c(x) = 0$ is $2\pi - x_0$. Can you show this directly?

(5 points) f) In terms of x_0, what are all the places where $c(x) = 0$ for $-2\pi \le x \le 4\pi$.

4. (35 points) Alone in your dim, unheated room you light one candle rather than curse the darkness. Disgusted by the mess, you walk directly away from the candle, cursing. The temperature (in degrees Fahrenheit) and illumination (in % of candle power) decrease as your distance (in feet) from the candle increases. In fact, you have tables showing this information!

distance(feet)	Temp.(°F)	distance(feet)	illumination
0	55	0	100
1	54.5	1	85
2	53.5	·2	75
3	52	3	67
4	50	4	60
5	47	5	56
6	43.5	6	53

You are cold when the temperature is below 40° (You are from California). You are in the dark when the illumination is at most 50% of one candle power.

(5 points) a) Two graphs are sketched below. One is temperature as a function of distance and one is illumination as a function of distance. Which is which? Explain.

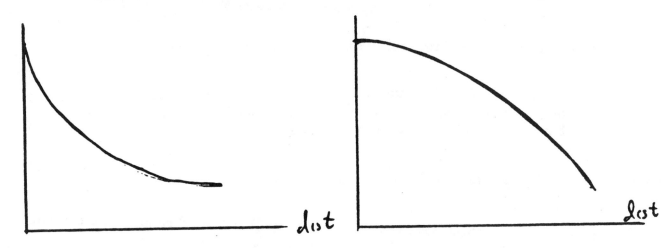

(5 points) b) What is the average rate at which the temperature is changing when the illumination drops from 75% to 56%?

(10 points) c) You can still read your watch when the illumination is about 65%, so somewhere between 3 and 4 feet. Can you read your watch at 3.5 feet? Explain.

(10 points) d) Suppose you know that at 6 feet the instantaneous rate of change of the temperature is −4.5° F/ft and the instantaneous rate of change of the illumination is −3% candle power/ft. Estimate the temperature and the illumination at 7 feet.

(5 points) e) Are you in the dark before you are cold, or vice-versa?

Breakfast at Wilbur

Below is the graph at the rate r in arrivals/minute at which students line up for breakfast. The first people arrive at 6:50 a.m. and the line opens at 7:00 a.m.

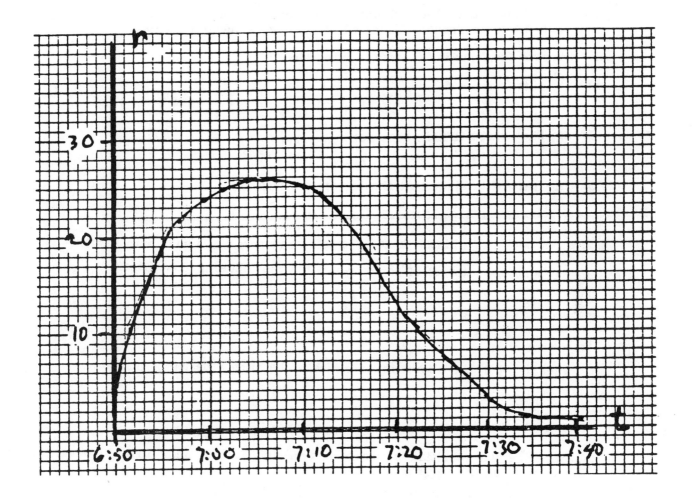

Suppose that once the line is open, checkers can check peoples' meal cards at a constant rate of 20 people per 10 minutes.

Use the graph and this information to find an estimate for the following:

a) The length of the line (i.e. number of people) at 7:00 when the checkers begin.

b) The length of the line at 7:10.

c) The length of the line at 7:20.

d) The rate at which the line is growing in length at 7:10.

e) The length of time a person who arrives at 7:00 has to stand in line.

f) The time at which the line disappears.

165

Math 114b
Jeff Tecosky-Feldman
Final Exam
Spring 1991

PART I: Answer 8 of the following 9 problems. Mark on the cover page which problem you wish not to be graded. Show all of your work for full credit.

1. Compute the following indefinite integrals:

a) $\int \sin x (\cos x + 5)^7 \, dx$

b) $\int \dfrac{\ln x \, dx}{x}$

c) $\int x \, e^{2x} \, dx$

2. a) Show that $\int_1^\infty (1/x)dx$ does not converge.

b) Use part a) to show that the harmonic series

$1 + 1/2 + 1/3 + 1/4 + 1/5 + 1/6 + \dots + 1/k + \dots$

does not converge. (Hint: Consider a left hand sum of $f(x)=1/x$ with $dx=1$).

3. a) Find the interval of convergence for the following power series

$$\sum_1^\infty \frac{2^k x^k}{k}$$

b) When x=1/4 in the above power series, it becomes a series of numbers:

$$\sum_1^\infty \frac{2^k(1/4)^k}{k}$$

By comparing the resulting series to a geometric series, show that it converges to some number less than 2.

4. This problem concerns the differential equation

$$dy/dx = 2x/y$$

Note: You can do part d) without parts a)-c).

a) On the axes below, sketch the direction field for the differential equation at the 14 points in the 1st and 2nd quadrants $-2 \le x \le 2$, $0 \le y \le 2$ (x and y are integers — don't include (0,0)).

b) Sketch in a solution curve passing through (1,2). Do you expect it to show any symmetry? Explain. You should find that it is concave up at (1,2). Will it remain concave up for all x, or will it eventually turn concave down? Explain.

c) Without plotting any more slopes in the 3rd and 4th quadrants, describe what the direction field must look like there, in terms of the direction field in the 1st and 2nd quadrants.

d) Find an equation for the solution to the differential equation dy/dx = 2x/y passing through (1,2). Is this consistent with your answer to part b)?

166

5. Suppose that a new office building is being planned. The architect wants to design a building that is thick at the base and eventually tapers to a graceful peak at the top. The building is to have 10 floors, and each floor is 15 feet high.
For the purposes of air conditioning the building, an estimate of the total volume of the building is needed. You have been hired as a consultant at an exorbitant salary to do this.

You have been provided with the following information which shows how much area, in units of 100 square feet, each of the 10 floors will contain:

Floor #	Gnd	1	2	3	4	5	6	7	8	9
Area	25	23	20	18	16	14	12	10	9	8

Earn your wage: find an approximate value for the volume of the entire building. Explain what you are doing.

6. Suppose there is a new kind of savings certificate that starts out by paying 3% interest/year and increases the interest rate by 1% each additional year that the money is left on deposit. (Assume that interest is compounded continuously and that the interest rate increases continuously).

a) Write a differential equation for dB/dt, where B(t) is the balance at time t.

b) Solve the equation that you found in part a) assuming an initial deposit of $1000.

c) When t = 7 years, the interest rate will have risen to 10%. Would it have been better to have invested $1000 at a <u>fixed</u> interest rate of 5% for 7 years than to use the variable rate savings certificate described in part a)? Explain your answer.

7. a) Find the Taylor polynomial of degree 3 about x=0 for the function

$$f(x) = \sqrt{1 - x}$$

b) Use your answer to part a) to give approximate values to $\sqrt{1/2}$ and $\sqrt{0.9}$.

c) Which approximation in part b) is more accurate? Explain why.

8. a) Write down the Taylor series for cos(x) at x=0. (You need not use the Σ notation.)

b) Use part a) to write down the Taylor series for cos($\sqrt{x}$) at x=0.

c) To what number does the series

$$1 - 2/2! + 4/4! - 8/6! + 16/8! - \ldots + (-1)^k 2^k/(2k)! + \ldots$$

converge?

9. A spherical raindrop evaporates at a rate proportional to its surface area. Note: You can do parts e) and f) WITHOUT doing parts a)-d).

a) If V=volume of the raindrop and S=surface area, write down a differential equation for dV/dt (this is EASY).

b) Your equation in a) should include an unspecified constant k. What is the sign of k? Why?

c) Since V=(4/3)Pi r³ for a sphere, write down an equation which relates dV/dt for a sphere to r and dr/dt.

d) Since S=4Pi r² for a sphere, you can write S in terms of r and dV/dt in terms of r and dr/dt and then the differential equation in part a) becomes dr/dt = k. Show how this happens.

e) Solve the differential equation dr/dt = k, where k is a constant.

f) If it takes 5 minutes for a spherical raindrop to evaporate to 1/8 of its original volume, how long will it take to completely evaporate?

Part II: TRUE/FALSE questions. Answer each question as TRUE or FALSE and provide a short explanation or counterexample. Each problem is worth 5 points.

a) If the Left Hand Sum, LEFT(n), for f(x)dx is too large for one value of n, it will be too large for all values of n.

b) y=x²+x is a solution to dy/dx=2(y−x²) + 1

c) If $\sum a_k$ is a series of numbers, and lim a_k=0 then the series converges.
$$k \to \infty$$

d) If a power series $\sum a_k x^k$ converges at x=1 and at x=2 then it converges at x= −1.

e) If the average value of f(x) on the interval 2≤x≤5 is between 0 and 1, then f is between 0 and 1 on the interval 2≤x≤5.

f) The solution of dy/dx=x+1 passing through (0,1) is the same as the solution passing through (0,0), except it has been shifted one unit ~~to the left.~~ upward

h) $\int_1^2 \sin(x^2) > 3.$

g) The solutions of dP/dt = kP(L−P) are always concave down.

i) If f' > g' for all a<x<b, then the Left Hand Sum approximation of $\int_a^b f \, dx$ will have larger error than the Left Hand Sum for $\int_a^b g \, dx.$

168

Mathematics 114b
Midterm Examination

Due 5 pm, Monday. March 25

Problem 1 (5 points)

a) Find the derivative of $\dfrac{x}{\sqrt{a^2+x^2}}$

Be sure to simplify your answer as much as possible.

b) Use part a) to find an antiderivative of $\dfrac{1}{(a^2+x^2)^{3/2}}$

Problem 2 (5 points each)

Evaluate each of the indefinite integrals below. Be sure to show your work.

a) $\displaystyle\int xe^x \, dx$

b) $\displaystyle\int \frac{e^x}{1 + e^{2x}} \, dx$

c) $\displaystyle\int \frac{1}{1 + e^x} \, dx$

d) $\displaystyle\int \frac{\sin x}{\cos x} \, dx$

e) $\displaystyle\int \frac{1}{\sqrt{1 - 4x^2}} \, dx$

Problem 3 (5 points each)

a) Does the integral

$$\int_0^\infty \frac{x^2}{e^{-x} + x} \, dx$$

converge? Why or why not?

b) If the following improper integral converges, find its value. Otherwise explain why it does not converge.

$$\int_{0}^{\infty} x^2 e^{-x} \, dx$$

Problem 4 (5 points each)

For each of the definite integrals below, approximate the values to within an error of less than .001. For each of your answers, explain carefully which method you used to obtain your result, and show how you know your answer is as accurate as required.

a) $\int_{0}^{10} e^{\sin x} \, dx$

b) $\int_{0}^{100} \ln(x^2+1) \, dx$

Problem 5 (5 points each)

TRUE/FALSE: For each statement, write whether it is true or false and give a short explanation. No explanation-->no credit.

a) For any given function, TRAP(n) is always <u>more</u> accurate than LEFT(n).

b) The Midpoint method gives EXACT answers for linear functions, no matter how many subdivisions are used.

c) $\int_{0}^{3} \cos^{36} x \, dx > Pi$

Problem 6 (10 points)

A flat metal plate is in the shape determined by the area under the graph of f(x) = 1/(1+x) between x=0 and x=5. The density of the plate x units from the y-axis is given by x² grams/cm².

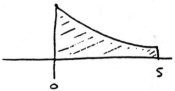

a) Write down a Riemann sum with 5 terms which approximates the total mass. Is your approximation an under or overestimate? Explain.

b)   Write down a definite integral which gives the exact value of the total mass of the plate.

c)   Evaluate the integral you found in part b).

Problem 7 (10 points)

The Great Cone of Haverford College is a monument built by Freshmen during a customs week long, long ago. It is 100 ft high and its base has a diameter of 100 ft. It has been built from bricks (purportedly made of straw) which weigh 2 lbs/ft³.   Use a definite integral to approximate the amount of Work required to build the Cone.

Problem 8 (5 points)

Given the graph of f below, draw a graph of the function

$$\int_{c}^{x} f(x)dx$$

Problem 9 (10 points)

We showed in class that the force of gravitational attraction between a thin
rod of mass M and length L and a particle of mass m lying in the same line as
the rod at a distance of A from one of the ends was

GmM

——

A(L+A)

Use this result to set up an integral for the total force due to gravity
between two thin rods, both of mass M and length L, lying in the same line
and separated by a distance A. You need not evaluate the integral. Explain
what you are doing.

Hint: Divide one of the rods up into small pieces, each of length dx and mass
(M/L)dx. Apply the formula above to each of the pieces, then form a Riemann
sum. You know the rest...

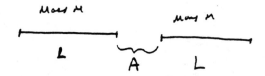

Math 113
Jeff Tecosky-Feldman
Final Exam
Fall 1990

1. If $f'' = 0$ at $x=0$, then the graph of f changes concavity at $x=0$.

2. If $f' > 0$ on an interval, the function is concave UP on the interval.

3. If f is always decreasing and concave down, then f must have at least one root.

4. The function described by the following table of values is exponential:

x	f(x)
5.2	27.8
5.3	29.2
5.4	30.6
5.5	32.0
5.6	33.4

5. $\int_{-1}^{1} \sqrt{1 - x^2}\, dx = \pi/2$

6. The 10th derivative of $f(x)=x^{10}$ is 0.

7. If a function is concave UP, then left-hand Riemann sums are always less than right hand sums with the same subdivisions, over the same interval.

8. An antiderivative of $2x\cos(x)$ is $x^2\sin(x)$.

9. If $\int_{a}^{b} f(x)dx = 0$, then f must have at least one root between a and b (assume $a \neq b$).

10. A quantity Q growing exponentially according to the formula $Q(t) = Q_0 5^t$ has a doubling time of $\ln(2)/\ln(5)$.

173

11. Suppose a function is given by a table of values as follows:

x	1.1	1.3	1.5	1.7	1.9	2.1
f(x)	12	15	21	23	24	25

a) Estimate the instantaneous rate of change of f at x=1.7

b) Write an equation for the tangent line to f at x=1.7 using your estimate found in a).

c) Use your answer in b) to predict a value for f at x=1.8. Is your prediction too large or too small? Why?

d) Is f'' positive or negative at x=1.7? How can you tell? Can you estimate its value?

12. Find derivatives of the following functions. You need not simplify:

a) $\cos(x^2+1)$

c) $\dfrac{e^{-x}}{1 + x^3}$

d) $2^e - (2/x) + \sqrt{1 - x}$

13. Evaluate the following indefinite integrals:

a) $\displaystyle\int 4x^5 \, dx$

b) $\displaystyle\int \dfrac{x^2 - x + 1}{x} \, dx$

c) $\displaystyle\int \cos(e^x)e^x \, dx$

14. Suppose the rate at which ice in a skating pond is melting is given by dV/dt = 4t + 2 ft³/minute.

a) Write a definite integral which represents the amount of ice that has melted in the first 4 minutes.

b) Evaluate the definite integral in part a).

15. Below is the graph of the second derivative, f'', of a function. Sketch graphs of f' and f, assuming $f'(0)=f(0)=0$.

16. A rectangle is inscribed in the region bounded by the curve $f(x)=x^2$, the x-axis and the line x=4. Find the dimensions of the rectangle with maximum area.

17. Consider the two functions

$f = -\cos^2(x)$ $g = \sin^2(x)$

a) Show that $f' = g'$.

b)   Use part a) to derive the famous trig identity $1 = \sin^2(x) + \cos^2(x)$.   Hint: what can you conclude about two functions whose derivatives are the same?

18. Consider the one-parameter family of functions given by

$e^{Ax} + e^{-Ax}$, where A > 0.

Use calculus to draw a graph of members of the family. Show what happens as A gets very small and very large. Be sure to label critical points and points of inflection, if any.

19.   Match the following graphs to the formulas.

Ⓐ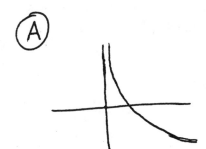

Ⓓ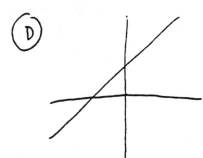

Ⓑ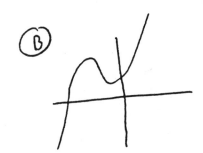

Ⓔ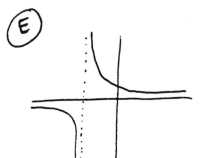

Ⓒ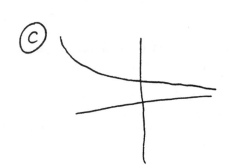

1. $\ln(e^x) + 1$

2. $-2 \ln x$

3. e^{-x}

4. $x^5 + 2x^4 - x^3 - 2x^2 + 5$

5. $\dfrac{1}{x+1}$

175

Mathematics 1b
Final Examination
May 24, 1991

1. (6 pts each) Find the following antiderivatives:

   (a) $\int \frac{4+x}{\sqrt{x}} dx$

   (b) $\int \frac{1+\sin(2x)}{2} dx$

   (c) $\int \frac{1}{(1+x)^2} dx$

   (d) $\int \frac{\ln(1+x)}{1+x} dx$

   (e) $\int \ln\left(\frac{1}{x}\right) dx$

2. (25 pts) A compressible liquid has density which varies with height. At the level of h meters above the bottom, the density is $40 \times (5-h)\mathrm{kg/m^3}$.

   (a) The liquid is put in the container depicted in the picture. The cross sections of the container are isosceles triangles. It has straight sides, and looks like a triangular prism. How many kg will it hold when placed as shown in Figure 1, resting on the triangular side?

   (b) How many kg will it hold if it is placed (with some support, of course) as shown in Figure 2?

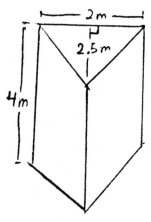

Figure 1

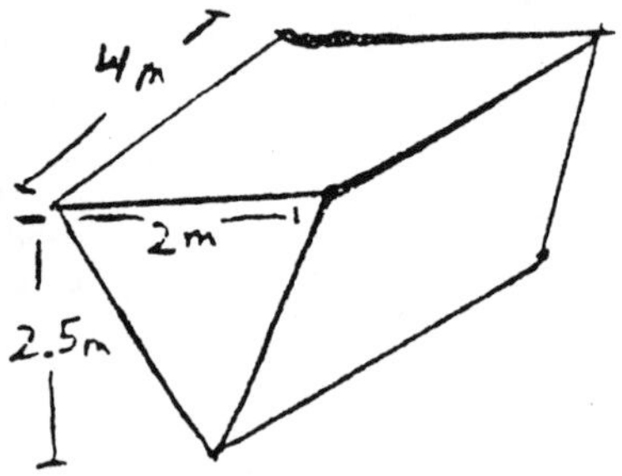

Figure 2

3. (15 pts) Let $S(t)$ be the number of daylight hours, in Cambridge, MA, at the t'th day of the year. During spring (from Vernal Equinox, $t = 80$, to Summer Solstice, $t = 173$), the graph of $S(t)$ is

concave down. In the table below we list some values of $S(t)$. What is the average length of the days in spring (in hours and minutes)? Please give an upper bound and a lower bound for the answer. These bounds should differ by less than 10 minutes.

t	$S(t)$
80	12 hours 12 minutes
111	13 hours 44 minutes
142	14 hours 50 minutes
173	15 hours 12 minutes

4. (26 pts) The interaction of two populations $x(t)$ and $y(t)$ is modeled by the system

$$\frac{1}{x}\frac{dx}{dt} = 1 - x - ky, \quad \frac{1}{y}\frac{dy}{dt} = 1 - y + kx,$$

where k is a positive constant.

(a) What type of interaction is modelled here (Symbiosis, Predator-Prey, Competition)?

(b) Do the Qualitative Phase Plane Analysis for the case $k > 1$. For example, try $k = 2$. What happens in the long run?

(c) Do the Qualitative Phase Plane Analysis for the case $k < 1$. For example, try $k = \frac{1}{2}$. What happens in the long run?

5. (8 pts) On a fine spring day you stand in the Square and throw a bean bag (or hockey puck) high into the air and catch it. On the axes below, sketch a trajectory which reflects the bean bag's trip. Label the points A, B and C on the trajectory where

A = the point corresponding to the instant the bag is tossed;

B = the bag reaches its highest altitude;

C = the point corresponding to the instant you catch the bag.

x = the altitude of the bean bag.

v = the velocity of the bag.

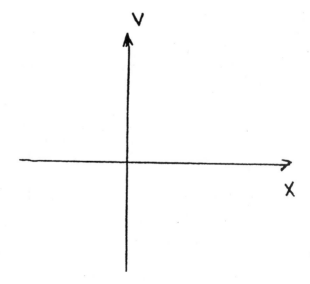

6. (16 pts) Below is a graph of position vs time. (a) Sketch a rough graph of v versus t.

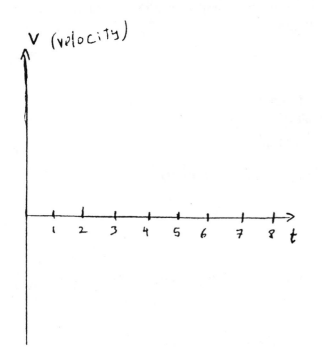

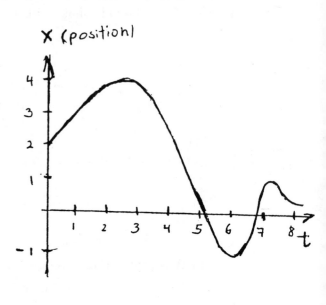

(b) Graph the corresponding trajectory in the xv plane.

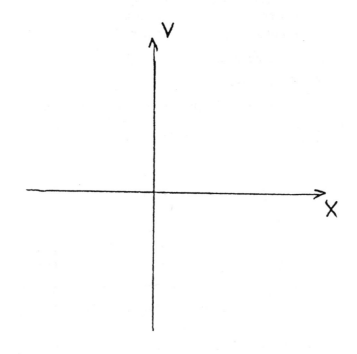

7. (30 pts) The acceleration of a moving object is given by

$$\frac{d^2x}{dt^2} = x\left(\frac{dx}{dt} - 1\right)$$

where $x(t)$ is the position at time t.

(a) Set up a system of first order differential equations for position x and velocity v.

(b) Do the qualitative phase plane analysis for this system indicating clearly the null clines and constant solutions. (Consider positive and negative values for x and v.)

(c) With the help of the TI-81, sketch two trajectories: one for initial values $x(0) = -3$, $v(0) = 3$ and the other for $x(0) = 3$, $v(0) = -2$.

(d) Consider the trajectory with initial values $x(0) = -3$ and $v(0) = 3$.
Approximate the maximum and minimum values of x (if such values exist).
Approximate the maximum and minimum values of v (if such values exist).

(e) Consider the trajectory with initial values $x(0) = 3$ and $v(0) = -2$.
Approximate the maximum and minimum values of x (if such values exist).
Approximate the maximum and minimum values of v (if such values exist).

(f) Draw some general conclusions about what happens to $x(t)$ and $v(t)$ for different initial values.

8. (25 pts) In a recent archeological expedition, a scroll was discovered containing a description of plans to build what appears to be the Tower of Babel. According to the manuscript, the tower was supposed to have circular cross sections and "go up to the heavens" (i.e., be infinitely high). A team of Harvard mathematicians was consulted to solve some of the questions posed by the archaeologists.

The mathematicians plotted half of the silhouette of the tower on a set of coordinate axis with the y-axis running through the center and discovered that it was approximated by the curve $y = -100\ln\left(\frac{x}{5}\right)$. Please answer the questions posed by the archaeologists:

(a) Would such a tower have finite volume? Justify your work completely.

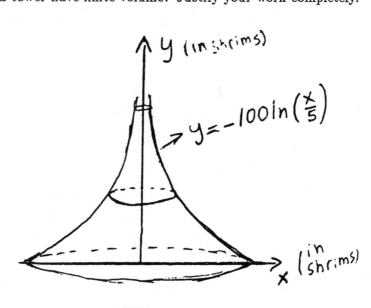

(b) The manuscript mentions that 4200 cubic "shrims" (Babel's unit of length) of stones were available to build the tower. Did they have enough? Explain.

9. (25 pts) Cesium 137 (Cs^{137}) is a short-lived radioactive isotope. It decays at a rate proportional to itself and has a half life of 30 years (i.e., the amount of Cs^{137} remaining t years after Ao milli-Curies of the radioactive isotope is released is given by $Aoe^{-(\frac{\ln 2}{30})t}$. We'll abbreviate milli-Curies by mCi).

As a result of its operations, a nuclear power plant releases Cs^{137} at a rate of .1 mCi per year. The plant began its operations in 1980, which we will designate as $t = 0$. Assume there is no other source of this particular isotope.

(a) Write an integral which gives the total amount of Cs^{137} T years after. (Note: The rest of the problem does not depend on correctly answering part (a).)

(b) Write a differential equation whose solution is $R(t)$, the amount (in mCi) of Cs^{137} in t years. (We are assuming $R(0) = 0$).

(c) After 20 years, approximately how much Cs^{137} will there be?

(d) In the long run, how much Cs^{137} will there be?

(e) Since Cs^{137} poses a great health risk, the government says that the maximum amount of Cs^{137} acceptable in the surrounding environment is 1 mCi (spread over the surrounds). What is the maximum rate at which the station can release the isotope and still be in compliance with the regulations?

1a) Constant solutions: 1 and 6 } see below
6 is stable

b)

points of inflection
at $y=0$ and $y=4$

2. at $(1,1)$, $\frac{dx}{dt}$ is positive
This is only the case in Ⓒ

3a) a) $\int_0^\infty \frac{1}{e^x}dx = \lim_{b\to\infty} \int_0^b e^{-x}dx = \lim_{b\to\infty}\left[-e^{-x}\right]_0^b$

$$= \lim_{b\to\infty}\left[e^{-b}+1\right] = 1$$

b) Since $1+x \geq 1$, for $x \geq 0$, we have $\frac{e^{-x}}{1+x} \leq e^{-x}$,

so $\int_0^\infty \frac{e^{-x}}{1+x}dx$ <u>converges</u>

On the calculator, the graph seems to merge with the x-axis at about 3. To be on the safe side, we estimate $\int_0^6 \frac{e^{-x}}{1+x}dx$

(Midpoints) $\boxed{.5957 < \int_0^6 (e^{-x}/1+x)\,dx < .5967}$ (Trapezoids) $\left(\begin{smallmatrix}100\\ \text{subdivs}\end{smallmatrix}\right)$

We estimate the tail: $\underline{\int_6^\infty \frac{e^{-x}}{1+x}dx} < \int_6^\infty e^{-x}dx = \lim_{b\to\infty}\int_6^b e^{-x}dx = e^{-6}\underline{< .0025}$

So $.5957 < \int_0^\infty \frac{e^{-x}}{1+x}dx < .5992$, or $\boxed{\int_0^\infty \frac{e^{-x}}{1+x}dx \approx .60}$

4a) 8% of 10,000, or $\boxed{800}$

b) For example, there are $92-80 = 12\%$ of the bulbs with a life span between 4 and 8 months. This is represented by a $\boxed{\text{rectangle of area 12}}$

c) $\underline{\text{average}} \approx \frac{1}{100}\left(2\cdot1 + 6\cdot3 + 12\cdot6 + 16\cdot9 + 24\cdot11 + 20\cdot13 + 16\cdot16 + 4\cdot19\right)$

$\approx \underline{10.9 \text{ months}}$

Here we assume, for example, that all bulbs with a lifespan of 4 to 8 months have a lifespan of $\frac{4+8}{2} = 6$ months

5a) $$\frac{dT}{dt} = \frac{1}{29}(10 - T)$$

b) "Flip": $\frac{dt}{dT} = \frac{29}{10-T}$ $\Rightarrow$ $t = -29\ln(10-T) + c$ $\Rightarrow$ $t - C = -29\ln(10-T)$

$\Rightarrow \ln(10-T) = -\frac{t}{29} + K$ $\Rightarrow$ $10-T = C\cdot e^{-\frac{t}{29}}$ $\Rightarrow T = 10 + K\cdot e^{-\frac{t}{29}}$

From the initial value $T(0) = 65$ we get $K = 55$, or $\underline{T = 10 + 55\cdot e^{-t/29}}$

$T(5) \approx 56.3$

$\boxed{\text{or}}$: Use EULER

c) $$\frac{dT}{dt} = 2 + \frac{1}{29}(10 - T)$$

d)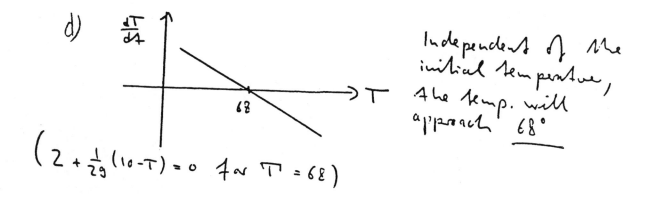

Independent of the initial temperature, the temp. will approach $\underline{68°}$

$\left(2 + \frac{1}{29}(10-T) = 0 \text{ for } T = 68\right)$

6a) $\dfrac{dT}{dt} = 3 - .3(T-M)$ $\qquad \dfrac{dM}{dt} = 3(T-M) - 3M$

$\qquad\qquad\qquad\qquad\qquad\qquad\qquad = 3(T - 2M)$

b) T

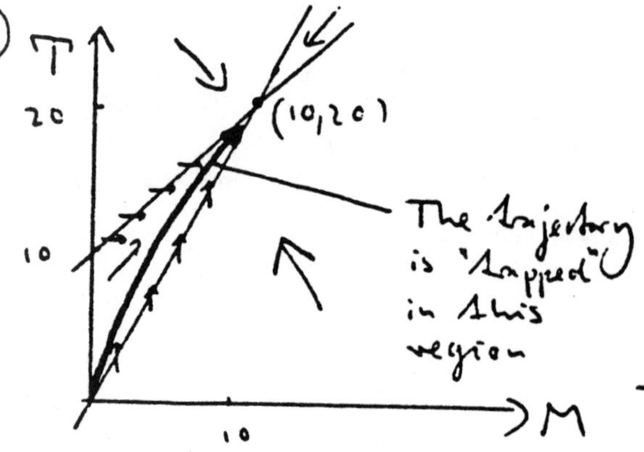

The trajectory is "trapped" in this region

Nullclines $\dfrac{dT}{dt} = 3 - .3(T-M) = 0$

$\qquad\qquad\qquad T - M = 10$

$\qquad\qquad\qquad \underline{T = M + 10}$

$\dfrac{dM}{dt} = 3(T - 2M) = 0$ for $\underline{T = 2M}$

Equilibrium: $M + 10 = 2M \Rightarrow \underline{M = 10}, \underline{T = 20}$

Trajectory approaches this point

c)

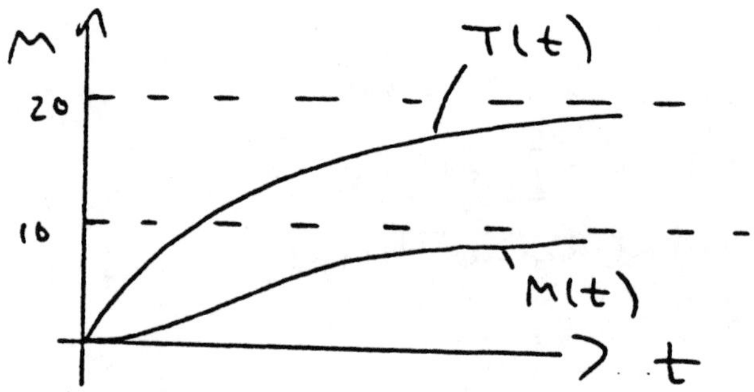

$T(t) \longrightarrow 20$ (as $t \to \infty$)

$M(t) \longrightarrow 10$ (as $t \to \infty$)

$T'(0) = 3$

$M'(0) = 0$

184

1. (8 pts) Consider the differential equation $\frac{dy}{dt} = g(y)$. The graph of g(y) is drawn below.

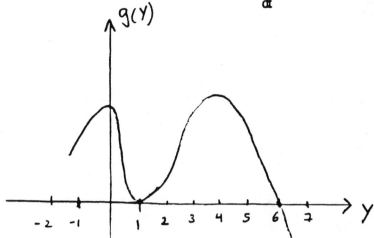

a) What are the constant solutions to the differential equation $\frac{dy}{dt} = g(y)$?
Which of them are stable?

b) Sketch a graph of y as a function of t for representative initial values of y. You do not have to provide a scale for t.

2. (8 pts.) Which system of equations would roughly have the given phase plane diagram?

a) $\frac{dx}{dt} = -10x+y$

$\frac{dy}{dt} = x-10y$

b) $\frac{dx}{dt} = x - 10y$

$\frac{dy}{dt} = 10x - y$

c) $\frac{dx}{dt} = -x+10y$

$\frac{dy}{dt} = -10x-y$

d) $\frac{dx}{dt} = x-10y$

$\frac{dy}{dt} = -10x-y$

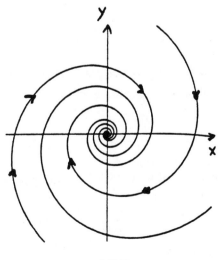

3. (18 pts.)   Are the following integrals convergent or divergent? Give reasons for your answers and if the integral is convergent, please give an approximation rounded off to two decimal places.   (Note: the function $f(x) = \dfrac{e^{-x}}{1+x}$ is concave up for $x \geq 0$.)

a) $\displaystyle\int_0^\infty \dfrac{1}{e^x}\, dx$

b) $\displaystyle\int_0^\infty \dfrac{e^{-x}}{1+x}\, dx$

4. (18 pts.) A lightbulb company is interested in the lifespan of their lightbulbs. They have 10,000 lightbulbs burning and have collected the following information.

   After 2 months, 98% of the bulbs were still working.

   After 8 months, 80% of the bulbs were still working.

We summarize all the data collected below: (Note: Read carefully: the data was not collected at regular intervals.)

# of months	% of bulbs still burning
2	98
4	92
8	80
10	64
12	40
14	20
18	4
20	0

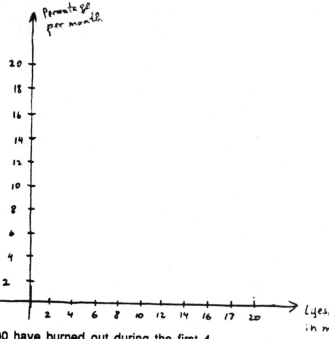

a) How many bulbs out of the original 10,000 have burned out during the first 4 months ?

b) Use the axes above to draw a histogram for the lifespan of a bulb reflecting all the information in the table. (Do not smooth out the graph.)

c) Approximate the average lifespan of a lightbulb. Explain your reasoning clearly.

5. (24 pts.) Consider the Hakosalo residence in Oulu, Finland. Assume that heat is lost from the house only through windows and the rate of change of temperature is proportional to the difference of temperature outside and inside. The constant of proportionality is $\dfrac{1}{29 \text{ hours}}$.

Assume that it is $10°$ F outside constantly.

On a thursday at noon the temperature inside the house was $65°$ F and the heat was turned off until 5 p.m.

a) Write a differential equation which reflects the rate of change of the temperature in the house between noon and 5 p.m..

b) Find the temperature in the house at 5 pm. (You may do this analytically or using your calculator to get a rough estimate.)

c) At 5 p.m. the heat is turned on. The heater generates an amount of energy that would raise the inside temperature by $2°$ F per hour if there were no heat loss. Write a differential equation that relects what happens to the inside temperature after the heat is turned on.

d) If the heat is left on indefinitely, what temperature will the inside of the house approach?

6. (24 pts.) One day when I came up to my chalet in the Swiss Alps, the temperature outdoors and indoors was just $0°$ C. I turned on the heat immediately. If no heat were lost to the outside, the heater would heat up the place at a rate of 3 degrees per hour. In fact, heat is lost to the outdoors despite the fact that I have double windows. Let T be the indoor temperature and M the temperature of the air between the windows. Due to the flow of heat through the inner window, T decreases at a rate proportional to T-M, with constant of proportionality .3(per hour). M increases at a rate proportional to T-M (due to heat flow through the inner window), and it decreases at a rate proportional to M (due to heat flow through the outer window). In both cases, the constant of proportionality is 3(per hour).

Assume that the outdoor temperature stays constant at $0°$ C and that the heat flow through the window is the only form of heat loss.

a) Set up a system of differential equations for the indoor temperature T and the temperature of the layer or air between the windows M.

b) For the system you established in a), sketch the " general directions " in the phase plane. Also, sketch the trajectory for the situation discussed above. What happens in the long run?

c) Sketch possible graphs for the two temperatures, as a function of time (you need not put a scale on the t-axis). Pay attention to the long term behavior of your graphs and to the behavior around t = 0. (t=0 is the moment when the heat is switched on.)

Math 1b
Exam 1
March 4, 1991

1. (8 points) Find elementary formulas for the following:

    (a) $\int (1+x)\sin(2x)dx$

    (b) $\int \frac{1+e^{2t}}{e^t}dt$

2. (8 points) Compute:

    (a) $\int_{-R}^{R} \frac{\sin x}{1+x^4}dx$

    (b) $\int_{0}^{R} \frac{1}{(4+x)^2}dx$

3. (8 points) Compute the following integrals. If you provide an approximation, it should be rounded to three decimal places and you must explain how you got it and how you know it has the desired accuracy.

    (a) $\int_{2}^{3} \frac{1}{\ln x}dx$

    (b) $\int_{0}^{3} x\sqrt{16+x^2}dx$

4. (18 points) A straight road goes through the center of a circular city of radius 5km. The density of the population at a distance r (in km) yfrom the road is well approximated by

$$D(r) = 20 - 4r$$

(in thousand people per km^2). Find the total population of the city.

5. (18 points) The price of crude oil in the recent past was well approximated by $P(t) = 40 - (t-4)^2$, where $P(t)$ is measured in US\$/barrel, and time t is measured in months, with $t = 0$ on July 1, 1990. In the same time period, Saudi Arabia produced oil at a rate well approximated by $R(t) = 160 + 30\arctan(t-3)$ (measured in million barrels per month). Assume that the oil is sold continuously two months after its production. How much did Saudi Arabia get for the oil it produced in the second half of 1990?

6. (20 points) The table below shows the speed $v(t)$ of a falling object at various times (time t measured in seconds, speed v measured in m/sec).

t	0	1	2	3
v	17	23	28	32

    (a) Due to air resistance, the object's acceleration is decreasing. What does this tell you about the shape of the graph of $v(t)$?

    (b) Find upper and lower bounds for the distance the object fell in these three seconds. The bounds should be less than three meters apart. Illustrate your reasoning on a sketch.

7. (20 points) A rectangular lake is 100km long and 60km wide. The depth of the water at any point of the surface is a tenth of the distance from the nearest shoreline. How much water does the lake contain (in km^3)?

188

1. (12 points) Find

    (a) $\int \sqrt{1 - 3x}\, dx$ (b) $\int x \ln x\, dx$

2. (10 points) Find the equation of the solution to the differential equation

$$y' = \frac{5}{1 + y}$$

satisfying $y(0) = 2$.

3. (12 points) (a) Using two subdivisions, find the left, right, trapezoid and midpoint approximations to

$$\int_0^1 1 - e^{-x} dx.$$

    (b) Draw sketches showing what each approximation represents.

    (c) Given only the information you found in (a), what is your best estimate for the value of this integral?

4. (12 points) For the differential equation represented by the slope field below, sketch the solution curve with $y(0) = 0$.

    (a)

    (b) On the same slope field, use $\Delta x = 0.5$ to sketch, as accurately as you can, two steps of Euler's approximation to this solution curve. (End at $x = 1$.)

5. (12 points)The *capital value* of an asset such as a machine is sometimes defined as the present value of all future net earnings of the asset. The actual lifetime of the asset may not be known, and since some assets last indefinitely, the capital value of the asset may be written in the form

$$\int_0^\infty K(t)e^{-rt}dt,$$

where $K(t)$ is the annual rate of earnings produced by the asset at time t, and r is the annual interest rate, compounded continuously. Find the capital value of an asset that generates income at a rate of $500 per year, with an interest rate of 10%.

6. (14 points) The density of cars (in cars per mile) down a 20 mile stretch of the Mass. Turnpike starting at a toll plaza is given by

$$\rho(x) = 500 + 100\sin(\pi x)$$

where x is the distance in miles from the toll plaza and $0 \le x \le 20$.

(a) Write a Riemann sum which estimates the total number of cars down the 20 mile stretch. Explain your reasoning.

(b) Convert this sum to an integral and evaluate it.

7. (12 points) Let $F(x) = \int_0^x \sin t\, dt$, and $G(x) = \int_0^x \sin^2 t\, dt$ and consider the quantities

$$G\left(\frac{\pi}{2}\right), \quad F(\pi), \quad G(\pi), \quad F(2\pi).$$

(a) Show how each quantity can be represented on a graph.

(b) Use the graph to rank these quantities in ascending (i.e., increasing) order.

8. (14 points) There is a theory that says the rate at which information spreads by word of mouth is proportional to the product of the number of people who have the information times the number that does not. Suppose the total population is N.

(a) If $p = f(t)$ is the number of people that have the information, what number does not have the information?

(b) Write a differential equation that describes the rate, $\frac{dp}{dt}$, at which the information spreads by word of mouth.

(c) Why does this theory make sense?

(d) Sketch the graph of $p = f(t)$ as a function of time.

190

1. (10 points) Rank in order of increasing present value, assuming 7% interest compounded continuously. No work need be shown.

    (a) $1000, paid today.

    (b) $1050, paid six months from now.

    (c) $1085, paid a year from now.

    (d) $1050, paid continuously over the next year.

2. (12 points) For $-1 \le x \le 1$, define

$$F(x) = \int_{-1}^{x} \sqrt{1 - t^2}\, dt.$$

    (a) What does $F(1)$ represent geometrically?

    (b) What is the value of $F(-1)$? $F(0)$?

    (c) Find $F'(x)$.

3. (12 points) Is

$$\int_{0}^{\infty} \frac{\sin^2 x}{(1 + x)^2}\, dx$$

convergent or divergent? Give reasons for your answer and if it is convergent, give an upper bound for its value.

4. (16 points) When an oil well burns, sediment is carried up into the air by the flames and is eventually deposited on the ground. The further away from the oil well, the less sediment is deposited. From experiments, it could be determined that the density (in tons/square mile) at a distance r from the burning oil well is given by

$$\frac{7}{1 + r^2}.$$

    (a) Find a Riemann sum which approximates the total amount of sediment which is deposited within 100 miles of the well. Explain your work.

    (b) Hence find and evaluate an integral which represents this total deposit.

1. (12 points) Find the following integrals. Show your work.

(a) $\int \left(\dfrac{1}{(x+1)} - \dfrac{1}{(x+1)^2} \right) dx$ (b) $\int x \cos 2x \, dx$

2. (12 points) Find by any method. Say briefly but clearly what you did.

(a) $\int_0^1 x^3 e^{x^2} dx$ (b) $\int_{-2}^2 f(x) dx$ where $f(x) = \begin{cases} 1 & \text{for } x \le 1 \\ x & \text{for } x > 1 \end{cases}$

3. (10 points) The following numbers are the left, right, trapezoidal and midpoint approximations to $\int_0^1 f(x) dx$, where $f(x)$ is as shown. (Each uses the same number of subdivisions.)

I) 0.36735
II) 0.39896
III) 0.36814
IV) 0.33575

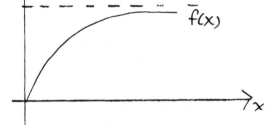

(a) Which is which? How do you know?

(b) Write $A < \int_0^1 f(x) dx < B$, where $B - A$ is as small as possible.

4. (16 points) A study of the costs to produce airplanes in World War II led to the theory of "learning curves," the idea of which is that the marginal cost per plane decreases over the duration of a production run. In other words, with experience, staff on an assembly line can produce planes with greater efficiency. The 90% learning curve describes a typical situation where the marginal cost, MC, to produce the x-th plane is given by

$$MC(x) = M_0 x^{\log_2 0.9},$$

where $M_0 =$ marginal cost to produce the first plane.

(a) If a plant produces planes with a 90% learning curve on production costs, and the marginal cost for the first plane is $500 thousand, then what is the marginal cost to produce the second plane? The fourth plane?

(b) Recall that marginal cost is related to total cost as follows:

$$MC(x) \approx C'(x),$$

where $C(x) =$ total cost to produce x units. Given this, and the formula for $MC(x)$ with $M_0 =$ \$500 thousand, find a formula for $C(x)$. What, physically, is the meaning of the constant in your formula for $C(x)$?

(c) If the constant in your formula for $C(x)$ is $20 million, and $M_0 = $500 thousand, then what, approximately, is $C(50)$?

1. (3 each) Find dy/dx if:

a) $y = xe^{-3x}$ b) $y = \cos^2(3x-1)$ c) $y = 1/(x^2+1)$

2. (3 each) Find formulas for the following indefinite integrals (anti-derivatives):

a) $\int (x+2)(x-2)\,dx$ b) $\int \frac{1+e^t}{e^t}\,dt$ c) $\int \frac{1-\ln(x)}{x}\,dx$ d) $\int (x-1)e^{-x}\,dx$

3. (3 each) Evaluate the following. Give both an exact, but possibly symbolic, value (e.g., 3/4, sin 3, ln 2, ...) and a decimal approximation accurate to two decimal places.

a) $\int_0^{1/2} \frac{1}{1-x^2}\,dx$ b) $\int_0^4 \frac{4x}{\sqrt{x^2+9}}\,dx$ c) $\int_1^3 \ln(x)\,dx$

4. (7) Give an upper bound U and a lower bound L for

$$\int_{-.5}^{.3} \frac{1}{1+x^4}\,dx$$

such that $U-L < 10^{-3}$. Explain your procedure.

5. (10) (a) A function g is known to be linear on the interval from $-\infty$ to 2 (inclusive) and also linear on the interval from 2 to ∞ (again inclusive.) Furthermore, $g(1) = 2$, $g(2) = 0$, $g(4) = 8$. What are $g(0)$, $g(3)$?

(b) Another function f satisfies $f(0) = 0$ and $f' = g$. What are $f(2)$, $f(3)$?

(c) Give formulas that express $f(t)$ directly in terms of t.

6. (10) Circle City is circular with a radius of four miles. Right in the center is a circular park with diameter one mile. No one lives in the park. Elsewhere the population density is $4000(5-r)$ people per square mile, where r is the distance from the center in miles.

(a) What is the total population of Circle City? Explain how you get your answer.

(b) What is the average density of population of the whole city?

7. (10) What point of the parabola whose equation is $y = x^2$ is nearest to the point (6,3)?

193

8. (10) The part of the graph of $\sin(x^2+y) = x$ that is near to

(0,π) defines y as a function of x implicitly.

(a) Is this function increasing or decreasing near 0? Explain how you know.

(b) Does the graph of this function lie above or below its tangent line at (0,π)? Explain how you know.

9. (15) When a bacterial cell is suspended in a fluid, the concentration of a certain drug within the cell will change toward the concentration in the surrounding fluid at a rate proportional to the difference between the two concentrations.

(a) Write the differential equation that expresses this relation. (Be sure to define the meaning of the literal quantities involved.)

(b) Assume that the concentration in the surrounding fluid is held constant. What is the general solution of the equation in (a)? (This solution will necessarily contain some unknown constants.)

9. cont. (c) Suppose that a patient's blood is infected with these bacteria, which initially contain none of the drug. The patient is given enough of the drug to bring (and hold) its concentration in his blood to .0001. After two hours, the concentration within the bacterial cells is found to be .00004.

Use this information to evaluate the unknown constants in (b).

(d) How long will it be before the concentration within the bacteria reaches .00008?

10. (10) Discuss the solutions of the differential equation

$$\frac{dy}{dx} = y(1-x-y).$$

Your discussion should include at least the following points.

Are there any constant solutions?

A sketch of several solution curves.

Explain why the solution function f for which f(-1) = 1 has a global maximum. What is the "long run" behavior of this function? (i.e., what can you say about lim f(x) as x $\longrightarrow \infty$?)

Many solution functions have global maxima. Where do these maximum points appear on the graph?

A discussion that includes other significant information may receive extra credit. Although you may use your calculator to get the picture, try to base your arguments on information taken directly from the differential equation.

Note: Solutions starting from negative values of y are likely to grow so fast that the calculator will overflow, causing it to stop and give an error message.

1. (3 points each) Differentiate:

a) $x^2\sqrt{1 - x}$

b) $\sin(\frac{1}{x})$

c) e^{e^x}

2. (3 points each)

a) $\displaystyle\int \frac{x^2 + 1}{\sqrt{x}} \, dx$

b) $\displaystyle\int (\sin^3 2\theta + 1)\cos 2\theta \, d\theta$

c) $\displaystyle\int \frac{3x^2 + \cos x}{x^3 + \sin x} \, dx$

d) $\displaystyle\int_0^{\frac{\sqrt{3}}{2}} \frac{dx}{\sqrt{1 - x^2}}$

e) $\displaystyle\int_0^{\ln 2} \frac{x}{e^x} \, dx$

3. (8 points) If the graph of $y = f(x)$ is shown below, arrange in ascending order (i.e., smallest first, largest last):

$f'(A)$, $f'(B)$, $f'(C)$, slope AB, 1, 0

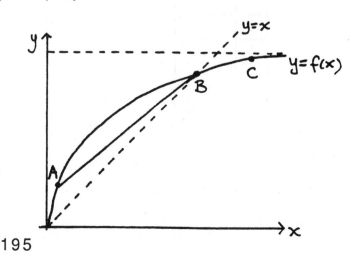

195

4. (10 points) Solve $\frac{dN}{dt} = 4 - .2N$, with $N(0) = 0$, and sketch the solution for $t \geq 0$. Label any intercepts or asymptotes clearly.

5. (10 points) A single cell of a bee's honey comb has the shape shown to the right. The surface area of this cell is given by

    $$A = 6hs + \frac{3}{2} s^2 \left(\frac{-\cos\theta}{\sin\theta} + \frac{\sqrt{3}}{\sin\theta}\right)$$

    where h, s, θ are as shown in the picture.

    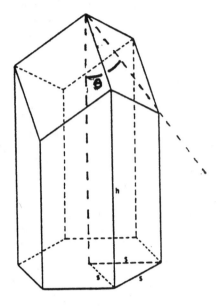

    a) Keeping h and s fixed, for what angle, θ, is the surface area minimal?

    b) Measurements on bee's cells have shown that the angle actually used by bees is about $\theta = 55°$. Comment

6. (10 points) Suppose $f(t)$ is given by the graph to the right. Complete the table of values of the function

    $$F(x) = \int_0^x f(t)dt .$$

x	F(x)
0	
1	
2	
3	
4	
5	
6	

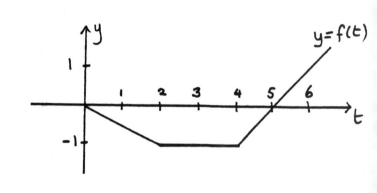

7. (8 points) Match the following four direction fields (slope fields) with four of the differential equations below. (One equation does not match!) No reasons are required.

A)

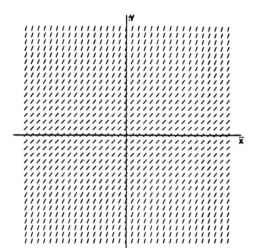

B)

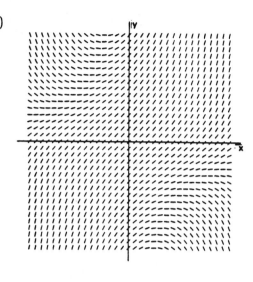

C)

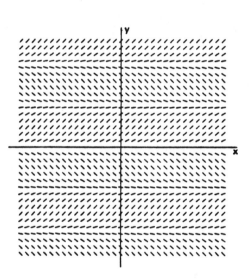

D)

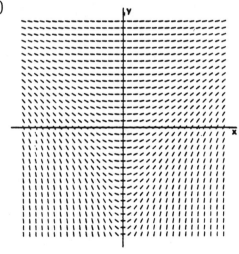

a) $y' = xy + 1$ is graph _____

b) $y' = \sin x$ is graph _____

c) $y' = xe^{-y}$ is graph _____

d) $y' = y^2 + 1$ is graph _____

e) $y' = \sin y$ is graph _____

Mathematics 1a
Final Exam: January 17, 1991

1. (9 points) Find, without simplifying your answers:

   (a) $\dfrac{d}{dx}\left(\ln(x^2 e^x)\right)$ (b) $\dfrac{d}{d\theta}\left(\dfrac{\cos\theta}{\sin\theta}\right)$ (c) $\dfrac{d}{dz}\left(\sqrt{1 + 2^{3z}}\right)$

2. (6 points) Find a function F such that:

   (a) $F'(x) = x^3 - \dfrac{1}{\sqrt{x}}$ (b) $F'(x) = \sin x + \dfrac{1}{x}$

3. (10 points) One of the functions below is a quadratic, one is a cubic, and one is a trigonometric function. Which is which? Why?
   [Note: You don't have to find formulas for these functions.]

x	$f(x)$		x	$g(x)$		x	$h(x)$
0.2	−0.42		1.3	0.41		0.5	−1.13
0.4	−0.65		1.7	0.81		1.2	0.13
0.6	0.96		2.5	0.65		1.8	0.03
0.8	−0.15		3.0	−0.10		2.0	0
1.2	0.84		3.5	−1.35		2.2	0.05

4. (12 points) If P dollars is invested at an annual interest rate of $r\%$, then in t years this investment grows to F dollars, where

$$F = P\left(1 + \frac{r}{100}\right)^t.$$

   (a) Assuming P and r are constant, find $\dfrac{dF}{dt}$. In practical terms (in terms of money), what does this derivative mean?

   (b) Solve the given equation for P. Assuming F and r are constant, find $\dfrac{dP}{dt}$. What is its sign? Why is this sign reasonable?

5. (15 points)

   (a) Sketch the graphs of $y = e^x$ and $y = ex$.

   (b) For which values of x is $e^x > ex$? Explain how you can be certain of your answer.

   (c) Find the average value of the difference between e^x and ex on the interval between $x = 0$ and $x = 2$.

6. (18 points) The police observe that the skidmarks made by a stopping car are 200 ft long. Assuming the car decelerated at a constant rate of 20 ft/sec², skidding all the way,, how fast was the car going when the brakes were applied?

7. (15 points)

Large cities in developing countries are growing much faster than cities in the industrialized world ever have. London, which in 1810 became the first industrial city to top 1 million, now has a population of 11 million. By contrast, Mexico City's population stood at only a million people just 50 years ago and is now at 20 million. [Adapted from the Population Crisis Committee, Washington, D.C.]

Assuming that the instantaneous percentage growth rates of London and Mexico City were each constant over the last two centuries,

(a) how many times greater is Mexico City's percentage growth rate than London's? Show your calculations and reasoning.

(b) When were the two cities the same size? Show your calculations and reasoning.

8. (15 points) The regular air fare between Boston and San Francisco is $500. An airline flying 747s with a capacity of 380 on this route observes that they fly with an average of 300 passengers. Market research tells the airlines' managers that each $20 fare reduction would attract, on average, 20 more passengers for each flight. How should they set the fare to maximize their revenue? Why?

9. (20 points) The Quabbin Reservoir in the western part of Massachusetts provides most of Boston's water. The graph below represents the flow of water in and out of the Quabbin Reservoir throughout 1989.

(a) Sketch a possible graph for the quantity of water in the reservoir, as a function of time.

(b) When, in the course of 1989, was the quantity of water in the reservoir most? Least? Mark and label these points on the given graph and on the graph you drew in (a).

(c) When was the quantity of water decreasing most rapidly? Again, mark and label this time on both graphs.

(d) By July 1990 the quantity of water in the reservoir was about the same as in January 1989. Draw plausible graphs for the flow into and the flow out of the reservoir for the first half of 1990. Explain your graph.

10. (20 points) When hyperventilating, a person breathes in and out extremely rapidly. A spirogram is a machine that draws a graph of the volume of air in a person's lungs as a function of time. During hyperventilation, the spirogram trace might be represented by

$$V = 3 - 0.05 \cos(200\pi t)$$

where V is the volume of the lungs in litres and t is in minutes.

(a) What are the maximum and minimum volumes of air in the lungs?

(b) What is the period of this function?

(c) Sketch the graph of one period of this function, starting at $t = 0$. Put scales on the V and t axes.

(d) Find the maximum rate (in liters/minute) of flow of air during inspiration (i.e., breathing in). This is called the *peak inspiratory flow*.

(e) Find the average rate of flow of air during inspiration. This is called the *mean inspiratory flow*.

11. (20 points)

(a) Find the family of all quadratic functions that have zeros at $x = 1$ and $x = 5$. (Your answer will contain one arbitrary constant.)

(b) Use your answer to (a) to find the family of all cubic functions, f, that have critical points at $x = 1$ and $x = 5$.

(c) For all cubics, f, in this family, find

(i) p, the x-coordinate of the point of inflection;

(ii) $f''(p)$, where p is the x-coordinate of the point of inflection;

(iii) $f'(1)$.

(d) From the list below, check off the data you would like to be told in order to specify the cubic f uniquely. Don't ask for more or less information than you need. (There are many possible answers. Just give one choice or set of choices.) Briefly explain your answer.

_____ $f(0)$
_____ $f(p)$ where p is the point of inflection
_____ $f'(p)$ where p is the point of inflection
_____ $f'(0)$

1. (10 points) Which of the functions below could be the derivative of which of the others? (Hint: Try all combinations.)

a)

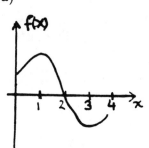

b)

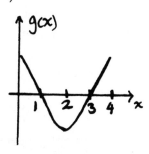

c)

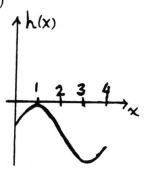

2. (10 points) (a) Find the derivatives:

(i) $\dfrac{d}{dt} e^{2(t-1)}$

(ii) $\dfrac{d}{d\theta} \left(\theta \sin(\theta^2) \right)$

(b) If P dollars is invested at an annual interest rate of $r\%$, then in t years this investment grows to F dollars, where

$$F = P \left(1 + \frac{r}{100} \right)^t.$$

Find $\frac{dF}{dr}$ (assuming P and t are constant). In terms of money, what does this derivative tell you?

3. (15 points) Each of the quantities below can be represented in the picture. For each quantity, state whether it is represented by a length, a slope or an area. Then using the letters on the picture, make clear exactly which length, slope or area represents it. [Note: The letters P, Q, R, etc., represents points.)

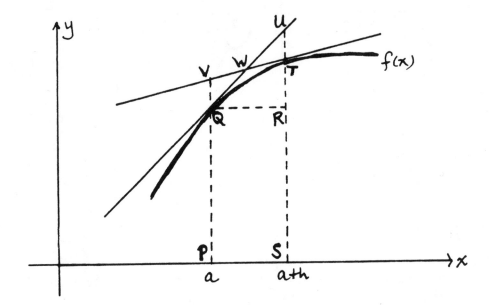

(a) $f(a+h) - f(a)$

(b) $f'(a+h)$

(c) $f'(a)h$

(d) $f(a)h$

(e) State whether the quantity

$$\frac{1}{h}\int_a^{a+h} f(x)dx$$

is represented by a length or area in the picture. Draw the length or shade the area in the picture above.

4. (15 points)

A car is moving along a straight road from A to B, starting from A at time t=0. Below is the velocity (positive direction is from A to B) plotted against time.

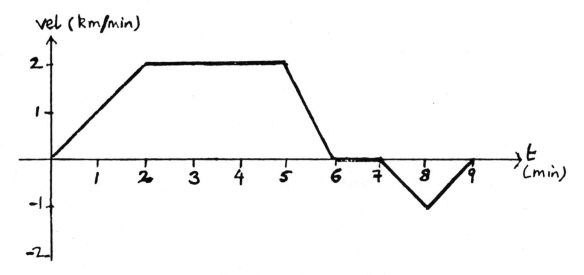

(a) How many kilometers away from A is the car at time t =2, 5, 6, 7, and 9?

4. (b) Carefully sketch a graph of the acceleration of the car against time. Label your axes.

5. (15 points) Esther is a swimmer who prides herself in having a smooth backstroke. Let $s(t)$ be her position in the Olympic size pool, as a function of time ($s(t)$ is measured in meters, t in seconds). (The Olympic size pool is 50 meters long.)

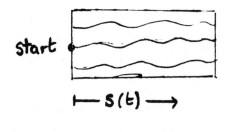

203

5. Below we list some values of $s(t)$, for a recent swim.

t	$s(t)$
0	0
3.0	10
8.6	20
14.6	30
20.8	40
27.6	50
31.9	40
38.1	30
45.8	20
53.9	10
60.0	0

5. (a) Sketch possible graphs for Esther's position and velocity. Put scales on your axes.

(b) Find Esther's average speed and average velocity over the whole swim.

(c) Based on the data, can you say whether or not Esther's instantaneous speed was ever greater than 3 meters/second? Why?

(d) Give a brief qualitative description of the graph of Esther's position (i.e., describe where the position is increasing, decreasing, concave up or down). Explain these qualitative features in terms of Esther's swimming behavior.

6. (15 points) Consider the region A that is bounded above by the graph of $f(x) = e^{-x^2}$, bounded below by the graph of $g(x) = e^{x^2} - 1$, and bounded on the left by the y-axis.

(a) Sketch and label the curves $f(x)$ and $g(x)$ and shade the region A. Find (approximately if necessary) and label the coordinates of the three corner points of A.

(b) By just looking at your sketch in (a), decide whether the area of A is more or less than 0.7. Is it more or less than 0.3? Give a graphical justification for your answers.

(c) Express the area of the region A as an integral, or as a sum or difference of integrals. Approximate the value(s) of the integral(s) with an accuracy that allows you to decide whether the area of A is more or less than 0.5. Explain what you are doing.

(d) Name the possible sources of error in your calculation of the area of A.

204

1. Find an equation for the line L shown below. Your answer will contain the positive constant b. Simplify your answer.

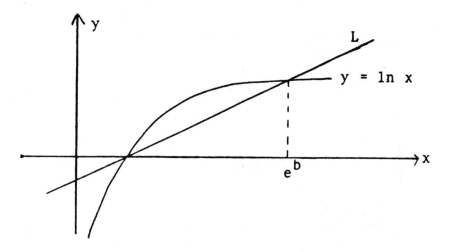

2. You are offered two jobs starting on July 1st of 1994. Firm A offers you $40,000 a year to start and you can expect an annual raise of 4% every July 1st. At firm B you would start at $30,000 but can expect an annual 6% increase every July 1st. On July 1st of which year would the job at firm B first pay more than the job at firm A?

3. Find a possible formula for each of the following functions. Check that your formula fits the data points.

   a)

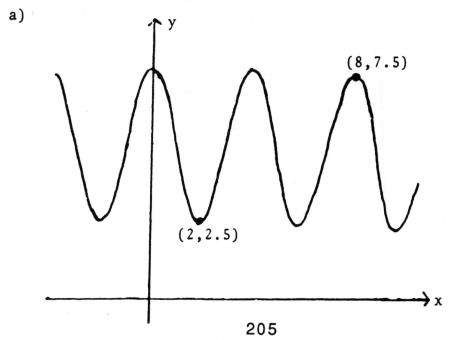

b)

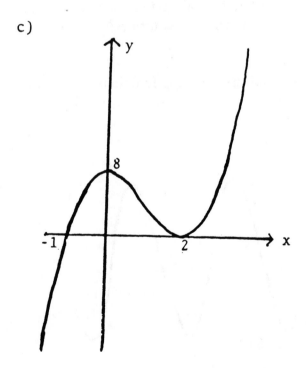

(4,39.0625)

(3,15.625)

(1,2.5)

(0,1)

c)

8

-1

2

x

4. For any number r, let $m(r)$ be the slope of the graph of the function $y = (2.1)^x$ at the point $x = r$.

(a) Complete the following table:

r	0	1	2	3	4
m(r)			3.27	6.87	14.43

(b) Explain in a few complete sentences what you did to fill in this table, and why you did it. (If you include pictures, make sure they are carefully labelled.)

(c) What you have done in part (a) gives you some points on the graph of the function $m(r)$. Graph the points and guess the general shape of the graph of the function $m(r)$ by "fitting a curve" through this data. Give the equation of the curve.

5. Here are some data from a recent Scientific American article on Old World monkeys.

(a) From the data presented give an approximate formula for

$$C = \text{cranial capacity (in cm}^3)$$

as a function of

$$A = \text{arc length of skull (in cm).}$$

Hint: Fit a line through the data points. Logarithms are to base 10.

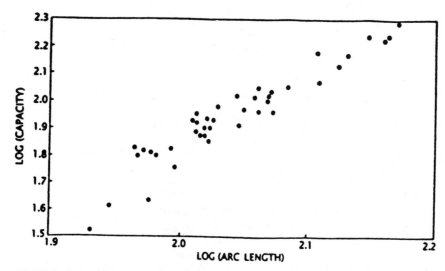

CRANIAL CAPACITY of contemporary Old World monkeys is related to arc length of skull as is shown.

SCIENTIFIC AMERICAN January 1989

5(b) What type of a function is $C = f(A)$ (logarithmic, exponential, trigonometric, power function,...)?

207

Points in parenthesis. Total is 150 points.

1. (24) Integrate:

    a) $\displaystyle\int \frac{x^3 + 1}{x^2}\, dx$

    b) $\displaystyle\int_0^2 \frac{x^2}{x^3 + 1}\, dx$

    c) $\displaystyle\int \frac{\sqrt{\ln x}}{x}\, dx$

    d) $\displaystyle\int \sin 3x\, e^{\cos 3x}\, dx$

2. (15) Differentiate:

    a) $f(x) = \dfrac{x^2 + 1}{x^2 - 1}$

    b) $f(x) = 2^x \tan x$

    c) $f(x) = \sqrt{(\ln x)^2 + 5}$

3. (16) Given below is the graph of a function f.

    a) Draw a graph of f', the derivative of f.

    b) Draw a graph of $\displaystyle\int_0^x f(t)dt$.

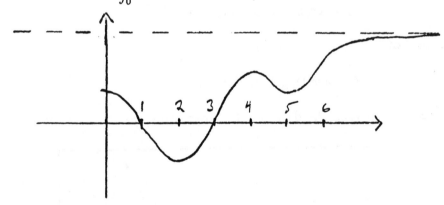

4. (35) Consider the function $f(x) = x + 2\cos x,\ 0 \le x \le 2\pi$.

    a) Find where f is increasing and where f is decreasing.
    b) Find the largest and smallest values of f in decimal form.
    c) Find all points of inflection.
    d) Find where f is increasing most rapidly.
    e) Sketch the graph of f.
    f) How many roots are there for $f(x) = 1$ in the given interval $0 \le x \le 2\pi$? How many for $f(x) = 2$? How many for $f(x) = 3$? Explain your answer with a picture.

5. (25) On a certain planet the gravitational constant g is -15 feet per second per second, that is for every second an object falls it picks up an extra 15 feet per second of velocity downward.

A ball is thrown upward at time $t = 0$ at 60 feet per second.

a) When does the ball reach the peak of its flight?

b) Find the peak height of the ball by giving equations for the ball's acceleration, then its velocity v (including computation of the antidifferentiation constant c), then its position s.

c) Find the peak height instead by left and right sums for $v(t)$. (First give a table of values for v.)

d) Find the peak height instead by graphing v versus t and recalling how distance traveled is related to the graph of velocity.

e) Suppose on another planet g is $\frac{1}{3}$ as much. Use the method (d) to find the peak height (same initial velocity of 60 feet per second).

6. (25) Consider the following table of data for the function f

x	5.0	5.1	5.2	5.3	5.4
$f(x)$	9.2	8.8	8.3	7.7	7.0

a) Estimate $f'(5.1)$.

b) Give an equation for the tangent at $x = 5.1$.

c) What is the sign of $f''(5.1)$? Explain your answer.

d) Is this table of data linear? Exponential? Quadratic? Explain your answer.

e) Suppose g is a function such that $g(5.1) = 10$ and $g'(5.1) = 3$. Find $h'(5.1)$ where

    i) $h(x) = f(x)g(x)$ ii) $h(x) = f(x)/g(x)$.

7. (10) The population of aphids on a rose plant increases at a rate proportional to the number present. In 3 days the population grew from 800 to 1400.

a) Write down an equation for the population of aphids at time t in days, where $t = 0$ is the day there were 800 aphids.

b) How long does it take for the population to get 10 times as large?

c) What was the population on the day before there were 800?

Math 111A, B - Third Hour Exam

April 16, 1991

Points in parenthesis.

1. (30) Consider $f(x) = x^2 e^{-x}$ for $-1 \le x \le 3$.

    a) Show that $f'(x) = e^{-x}(2x - x^2)$ and that $f''(x) = e^{-x}(x^2 - 4x + 2)$.
    b) For which x is f increasing? For which is f decreasing?
    c) Find the values of x where $f(x)$ is the greatest; where $f(x)$ is the least.
    d) Find all values of x where there is a point of inflection.
    e) Find the values of x where f is increasing most rapidly; where f is decreasing most rapidly.
    f) Sketch the graph of f.

2. (20) Let $f(x) = x^4 - 4x + 2$

    a) How many zeroes does f have? Justify your answer.
    b) Approximate one of the zeroes by first getting an initial estimate and then improving it by using Newton's Method <u>one time</u>.
    c) An initial estimate of $x = 1$, or x very near 1, doesn't work well for Newton's Method. Why?
    d) Suppose we wished to solve $f(x) = b$ instead (same f). For which values of b would there be no solutions? For which values of b would there be one solution? For which two solutions? For which more than two solutions?

3. (18) A car is going 80 feet per second and the driver puts on the brakes bringing the car to a stop in 5 seconds. Assume the deceleration of the car is constant while the brakes are on.

    a) What is the acceleration (really deceleration) of the car?
    b) How far does the car travel from the time the brakes are applied until it stops?
    c) Suppose the car is traveling twice as fast and the brakes are applied with the same force as before. How far does the car travel before it stops?
    d) Suppose the brakes are twice as strong (can stop the car twice as fast). How far does the car travel if its speed is 80 feet per second? How far if its speed is 160 feet per second?

4. (15) a) Find a function $F(x)$ such that $F'(x) = x^4 + \sin x$ and $F(0) = 5$.
    b) Sketch the graph of the function $G(x)$ whose <u>derivative</u> $G'(x) = g(x)$ has the graph drawn below.

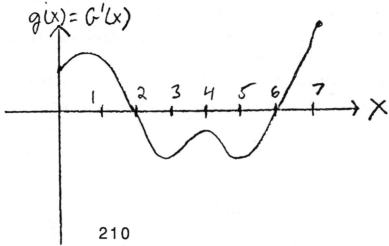

210

5. (17) Given below is the graph of the cost $C(q)$ of producing the quantity q and the revenue $R(q) = pq$ of selling the quantity q, where p is the price per unit (p is a constant).

   a) Show graphically where the quantity q_0 is such that the average cost per unit, $a(q) = \dfrac{C(q)}{q}$, is a minimum. Explain what you are doing.

   b) Show graphically where the quantity q_1 is such that your profit $R(q) - C(q)$ is a maximum. Explain the relationship between $C'(q_1)$ and p that should be evident in your picture.

   c) Which is larger $C'(q_0)$ or $C'(q_1)$? If you want to maximize profit, should you minimize your average cost? Explain your answer.

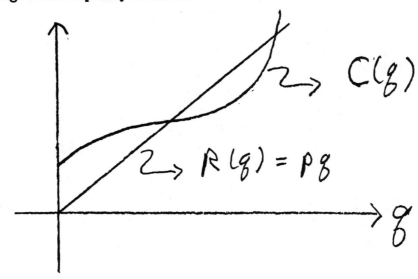

Points in parenthesis.

1. (12) Sketch the graph of the derivative, $y = f'(x)$, for each of the functions $y = f(x)$ whose graphs are given on the next page.

2. (12) Estimate $\int_8^{10} \ln x \, dx$ with accuracy .1. Show why you chose the Δx that you did.

3. (14) On the next page is given the graph of the <u>velocity</u> (in feet per second) of a hat that is thrown up in the air. Positive velocity means upward motion.

    a) When does the hat reach the top of its flight and about how high is it then?
    b) About how high is the hat at time $t = 4$?
    c) About what is the average velocity, $0 \le t \le 4$?
    d) Write an expression, involving v, for the average <u>speed</u>, $0 \le t \le 4$.

4. (15) Find $f'(x)$.

    a) $f(x) = e^{3x} \cos 5x$
    b) $f(x) = \sin\left(\sqrt{\ln x + 7}\right)$
    c) $f(x) = \dfrac{x + 1}{x^2 + 3}$

5. (15) On the next page are given a table of values for a function F near $x = 3$ and tables of values for a function G near $x = 3$ and near $x = 7$.

    a) Find $F'(3)$, $G'(3)$, $G'(7)$.
    b) If $H(x) = F(x)G(x)$, find $H'(3)$.
    c) If $H(x) = G(x)/F(x)$, find $H'(3)$.
    d) If $H(x) = G(F(x))$, find $H'(3)$.

6. (14) Consider the function $f(x) = x^3 - 4x^2 + 9$
    a) Give the equations of the tangent line at $x = 1$ and the tangent line at $x = 2$.
    b) Estimate $f'(1.5)$ using first the tangent line at $x = 1$ and then the tangent line at $x = 2$.
    c) The estimate using $x = 1$ is slightly better. Explain why.

7. (10) Suppose that $xy^2 + \sin y + x^3 = 8$.
    a) Find $\frac{dy}{dx}$
    b) Give a table of values for x and y near $(2, 0)$. (Use $x = 1.8, 1.9, 2.0, 2.1$)

8. (8) The volume of a certain tree is given by $V = \frac{1}{12\pi} C^2 h$, where C is the circumference of the tree at ground level and h is the height of the tree. If C is 5 feet and growing at the rate of .2 feet per year, and if h is 22 feet and growing at 4 feet per year, find the rate of growth of the volume V.

Graphs

For Problem !

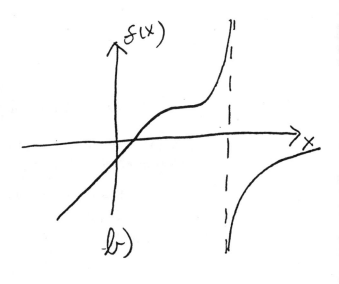

a)

b)

For Problem 3

Note that this is the graph of <u>velocity</u>, not distance

Points shown: (1, 15), (3, -10), (4, -15)

Tables for Problem 5

x	2.9	3.0	3.1
F(x)	6.7	7.0	7.3

x	2.9	3.0	3.1
G(x)	5.2	5.0	4.8

x	6.9	7.0	7.1
G(x)	1.95	2.0	2.05

Math 111a&b
First Hour Exam
February 11, 1991
Points for each problem in parenthesis. Total of 100 points.

1. (5) Give rough sketches, for $x > 0$, of the graphs of $y = x^5$, $y = x$, $y = x^{\frac{1}{3}}$, $y = x^0$, and $y = x^{-2}$.

2. (15) Give rough sketches of the graphs of the following functions. In each case, give me a scale along the x-axis and y- axis.
   (a) $y = 4 + 3\sin 2x$ (b) $y = \log_2(x - 3)$ (c) $y = -5(x + 2)x^2(x - 1)$

3. (20) Give a possible function for each curve.
   (a)   (b)

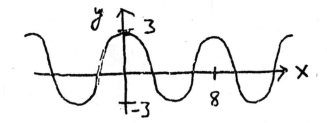

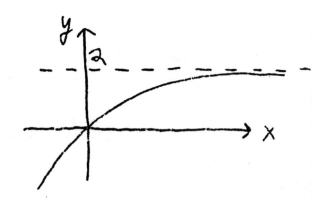

   (c)   (d)

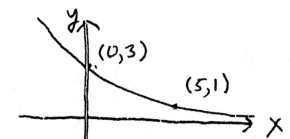

214

4. (12) One of the following tables of data is linear and one is exponential. Say which is which and give an equation that best fits each table. For the exponential table you do not have to use e if you do not want. An answer like $y = (3.73)(1.92)^{\frac{x}{6}}$ is fine.

(a)

x	0	0.50	1.00	2.50	2.00
y	3.12	2.62	2.20	1.85	1.55

(b)

x	0	0.50	1.00	1.50	2.00
y	2.71	3.94	5.17	6.40	7.63

5. (12) You have $500 invested in a bank account earning 8.2% compounded annually.

(a) Write an equation for the money M in your account after t years.

(b) How long will it take to triple your money?

(c) Suppose the interest were compounded monthly instead, that is you earned $\frac{8.2}{12}$% interest each month. What interest would you earn then for 1 year?

6. (10) Suppose that $f(T)$ is the cost to heat my house, in dollars per day, when the outside temperature is T degrees.

(a) What does $f'(23) = -0.17$ mean?

(b) If $f(23) = 7.54$ and $f'(23) = -0.17$, approximately what is the cost to heat my house when the outside temperature is 20°?

7. (12) Given the following data about a function f,

x	3.0	3.2	3.4	3.6	3.8
$f(x)$	8.2	9.5	10.5	11.0	13.2

(a) estimate $f'(3.2)$, $f'(3.5)$.

(b) Give the average rate of change of f between $x = 3.0$ and $x = 3.8$.

(c) Give the equation of the tangent line at $x = 3.2$.

8. (14) A certain function f is decreasing and concave down. In addition, $f'(3) = -2$ and $f(3) = 5$.

(a) Sketch the graph of f.

(b) Estimate $f(2)$, namely give two values you're sure $f(2)$ is between.

(c) Estimate the zeroes of f. (First say how many there are and why.)

Mother Goose & Grimm   **By Mike Peters**

1. Draw a graph of speed against time which accurately describes the cartoon above. Pay close attention to concavity! Explain your graph in two sentences. Could the cartoon be accurate?

2. Find antiderivatives of the following functions:

    (a) $x^2 - \dfrac{3}{x} + \dfrac{2}{x^3}$

    (b) $\left(x + \sqrt{\sin(2x) + 3}\right)\left(x - \sqrt{\sin(2x) + 3}\right)$

3. Find the derivative of the following functions:

    $f(x) = x^2 \ln(x^2)$

    $g(x) = \frac{x^2+4}{x^2-4}$

    $h(x) = (x^2 + 1)\tan^{-1} x$

    $m(x) = \sin\left(\cos(e^{3x})\right)$

4. Draw a graph which accurately represents the temperature of the contents of a cup left overnight in this room. Assume the room is $70°$ and the cup is originally filled with ice water.

5. Give expressions for $f(x)$, $g(x)$ and $h(x)$ which agree with the following table of values.

x	$f(x)$	$g(x)$	$h(x)$
0	-7	0	$-$
1	-4	2	5
2	-1	8	2.50
3	2	18	1.66...
4	5	32	1.20
5	8	50	1

6. The graph below is of $y = f(x)$. Draw $f'(x)$ and $f^{-1}(x)$ on the same axes.

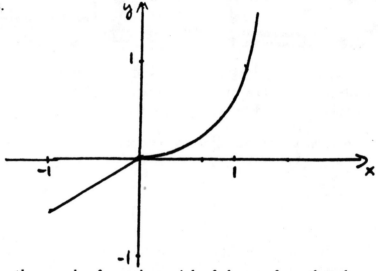

7. Draw the graph of a polynomial of degree four that has a relative minimum at $(-3, -2)$ and inflection points at $(-1, -1)$ and the origin.

8. Using the graph below:

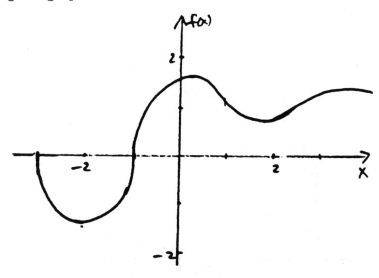

(a) list in increasing order (from smallest to largest) $f'(2)$, $f''(1)$, $f(0)$, $f'(0)$, $f''(0)$, $f'(-0.9)$, $f'(-2.9)$.

(b) Suppose you know the precise values of $f(x)$ for $x =$ an integer, and you want to use a tangent line approximation to calculate $f(x)$ for $x = -\dfrac{5}{2} + n$, $n = 0, 1, 2, 3, 4, 5$. Which of these values of x can you calculate the resulting $f(x)$ with the most accuracy? Illustrate on the graph.

9. Find a point on the graph of $y = e^{3x}$ at which the tangent line passes through the origin.

10. (a) Sketch the graph of a continuous function with the following properties: $f(0) = 1$, $|f'(x)| < 0.5$, $f''(x) < 0$ for $x < 0$, $f'(2) = 0$. (There are an infinite number of possible graphs.)

(b) Does your graph in (a) have a local maxima for $x < 0$?

(c) Could the graph of f have a local maxima for $x < 0$ and still satisfy the given four conditions? If so, draw such a graph. If not, explain why not.

(d) Which of the following are inconsistent with (a) (explain why!)?

$$\lim_{x \to -\infty} f(x) = 0 , \quad f(2) = 3 , \quad f''(2) = 0.$$

11. (a) Sketch the graph of $f'(x)$ on the same axis.

(b) Where does $f'(x)$ change its sign?

(c) Where does $f'(x)$ have a local extremum?

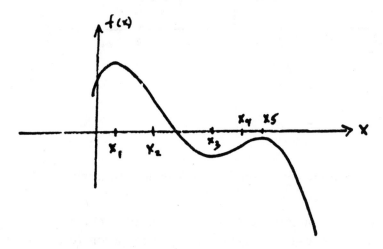

12. Let f be a function with positive values and let $g = \sqrt{f}$.

(a) If f is increasing at $x = x_0$, what about g?

(b) If f is concave down at $x = x_1$, what about g?

(c) If f has a local maximum at $x = x_2$, what about g?

13. For the function $y = axe^{-bx}$, choose a and b so that y has a critical point at $x = 2$ and a maximum value of 7.

14. If f is given as below, sketch two functions F, such that $F' = f$. In one case, have $F(0) = 0$ and in the other, let $F(0) = -1$.

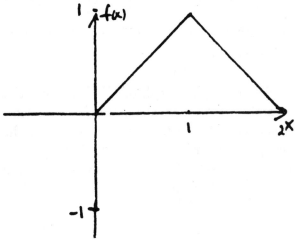

15. A rectangular sheet of paper is to contain 72 square inches of printed matter with 2 inch margins at top and bottom and 1 inch margins on the sides. What dimensions for the sheet will use the least paper?

16. Assuming the 440 ft. is accurate and you neglect air resistance, determine the accuracy of the following paragraph:

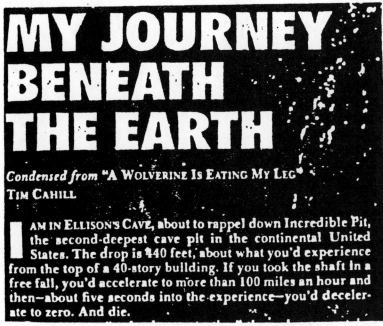

17. Consider the following three equations:

$$y^2 - 2\cos(x) = 2 , \quad x\sin(y) + y = 2 , \quad \ln|(y/(1-y)| = .71x + \ln 2.$$

Assuming each of the above equations implicitly defines y as a function of x, find $\dfrac{dy}{dx}$ for each equation.

18. Note that the point $(0,2)$ is on the graph of all three equations in the previous problem. On the next pages are slope fields consistent with two of your three equations. Identify which two equations have these slope fields. (Label each graph with the letter A, B, or C.) and explain why you made each choice. On each graph, draw the curve described by the appropriate equation (A, B, or C).

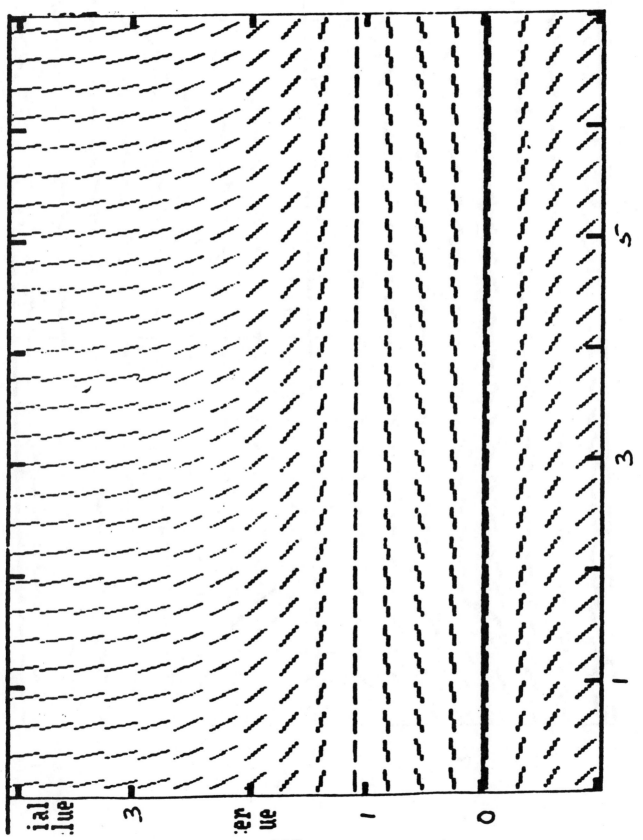

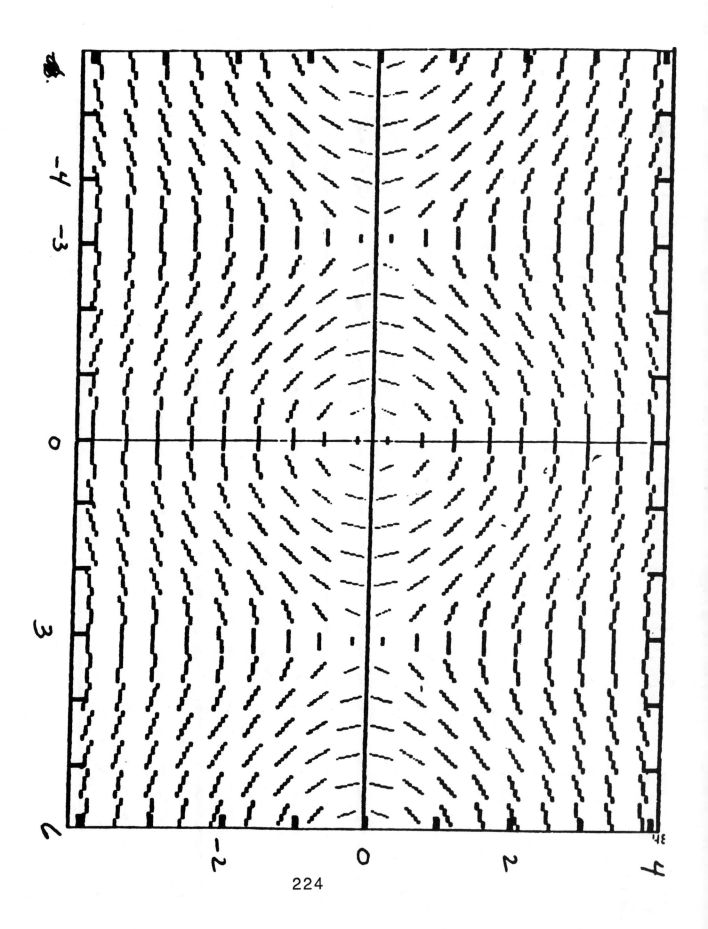

Math 125a, Section 2, Fall 1990
Final Exam

William G. McCallum

December 14, 1990

(20 points)   1. There is a function used by statisticians, called the error function, which is written

$$y = \mathrm{erf}(x).$$

Suppose you have a statistical calculator, which has a button for this function. Playing with your calculator, you find that

$$\mathrm{erf}(0) = 0$$

and

$$
\begin{aligned}
\mathrm{erf}(1) &= .29793972 \\
\mathrm{erf}(.1) &= .03976165 \\
\mathrm{erf}(.01) &= .00398929.
\end{aligned}
$$

(a) Using this information alone, give an estimate for $\mathrm{erf}'(0)$, the derivative of erf at $x = 0$. Only give as many decimal places as you feel reasonably sure of, and explain why you gave that many decimal places.

(b) Suppose that you go back to your calculator, and find that

$$\mathrm{erf}(.001) = 0.000398942.$$

With this extra information, would you refine the answer you gave in (a)? Explain.

225

(30 points) 2. To study traffic flow along Speedway, the city installs a device in front of the Plaza Hotel at 4.00 a.m. The device counts the cars driving past, and records the total periodically. The resulting data is plotted on a graph, with time (in hours) on the horizontal axis and the number of cars (in thousands) on the vertical axis. The graph is shown below; it is the graph of the function

$$C(t) = \text{Total number of cars that have passed by after } t \text{ hours.}$$

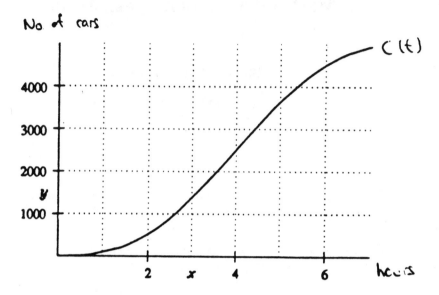

Figure 1: Traffic along Speedway.

(a) When is the traffic flow greatest?

(b) From the graph, estimate $C'(3)$.

(c) What is the meaning of $C'(3)$? What are its units? What does the value of $C'(3)$ you obtained in (b) mean in practical terms?

(20 points) 3. A ball is dropped from a window 100 feet above the ground. Assume that its acceleration is $a(t) = -32 \, \text{ft/sec}^2$ for $t \geq 0$.

(a) Find the velocity of the ball as a function of time t.

(b) Find the height of the ball above the ground as a function of time t.

(c) After how many seconds does the ball hit the ground?

(20 points) 4. Let a be a positive constant (i.e, $a > 0$). The equation

$$a^x = 1 + x$$

has the solution $x = 0$, for all a. Are there any solutions for $x > 0$? How does your answer depend on the value of a? You may explore with the computer by trying various different values of a to help answer this question, and you will get partial credit for an answer which simply reports on the results of this exploration, but to receive full credit you must include an exact answer with justifaction.

226

(30 points)   5. Below is the graph of the *derivative* of a function f, i.e., it is a graph of $y = f'(x)$.

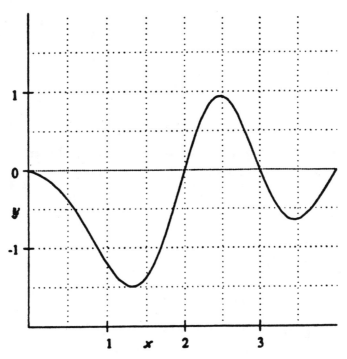

Figure 2: Graph of $y = f'(x)$.

(a) State the intervals on which f is increasing and on which it is decreasing.

(b) Say where the local extrema of f occur, and for each one say whether it is a local maximum or a local minimum.

(c) Where in the interval $0 \leq x \leq 4$ does f achieve its global maximum?

(d) Suppose you are told that $f(0) = 1$. Estimate $f(2)$.

(e) Still assuming that $f(0) = 1$, write down an exact expression for $f(2)$.

(30 points)   6. A function defined for all x has the following properties:

- f is increasing.
- f is concave down.
- $f(5) = 2$.
- $f'(5) = 1/2$.

(a) Sketch a possible graph for $f(x)$.

(b) How many zeroes does $f(x)$ have and where are they located? Justify your answer.

(c) Is it possible that $f'(1) = 1/4$? Justify your answer.

227

(30 points)   7. Find the derivatives of the following functions.

(a) $f(x) = \sin(2x) \cdot \sin(3x)$

(b) $f(x) = e^{-(1-x)^2}$

(c) $f(x) = \dfrac{1 + x}{2 + 3x + 4x^2}$

(d) $f(x) = \ln(\cos x)$

(20 points)   8. The cost $C(q)$ (in dollars) of producing a quantity q of a certain product is shown in the graph below.

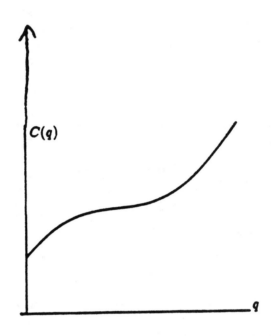

Figure 3: A cost function

The *average cost* is
$$a(q) = \frac{C(q)}{q}.$$

(a) Interpret $a(q)$ graphically, as the slope of a line in the sketch above.

(b) Based on the graphical interpretation in (a), find on the graph the quantity q_0 where $a(q)$ is minimal.

(c) Now suppose that the fixed costs (i.e., the costs of setting up before production starts) are doubled. How does this affect the cost function? Sketch the new cost function on the same set of axes as the original one.

(d) Let q_1 be the quantity where the new $a(q)$ is minimal. Where is q_1 in relation to q_0? Does your answer make sense in terms of economics?

228

MATH 125A, Section 2, Fall 1990
Test 3

William G. McCallum

November 27, 1990

(20 points) (1) Find the derivatives of the following functions.

(a) $f(x) = x \ln x - x$

(b) $g(t) = \sin 3t - \cos 5t$

(c) $R(p) = \dfrac{e^p}{1 + e^p}$

(d) $H(x) = \sqrt{1 - x^2}$

30 points) (2) Let
$$f(x) = e^{-x^2/b},$$
where b is a positive constant.

(a) Using the computer, sketch a graph of f. By choosing various different values of b, observe how the shape of the graph changes when b is made larger or smaller. Describe your observation in a clear, concise sentence that would make sense to someone who cannot see your graph.

(b) Find the inflection points of f, in terms of b.

(c) Use your answer to (b) to explain mathematically the effect of varying b that you observed in (a).

10 points) (3) Let f be a function. Is the following sentence true or false?

The inflection points of f are the local extrema of f'.

Explain your answer in a couple of short, clear sentences. You may assume that the second derivative of f is defined and continuous everywhere.

20 points) (4) Find the best possible upper and lower bounds for the function $f(x) = xe^{-x}$ for $x \geq 0$, i.e., find numbers A and B such that
$$A \leq xe^{-x} \leq B, \quad x \geq 0.$$
The numbers A and B should be as close together as possible.

229

(20 points) (5) The cost $C(q)$ (in dollars) of producing a quantity q of a certain product is shown in the graph below.

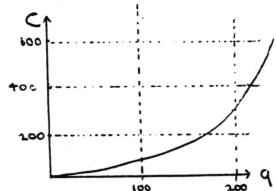

Suppose that the manufacturer can sell the product for $2 each (regardless of how many are sold), so that the total revenue from selling a quantity q is $R(q) = 2q$. The difference

$$\pi(q) = R(q) - C(q)$$

is the total profit. Let q_0 be the quantity that will produce the maximum profit.

You are told that q_0 can be found by finding the point on the graph where $C'(q_0) = 2$.

(a) Draw the graph of R on the figure above and then explain why this rule makes sense graphically.

(b) Now give a mathematical explanation of the rule, using what you know about maxima and minima.

230

1) Below is the graph of a function f. Sketch the graph of its derivative f' on the same axes.

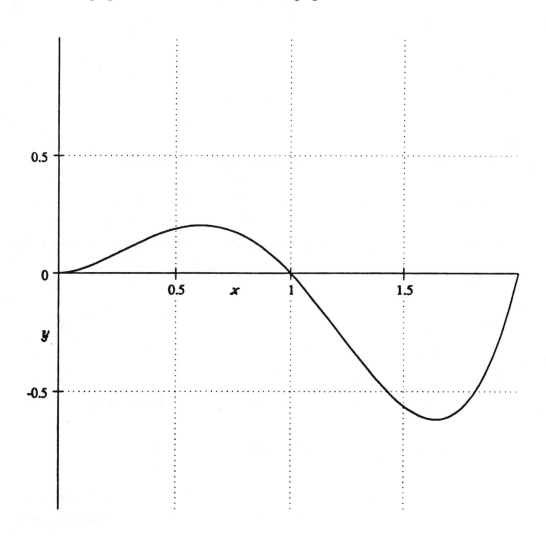

2) The graph below represents the *rate of change* of a function f with respect to t; i.e., it is a graph of f '.

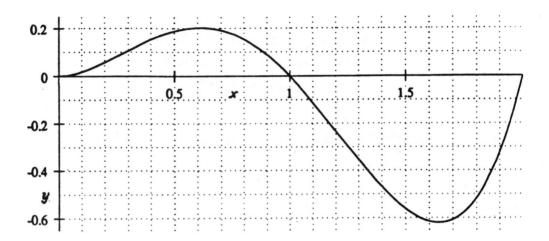

You are told that f(0) = 0.

On what intervals is f increasing?   On what intervals decreasing?

On what intervals is the graph of f concave up?   Concave down?

2)(cont.) Is there any value x = a other than x = 0 in the interval $0 \le x \le 5$ where f(a) = 0? If not, explain why not, and if so, give the approximate value of a.

3) Let $f(x) = x^{\sin(x)}$.
   a) Using your calculator, estimate f '(2).
   DON'T FORGET TO SET YOUR CALCULATOR TO RADIAN MODE.

   b) Find the linear approximation for f(x) near x = 2.

   c) Using the computer, graph f(x) and its linear approximation together on the same screen. For what range of values do you think your approximation is reasonably accurate? Explain how you chose your answer.

   d) Now graph f(x) and $g(x) = x^x$ on the same axes. Describe what you see, including any particularly interesting features. Can you explain those features?

4) Census figures for the US population (in millions) are listed in the following table.

Year	Population	Year	Population
1790	3.9	1890	62.9
1800	5.3	1900	76.0
1810	7.2	1910	92.0
1820	9.6	1920	105.7
1830	12.9	1930	122.8
1840	17.1	1940	131.7
1850	23.1	1950	150.7
1860	31.4	1960	179.0
1870	38.6	1970	205.0
1880	50.2	1980	226.5

Let $P = f(t)$ be the US population (in millions) at time t (in years). Since the population varies with time, there is a function f such that $P = f(t)$. Assume that f is increasing (as the values in the table suggest). Then f is invertible.

(a) What is the meaning of $f^{-1}(100)$?

(b) What is the practical significance of the derivative of $f^{-1}(x)$ at $x = 100$?

(c) Estimate $f^{-1}(100)$.

(d) Estimate the derivative of $f^{-1}(x)$ at $x = 100$.